To Hell or to Hobart

Stephen and Ellen Howard with two of their daughters at Geeveston in the 1890s
(*Author's collection*)

To Hell or to Hobart

Patrick Howard

Kangaroo Press

Cover illustration: *Constant* outside Sydney Heads, c 1845 (*Courtesy of Mr P. Hemery*)

©Patrick Howard 1993

First published in 1993 by Kangaroo Press Pty Ltd
3 Whitehall Road Kenthurst NSW 2156
PO Box 6125 Dural Delivery Centre NSW 2158 Australia
Typeset by Midland Typesetters Pty Ltd
Printed in Singapore by Fong & Sons Printers Pte Ltd

ISBN 0 86417 550 7

Contents

Preface

When I started work on this book in 1982, I did not foresee the problems I would encounter. However, when researching this project my rule was simple. I never hesitated to travel to the most distant areas in my quest for information, and I tried to locate any possible source, however remote.

The Irish end of the research proved to be much more difficult than I had expected, due primarily to the destruction of 92 per cent of the nation's records in the Civil War of 1922. As if this was not enough, terrible damage was done elsewhere. A whole library was lost when the Black and Tans burnt the Cork Town Hall in 1920; the Cork legal records were lost when the Cork Courthouse was extensively damaged at the end of the last century; in 1916 the Royal Academy of Arts lost two centuries of art treasures when the repository in Sackville Place was destroyed during the uprising, although the caretaker managed to escape with the president's chain of office around his neck.

When researching the parliamentary papers I found myself working off two sets of papers—the original set held by the National Library of Ireland and the abridged version published by the Irish University Press. In every case the references in the chapter notes relate to the original volumes.

Unfortunately there were virtually no records of the early members of our family. The convict background of my great-grandparents was something people never spoke about, and I only learnt about it through my own research. In fact much more research on the Australian end of the project remains to be done.

Gratitude must be expressed to the staff of the following organisations: the Archives Office of Tasmania; the State Library Hobart—Tasmanian Allport and Special collections; West Coast Pioneers Memorial Museum, Zeehan; the Battye Library, Perth; the Mitchell Library, Sydney; La Trobe Library, Melbourne; Public Records Office, National Army Museum, and Guild Hall Library, London; Tyne and Wear Archives, Newcastle; British Newspaper Library; the Museum of the Duke of

Edinburgh's Royal Regiment, Salisbury; the National Library of Ireland, State Papers Office, and Public Records Office, Dublin; Limerick City Library; Kerry County Library, Tralee; Tipperary County Library, Thurles; Cork County Library, Cork; Galway County Library, Galway; in addition, special thanks are due to Mrs R. Willoughby of Salruck, and Mrs Bridget Clesham of The Neale, who gave me access to the Thomson family papers; Mr P. Hemery of Kings Lynn; Mr L. A. C. Dopping-Hepenstal of Hindhead, Surrey; my brother Julian, who gave me a lot of assistance with the Tasmanian end of the research; and Christine Cave of Griffith, who typed the manuscript.

Thanks are also due to Lord R. Plunket, Lieutenant-Colonel W. M. C. Wall, and Commander Guy Kilroy who gave me permission to publish the portraits of their ancestors.

I am also grateful to the following publishers who allowed me to quote from their publications: Penguin Books Australia Ltd; Collins/Angus & Robertson; Brown, Son & Ferguson Ltd; Gill & Macmillan; J. Walch & Sons; Hamish Hamilton Ltd; Methuen London; and Ayer Co. Pubs. Inc.

The vast majority of those who left in the convict ships never returned, but became the essential bricks and mortar in building the new nation of Australia. To them this book is dedicated.

Patrick Howard
January 1993

Introduction

Like most Australians of Irish origin, I learned a lot about British and Australian History while at school, but I was blissfully unaware of Irish history. As I was brought up a Catholic, I was aware some members of the Irish clergy had a deep-seated antipathy towards 'the English', as they called them, and this puzzled me. But during my school days the hostility of the Irish clergy was more than balanced by the influence of my main teachers, who were New Zealanders and more inclined towards the British side of the story.

As time went on I became aware of Brian Boru, the legendary High King of Ireland, and the Battle of the Boyne, but I still had no idea what they meant to Ireland. Like most Australians I used the term 'beyond the pale' without knowing its Irish origin or original meaning.

My father felt his grandfather had been a remittance man who had been sent to Australia as a wayward son of a wealthy family. As time went on I learned my great-grandfather was a convict, and this only made me more curious than ever to investigate my origins. A substantial legacy from my father's estate enabled me to obtain a literary education and to carry out research in Ireland with the aim of writing a book. Originally I planned to write a novel based on my research. However, I decided a factual account of the experiences of my great-grandfather Stephen Howard who was transported in 1843, and my great-grandmother Ellen Lydon who was transported in 1849, would be more exciting. Through five years full-time research, I have been able to reconstruct their story, of which few details remain, by reconstructing the causeway along which they travelled. The lack of oral family history and the almost total destruction of the Irish records left me with no choice but to reconstruct the era in which they lived. As a result, the story is not merely the story of my great-grandparents, but also that of many other Irish convicts who travelled the same causeway.

My account begins with the historical background against which the Irish people evolved. During my research I virtually lived in the nineteenth century, and historical sections of Dublin, Cork and Limerick assumed a meaning for me they could not have had otherwise. In short, I learned the Irish side of history with a vengeance and soon began to understand the deep-seated distrust and even hatred that many Irish people have for those they term 'the English'. From the Norman Invasion of Ireland in 1166–72 until 1921, when the Anglo-Irish treaty was signed in London, Irish experiences at the hands of the English were fearful. They experienced not only oppression, but the dispossession of their lands, the destruction of their language and culture, religious persecution and even outright genocide.

After Chapter 1, the story of Stephen Howard and Ellen Lydon unfolds. It begins with their humble origins in Limerick and Galway and then goes on to describe their offences, arrest, imprisonment and trials. The story has been reconstructed through newspaper accounts of the trials and biographical material concerning the legal figures involved in their trial. In a similar vein, it continues until they leave Ireland aboard convict transports and reach Van Dieman's Land, never to return to their native land. After serving their probation, Stephen and Ellen met and married in Hobart and settled in the Huon Valley. The final chapter deals with the family's progress after the second generation moved to the west coast of Tasmania to take part in the mining boom at Zeehan.

1

An Irish Heritage

The Irish people are the last remnant of a great Celtic empire which once stretched across Europe into what is now Germany, but was pushed back towards the Atlantic seaboard by the westward thrust of the Germanic peoples in the early centuries of the Christian era. Ireland missed out on the rule of Imperial Rome, which did not show any interest in Ireland. But while it is a proud boast of the Irish that not one Roman soldier ever put foot on Irish soil, the country was the poorer for not undergoing the Roman apprenticeship. Ireland missed out on the Roman rule of law (derived from the Greek), on Roman civil engineering, Roman military organisation, and finally on Plato's famous division of labour (for example, the philosophers who rule, the soldiers who defend, and the helots who do the work).

In 431 Pope Celestine I sent Palladius to the Irish as their first bishop. Palladius died soon after, and was succeeded by St Patrick. Born in Roman Britain in 389, the son of an alderman, Patrick was captured by Irish raiders at the age of sixteen and sold as a slave in Ireland. He escaped after six years of servitude and went to Gaul, where he trained as a priest. Legend has it that Patrick had a vivid dream in which he heard the Irish calling him to return and to walk amongst them. He volunteered his services as a missionary, and in 432 he was sent to succeed Palladius. Patrick soon showed himself to be a man of action and in his missionary work, which was extraordinarily successful, he had to face dangers to his freedom, and even to his life, mostly from the Druids who were his chief opponents. He was also involved in clashes with the English, whose clergy severely criticised him as a zealous but unlearned man. Patrick demanded the excommunication of the British prince Croticus, who had killed some of Patrick's converts and sold others into slavery during a retaliatory raid in Ireland. In the *Confession*, written when he was an old man, Patrick replied to his critics by pointing to the success of his energetic mission crusade. He had laid the foundations of the Irish Church and established its centre at Armagh, which later became the primatial see of all

Ireland. When he died in 461, he had achieved his dream of introducing both Roman civilisation and the Christian Church to Ireland.

In 521 Columba, or Colum Cille, the 'Dove of the Church', was born at Gartan in Tyreconnell. After being ordained a priest he founded a church at Derry and became its first abbot. He later drew up the Columban rule, which put a strong emphasis on both scholarship and missionary endeavour, and attracted numerous recruits to his houses. While staying with another abbot Columba secretly copied out a portion of the Bible, thus causing a dispute with his host, who wished to keep the precious book to himself. The High King Diarmait was appealed to, and he gave a famous ruling: 'To every cow her calf, to every book its copy'. Columba angrily rejected the decision, others joined in the dispute, and this led to the battle of Culdremna in 561, in which thousands were killed. Widely condemned, and appalled at the slaughter himself, Columba decided to redeem himself by missionary work in a foreign land to win as many souls for Christ as had perished at Culdremna. In 563 he sailed to Iona, making it a famous seat of learning and of piety, and from which his monks christianised Scotland and much of England. When he died in 597, Columba's name was the greatest in the Irish Church and he had demonstrated an Irish genius for missionary work, which has been followed by Irish missionaries ever since.

By the end of the eighth century Ireland had become united in language, religion, customary law and cultural tradition. However, it was divided into two regions dominated by the UiNeill kings in the north, who had their royal centre at Tara, and the Eoganachta in the south, whose royal centre was at Cashel. There was little direct conflict between the two groups. In 795 the first Viking fleets came from Norway, raided many monasteries, and expanded their foothold wherever they could on the eastern seaboard. In 908 the Eoganachta were defeated when they tried to subject Leinster to Cashel's rule. Their king Cormac MacCullenan was killed, and this so weakened the Eoganachta that the southern part of Ireland also became prey to the Vikings, who established settlements at Waterford in 914, Dublin in 916 and Limerick in 920. A chain of Viking fortresses was established round the coast, from the Liffey to the Shannon, and for a century Norse tyranny was the dominant factor in Irish life.

In 940 Brian Boru was born, the son of a leader of one of the royal free tribes of Munster. Brian's brother Mahon had already wrested Munster, in the south of Ireland, from the Norsemen and established himself as King of Cashel, but he was slain by treachery. Brian succeeded him in 976, killed his enemies and reigned as King of Munster until 1014. In 1002, after subjecting the whole of southern Ireland to his rule, Brian became High King, or Ard Ri, of all Ireland after Malachy surrendered the kingdom of Tara to him. Twelve years later the Irish army, commanded by Brian Boru, defeated the Norsemen led by Sitric and Maelmora in the battle of Clontarf. Brian was killed by the fleeing Norsemen, as he was left unguarded in his tent behind the Irish lines, but the battle ended Norse rule in Ireland.

Due to power of local kings, the successors of Brian Boru still had great difficulty unifying Ireland politically. In the meantime, powerful forces were moving inside the Church. In the seventh century the Irish Church had come into conflict with Rome over customs observed by the monks and, more importantly, over the Irish liturgical calendar which fixed Easter at a different date from that of the Roman calendar. By the eleventh century it was shown that more serious differences remained, as the Irish Church was essentially a monastic one and the bishops had no real power or authority. In 1156 Turloch More O'Connor, a king of Connacht who had become High King in 1119 and was the greatest of Brian Boru's successors, died. His successor lacked the Turloch's strength and the later Norman invasion found Ireland lacking a strong central government. Considerable controversy has raged over Henry II's invasion of Ireland in 1171 as it is claimed, possibly inaccurately, that he was commissioned to do so by Pope Adrian IV, in order to reform the Church.

The first Norman intervention was brought about by the banishment of Dermot MacMurrough, the King of Leinster. A strong but brutal king, Dermot was driven out by the rebellion of his chiefs and the intervention of Tiernan O'Ruairc, who was the Lord of Brefni, a vassal state in north-east Connacht. O'Ruairc immediately sailed for Bristol to seek the support of the Norman princes. With the assistance of his beautiful daughter Eva, whom he married off to Richard de Clare, the Earl of Pembroke, better known as Strongbow, he was only too successful. In May 1169 a small advance guard of Normans arrived in South Wexford. These consisted of thirty knights, sixty men at arms and 300 archers. In August the following year they were joined by Strongbow, Eva, and 1,000 men at arms. They immediately attacked and took Dublin, which became the seat of English power in Ireland. As Dermot MacMurrough died shortly afterwards, Strongbow became King of Leinster.

This first confrontation between the Irish and the Normans not only highlighted the political weakness and technological backwardness of the Irish, but it set the pattern for virtually all later confrontations. The warlike and courageous Irish, clad only in linen tunics and armed with light axes, swords and spears, fought mounted soldiers who were protected by long mail shirts and iron helmets with a guard for the nose and a chain covering for the back and the neck. Their horses were unprotected, but speedy. These Norman soldiers may be considered to be the forerunners of the legendary knights in shining armour, as by 1200 it had become customary for both horses and men to be protected by a more comprehensive set of armour. Perhaps even more important, these soldiers functioned as cavalry, and as such were supported by bowmen and foot soldiers. Although brave, the Irish had little chance against such highly organised modern armies. The Norman right of succession, in which son succeeded father, also made the Normans much stronger, as they were not troubled by the disputed successions that bedevilled Irish politics.

Henry II of England landed at Waterford in October 1171, with an army of 4,000 men. His main purpose was to formalise Strongbow's position in Leinster and to establish English sovereignty in Ireland. He toured all the conquered parts of Leinster, received the submission of the native chiefs, and also the church leaders, who probably saw Henry as the agent of reform and revival. Henry was only in Ireland for six months, but while he was there the Synod of Cashel met at the end of 1171. It was attended by most of the church leaders, who despaired of achieving regimentation of the Irish Church without the protection of a powerful monarch. Much was accomplished. The Synod submitted to the King of England and passed decrees approving tithes for the clergy, Peter's pence for Rome, regulations for marriage and baptism, and freeing churches from secular demands. It affirmed Armagh as the primatial see of all Ireland, with final obedience to Rome, and ignored the claims of Canterbury over the Irish Church, which was divided into four provinces and reorganised along episcopal lines, with a structured hierarchy. Henry's sovereignty over Ireland was approved by the Pope in September 1172.

English expansion into Ireland continued. In 1235 Richard de Burgo conquered Connacht, and in 1264 Walter de Burgo was made Earl of Ulster. By 1272 the English had conquered Ulster east of Lough Neagh, in Meath, along with most of Connacht and of Munster. In 1315 the Scot Edward Bruce arrived at Larne harbour with an army of 6,000 veterans to assist the Irish. He fought his way successfully down to Leinster, where he was later joined by his brother Robert, King of the Scots, and their victories were a great inspiration to the native Irish. Robert returned to Scotland, while Edward was later killed by the English in 1318, near Dundalk, after having failed to become the Ard Ri so long sought after by the Irish. The English hold on Ireland was reaffirmed, but powerful and rebellious provincial kings proved to be a continuous source of trouble, despite the lack of a central command and the inability of the Irish to fill the position of Ard Ri. Soon the English were to make a series of political decisions which would divide the country for centuries. In 1361 an edict banned pure-blooded Irishmen from becoming mayors, bailiffs, officers of the king or clergymen serving the English. Five years later, Lionel, Duke of Clarence, tired of the struggle against the local Irish kings, enacted the Statutes of Kilkenny. Edmund Curtis writes of Clarence that, 'His one lasting contribution to the Irish history was to be the division and estrangement of the two races in Ireland for nearly three centuries'.[1]

Under the thirty-five Statutes of Kilkenny, the English were forbidden all normal communication with the Irish such as intermarriage, the fosterage of Irish children, conversation, uses of Irish law and the sale of horses or armour to the Irish. They had to use English surnames, language and customs. The Irish language in English communities was strictly forbidden, and the Irish were excluded from cathedrals, abbeys and clerical positions amongst the English. The English were ordered to be in a high state of readiness for war, and to train for it in the English fashion. These statutes were enforced by severe penalties and remained in force from 1366 until 1613.

In October 1394, King Richard II landed at Waterford with a large army and then marched up to Dublin, where he spent Christmas in the Castle. Richard received great homage from many Irish chiefs, and developed a policy which had four objects, among them the creation of an 'English land' in eastern Ireland. This land, which was known as the 'Pale', had its western borders in a line from Dundalk to the Boyne River, then down the Barrow River to Waterford, while its eastern borders were on the coast. This then completed a program of what has come to be known, in modern terminology, as apartheid or separate development. As with so many inhuman cruelties to be suffered by other nationalities, the Irish were to experience them first. However, by the middle of the fifteenth century, the Gaelic and the Norman lords were drawing so close together the Statutes of Kilkenny began to be ignored. Marriage and fosterage became common, the Irish language became widely used, and both races showed a love of Irish minstrels, poets and storytellers. Unfortunately, this uneasy cooperation was not to last.

During the Reformation Parliament of England, 1529–36, Henry VIII made his great breach with Rome and set himself up as head of the Church in England. For Ireland this was to have dreadful consequences, as Henry also set himself up as the spiritual head of the Irish Church. He supplanted the native lords with English deputies at the highest levels and ruled the country through them, though he generally left the less influential Irish and the Norman lords alone, preferring to base his rule on treaties rather than conquest. Greatly in favour of English speech and customs, he tried to suppress the Irish language and culture wherever possible. Although Henry's sovereignty was extended from Leinster into Munster, he was content to rule through chiefs, who governed their people through Irish law and customs, provided of course these chiefs submitted to him. When Henry VIII died in 1547 he was succeeded by the boy King Edward VI and England and Ireland were ruled by the senior nobility of England. In 1553 Mary ascended the throne and the Catholic restoration began. Despite this, two-thirds of the counties of Leix and Offaly were made available to planters who were 'English subjects born either in England or Ireland'.[2] Predictably, the injustice of this appropriation of Irish land brought about a rebellion by the native clans which continued for nearly fifty years.

Ireland was now entering the most difficult and dangerous period of its history, and the traditions of the old Gaelic world were of little help. Tradition demanded that leaders must first be warriors, who excelled or made heroes of themselves in battle. The Irish did not grasp the advantages offered their enemies by professional soldiers, generals who directed their armies from behind the lines, or statesmen who directed the generals from the capital. Many able Irish leaders died in battle, and there were few statesmen or shrewd politicians left. Upon Elizabeth's succession to the throne in 1553, the schism with Rome deepened when the new *Book of Common Prayer* became the official service book of the Church of England. The English language replaced Latin and attendance at the state church was made compulsory. Ireland was soon reduced to a state of insurrection, because of religious grievance, coupled with insecurity of land tenure on the part of the Normans of Leinster and Munster and the encroachment of the planters. Local rebellions and sporadic fighting began to break out. Most of the Irish and old English wished to remain loyal to the Pope on spiritual matters and to the Queen on temporal ones, but the widening rift between Rome and Elizabeth threw them into a state of great confusion. Traditionally, the Irish had gained great comfort from the Mass and the Sacraments. The new service in the English language seemed to be foreign and offered them little such comfort.

The resentment caused by the new English colonists was greatly increased by the plantation of Munster in 1586. When the Earl of Desmond fell from the Queen's favour, Elizabeth approved the confiscation of his lands and it was planned that some of the 500,000 acres in Munster would be acquired. Finally, 210,000 acres were granted to new settlers who were required to be English, but not necessarily Protestant. Both the old English and the Irish hated the planters, who they regarded as interlopers. Further to this, the planters were a great disappointment to Elizabeth, as they did not fulfil the conditions under which they were settled on the land, and little revenue was received from them.

While this land grievance grew more complex and serious, the religious atmosphere became tenser as wars raged on the Continent between the Reformation and Counter-Reformation forces. The Council of Trent (1545–63) gave Roman Catholics a greater sense of purpose and zeal and a greater awareness of their religious heritage, and the Jesuits who led the Counter-Reformation in Europe paid considerable attention to Ireland.

In 1588 the Spanish Armada was sent by Philip of Spain to conquer England. Although thought to be invincible, the large clumsy galleons were easily defeated by the small and manoeuvrable British ships. Many of the surviving galleons were wrecked on the north and west coast of Ireland, and they contained so many soldiers that, had they been able to land safely, they could have provided the local chiefs with a first-rate fighting force. However, stormy weather drove them on to the rocks, where they were hopelessly wrecked and the survivors, who could have numbered as many as 10,000 men, were executed by English officials as they came ashore. The Ulster chiefs did not mete out such treatment, and thousands of Spaniards were sent safely to Scotland. Had the Armada triumphed, there is no doubt a Spanish victory would have been very acceptable to the Irish.

The late sixteenth century also saw the rise of Hugh O'Neill, who was both a soldier and a statesman. More modern in outlook than the traditional Gaelic leaders, O'Neill proceeded cautiously, managed to unite the northern Gaelic chiefs, and in August 1594 defeated a small English force at the Ford of Biscuits near Enniskillen. On 15 August 1598, at the Yellow Ford, on the Blackwater River, a much stronger English force of 4,000 men was defeated and its commander killed. The Irish by this time had also solicited and won Spanish assistance and were ready for bigger things. O'Neill successfully pursued what was later to become known as a war of attrition, reducing Lord Mountjoy's English forces of 20,000 men to 6,500. In 1601 the Spaniards landed 4,000 men at Kinsale, in the south, but under a commander called D'Aguila who inspired neither the confidence nor the sympathy of the Irish. On 24 December 1601 the decisive battle of Kinsale took place. The Spanish and Irish forces were superior in numbers, but poor leadership lost them the battle. This defeat, after nine years of successful warfare, was a terrible blow to the Irish cause. It meant the end of the Gaelic order and the end of Irish hopes. Had O'Neill won, his forces would have been greatly augmented by sympathisers from all over Ireland and by further help from Spain. Instead, O'Neill submitted to Mountjoy, not knowing Elizabeth had died and that James I was on the throne. Red Hugh O'Donnell, who was O'Neill's lieutenant and an outstanding military commander, escaped to Spain and died at Salamanca a year later, probably poisoned by an English agent. Ulster was now a conquered province and wide open for colonists of the new English order.

After the battle of Kinsale, the Irish became more united as the old English and the Gael became both racially blended and more Catholic than ever before. The English rulers were faced with the problem of accommodating this Catholic nation while also coping with the encroachments of a rapacious, fast-expanding Protestant Ascendency who were to become the ruling class of Ireland for nearly three centuries. This problem was not helped when 500,000 acres of good land were thrown open to English and Scottish settlers, known as Undertakers, in May 1609. This time, unlike the plantation of Munster, it was stipulated that the planters had to be Protestants. A second class of grantees, who were generally Scots, were given less favourable terms and had to take the Oath of Supremacy, which admitted the English king to be head over the church. A third or lower class consisted of native Irish, who were not requested to take the oath. The native gentry soon became a minority in their own province, and the best lands were monopolised by the Undertakers. Although the plantation of Ulster was not an overall Protestant success, Ulster became England's only successful colony in Ireland. This was due in large part to the shrewdness, tenacity and resourcefulness of the large Scottish element.

Although many members of the old Gaelic aristocracy were left in Ulster, few survived Oliver Cromwell's rampage through Ireland between 1649 and 1658. Cromwell's domination of the English parliament and his execution of Charles I in January 1649 had an unsettling effect upon Ireland, and brought about new alignments everywhere. The Scottish Presbyterians in Ulster and Scotland, and the English in Ireland, united to save the monarchy. As for the Catholics, they feared the Puritans and would have much preferred a moderate Protestant government. An advance guard of 8,000 Roundheads reached Dublin on 28 July 1647, and on 15 August 1649 Oliver Cromwell arrived in Dublin as 'Lord Lieutenant and General for the Parliament of England'. Curtis notes that Cromwell 'commanded an army of 20,000 men, all determined and enthusiastic members of various sects, highly disciplined, perfectly equipped, and inspired by Old Testament Christianity. Their commander, however, as well as being a Protestant zealot, was a sturdy English nationalist, a great soldier, and a cool-headed politician.'[3]

The sufferings of the Irish under the Puritans can scarcely be imagined. Some idea of the feelings of the Puritans against the Catholics of Ireland, and the sentiments which inspired their soldiers, may be gained from the following excerpt taken from a Puritan political pamphlet of the period:

I beg upon my hands and knees that the expedition against them may be undertaken whilst the hearts and hands of our soldiery are hot, to whom I will be bold to say, briefly: 'happy is he that shall reward them as they have served us; and cursed is he that shall do the work of the Lord negligently'. Cursed be he that holdeth back his sword from blood; yea, cursed be he that maketh not his sword stark drunk with Irish blood—that maketh them not heaps upon heaps, and their country a dwelling-place for dragons, an astonishment to nations. Let not that eye look for pity, nor that hand be spared that pities or spares them; and let him be accursed that curseth them not bitterly.[4]

Early in September 1649, Cromwell turned northwards and attacked Drogheda, where a general massacre of the townsfolk of both sexes took place: 'Cromwell himself reckoned that less than thirty of the defendants were *not massacred, and these*, he adds, *are in safe custody for the Barbadoes*'.[5]

Turning south, Cromwell laid siege to Wexford, which was well fortified and well equipped in food and arms to stand a prolonged siege. However, a traitor opened the gate and the Cromwellian army had control before the defenders realised what was going on. The Puritans again massacred the inhabitants of Wexford, displaying a fanaticism worthy of Hitler's Nazis as they spared neither women nor children. Catholic clergy were prime targets of the invading army and very few survived. Cromwell's writings show he could justify almost anything in the service of his religious beliefs, and although he left Ireland in 1650, his work was carried on by his lieutenants. Most of the large towns suffered the ravages of his troops, although Clonmel and Limerick put up an unusually gallant resistance. Local resistance to Cromwellian troops continued until 1652, at which time most of the local armies submitted to the Cromwellian army under Ireton. Over 30,000 of these soldiers were allowed to leave the country for France and Spain, but once they had departed, the Puritans turned upon the common people who displeased them, and many thousands were sent to the West Indies as slaves.

In 1656 it was estimated that 60,000 Catholics had been sent as slaves to Barbados and other islands in the Caribbean. One observer, writing in 1672, stated that 6,000 boys and women were sold as slaves since England gained control of Jamaica and the adjoining islands. In 1666 a visiting cleric found 12,000 Irish slaves scattered about the islands, while another observer estimated the total number of Irish exiles as being 100,000, of whom many were transported to the West Indies. When Colonel Stubbers, the Governor of Galway, became alarmed at the multitude of vagabonds and idlers in the country, he had 2,000 of them transported to Barbados as slaves. Many people who were on the waterfront at the time the ships were leaving were also pressed on board and transported. The persecution under Elizabeth had been mild, compared with the Cromwellian scourge, and an observer noted that 'whole towns are transported to the Barbadoes'.[6]

Having rid themselves of opposing soldiers by sending them to the Continent, and of troublesome commoners by sending them into slavery to the West Indies, the Puritans still had to deal with the Irish aristocracy. Further to this, new land had to be made available to those soldiers who had become eligible for grants as planters. The problem was solved by transplanting the Irish gentry and landowners into a large strip of land in the province of Connaught between the Shannon River and the western coast: As the services of the peasants were needed as labourers, they were usually left alone. P. F. Moran notes:

> The province of Connaught was chosen, the most desolate and devastated in the whole kingdom, and thither, by public proclamation, all Catholics were commanded to repair. This was, in fact, nothing less than a frightful imprisonment of all the survivors of the nation. To Connaught or the scaffold was the fiendish cry of the persecutors throughout the country; and yet it was not even the province of Connaught, but only the barren portions of it, that the bounty of the Puritans set aside for the Irish Catholics. The heretics retained for themselves a breadth of four miles along the shores of the Atlantic, and of two miles along the rich banks of the Shannon. The Irish, moreover, were not allowed to reside in the capital province or in any of the market towns. Pent up within these precincts, it was expected that the Catholic race would soon become extinct by famine and disease.[7]

As if Cromwell and his soldiers were not enough, Ireland was also ravaged by famine and plague. According to one observer: 'in the years 1652 and 1653, the plague and famine had swept away whole counties, that a man might travel twenty or thirty miles and not see a living creature'.[8] The population of Ireland, estimated at 1,500,000 before the Cromwellian intervention, was reduced by two-thirds to 500,000 at Cromwell's death in 1658.

After the restoration of the monarchy and the state church in Britain, the Duke of Ormond ruled Ireland as viceroy between 1661 and 1668, and again between 1677 and 1683. Much was achieved in revising the more extreme outrages of Cromwell's persecution, but the two great grievances of land and religion remained.

Known as the 'Merry Monarch' because of his profligacy, Charles II set up a court of claims which was responsible for restoring large numbers of the Catholic gentry to their former estates. Although good work was done in this area, the Protestant backlash was such that the court had to stop its operations and more that 3,000 former members of the landowning class were prevented from having their estates restored to them. The new Cromwellian settlers owned more than a third of the best farming land in Ireland. In 1685 Charles was succeeded by James II, a Catholic king who had the support of both the Church of England and the Tories. As part of his Irish policy, he instructed the viceroy, Earl Clarendon, to raise a Catholic army in addition to the Protestant militia, and to restore Catholics to public office in the judiciary, the civil service and the town councils. These measures were carried through, and the way was greatly smoothed by the influence of the Earl of Tyreconnell, who had command of the army in Ireland. But just when things were proceeding smoothly, and it appeared all would be well for Ireland, James fell out badly with both parliament and the Church of England. William of Orange was invited over to reign in his stead.

After his defeat at Killiecrankie in 1689, James came to Ireland, seeing the Catholic army under Tyreconnell as his last hope. Tyreconnell had most of Ireland under the control of his army, but Derry and Enniskillen had held out against him. The war began with the siege of Derry, which was relieved on 1 August 1689. The loss of Ulster followed, and on 1 July 1690 the Battle of the Boyne took place between the two kings William and James. William had about 35,000 men, mostly French Huguenots and mercenaries from Denmark, Prussia, Finland and Switzerland. James had an army of 21,000 men, mostly Irish peasants who were stiffened with 7,000 French regulars. The battle was decisively won by William's forces, James contributing to his loss by interfering with his generals' councils at critical moments during the battle. Fearing encirclement by William's cavalry, James fled from the battle and from the country. Led by a great cavalry commander, Patrick Sarsfield, the Irish fell back on Limerick. Although the Irish peasants were hardy natural soldiers, they were inferior to William's army in numbers, training, and equipment. Still, the Battle of the Boyne, together with the name of Brian Boru, was to become part of the collective unconscious of those who are descended from Irish emigrant stock. Edmund Curtis remarked:

> The importance in history of the Battle of the Boyne is beyond all comparison with its interest as a clash of two armies. As a European event it was part of the coming and the final triumph of Louis' European enemies . . . In the history of Ireland it is one of the half-dozen events that have completely changed her destiny. Kinsale in 1603 had spelled the downfall of the Gaelic order. The Boyne marked the doom of the Old English loyalist aristocracy.[9]

Limerick became the city of refuge for the Irish troops, with Athlone, County Westmeath, its bridgehead. A valiant French general, Marshall St Ruth, rallied the Irish, and after being forced out of Athlone they fought a gallant battle at Augrim. They had almost carried the day when St Ruth was killed and the now leaderless Irish were routed. All Sarsfield could do was to regroup what was left and fall back on Limerick once more. William now controlled all of Ireland except Limerick.

William attempted to take Limerick soon after the Boyne. When he failed he sent for a wagon train full of artillery and ammunition with which he intended to force his way in. In August 1690 Sarsfield led 600 men out of the city by night, and following a circuitous route of sixty miles, he intercepted the wagon train at Ballyneety, six miles from Limerick. By a remarkable coincidence, the password for the troops guarding William's artillery was Sarsfield. Once he had learnt this from his spies, Sarsfield attacked the wagon train with the cry, 'Sarsfield is the word, and Sarsfield is the man'.[10] The munitions and artillery were blown up, whereupon William raised his siege and left Ireland.

In September 1691 William's army again put Limerick under siege. The city held out stubbornly for a month and Sarsfield, believing the French were no longer interested in Ireland, decided to come to terms with the enemy. No sooner had he signed the Treaty of Limerick, the terms of which were reasonable enough from the Irish viewpoint, than a French fleet sailed up the Shannon with a large army on board. Sarsfield could not go back on his word and the great bulk of his army of 11,000 men sailed for France, believing themselves to be honour-bound to the worthless James. Sarsfield himself was killed fighting for France two years later.

The Irish parliament was now entirely controlled by the Protestant Ascendency, many of them Cromwellians. The Treaty of Limerick was dishonoured, and the parliament passed a series of extremely repressive acts against Catholics in the years 1692, 1695 and 1697–98. The Penal Laws were summed up by John Mitchell as follows:

> They took charge of every Catholic from his cradle and attended him to his grave— Catholic children could only be educated by Protestant teachers at home; and it was highly penal to send them abroad for education.
>
> Catholics were excluded from every profession, except the medical, and from all official stations without exception.
>
> Catholics were forbidden to exercise trade or commerce in any corporate town.
>
> Catholics were legally disqualified to hold leases of land for a longer tenure than thirty-one years; and also disqualified to inherit the lands of Protestant relatives.
>
> A Catholic could not legally possess a horse of greater value than five pounds; and any true Protestant meeting a Catholic with a horse of fifty or sixty pounds in value, might lay down the legal price of five pounds, unhorse the idolator, mount in his place and ride away.
>
> A Catholic child, turning Protestant, could sue his parents for maintenance; to be determined by the Protestant Court of Chancery.
>
> A Catholic's eldest son, turning Protestant, reduced his father to a tenant for life, the reversion to the convert.
>
> A Catholic priest could not celebrate Mass, under severe penalties; but any priest who recanted was secured a stipend by law.[11]

The Protestant Ascendency was now supreme, although divided within itself. The last act of the penal code which disenfranchised Catholics was passed in 1727, and was not repealed until 1829. For a good part of the eighteenth century, Ireland was dormant politically. In October 1791 the United Irishmen movement was founded by Wolf Tone. Many of its leaders were executed in the rebellion of 1798 and Tone himself was sentenced to death, although he suicided before he was hanged. In 1795 serious clashes in Armagh between Protestants and Catholics led to the disarming of Ulster in 1797, by General Lake. The following year Lake and his troops were again in action, suppressing a serious rebellion led by the militant priest and inspiring leader, Father Murphy. Serious fighting took place at Gorey and New Ross before the whole county of Wexford erupted in rebellion. General Lake finally quelled the rebellion when he stormed the rebel headquarters at Enniscorthy with 13,000 soldiers. In the meantime, three small Presbyterian rebellions at Antrim and Down were also suppressed.

The army in Ireland at the time was utterly undisciplined, and the atrocities they committed against the civilian population under General Lake alienated the Irish people yet again. At the same time the magnitude and desperation of the rebellion in Wexford alarmed the English parliament and the prime minister, William Pitt the younger, decided the only thing that could be done was to prorogue the Irish Parliament and bring about a union with Britain. This was formalised by the Act of Union in 1800, which was carried despite opposition from a large section of the Irish parliament led by the enlightened Henry Grattan. The Act of Union provided the Irish would have one-fifth of the representation of Britain, with 100 members in the House of Commons.

The negative tone with which the nineteenth century began was to continue. From 1791 to 1841 the Irish population almost doubled, rising from 4,206,612 to 8,175,124. But while it was a British boast that they could hold India with 60,000 troops, they were struggling to hold Ireland with 100,000 troops. At any time the garrison in Ireland was bigger than the one in India.

The population of Ireland was primarily a peasant one, and the Irish peasant faced a number of demands, the most hated of which were tithes for the Protestant clergy and a fair rent from the landlord. Not surprisingly, the peasants hit back by forming secret societies which later developed into peasant guerilla movements that were known by a variety of names, the most common of which was Whiteboys. For nearly ninety years from 1760 up until after the famine, they kept the countryside in a state of turmoil through their assaults on property and on the people belonging to, or in the service of, the Protestant Ascendancy.

The nineteenth century also saw the rise of Daniel O'Connell, who was born at Derrynane, County Kerry, in 1775. As a young boy he was fostered with a peasant family and developed an affinity for the common Irish that he was never to lose. He received his early schooling from the parish priest and itinerant teachers, and as Catholics were banned from education, he was sent to France to receive further instruction at St Omer and Douai. When he returned home the acts of 1792–93 had relaxed the law enough for Catholics to be able to hold a commission in the army, or to take a degree at Trinity College. O'Connell was admitted to the Bar in 1798, and soon made his mark as a successful barrister. A brilliant orator, with a magnificent presence, he soon became the leader of the Catholic Association, which fought successfully for Catholic Emancipation. After emancipation had been granted in 1829, O'Connell threw himself into the cause of the repeal of the Act of Union. He organised huge meetings all over the country and became known throughout Ireland as 'The Liberator'. O'Connell was elected to parliament as the Member for Clare in 1828, but was unable to take his seat because the oath was objectionable to Catholics. In 1829 he was re-elected, and because a new oath that was acceptable to Catholics had been prepared, he took his seat.

The mid-nineteenth century was a nervous period for the British in Ireland, even though O'Connell was dedicated to non-violence. On 14 October 1843 O'Connell and nine of his associates, including his son, were charged 'with conspiring to change the government by intimidation, and demonstrations of great physical force'.[12] O'Connell was brought to trial in January 1844 and was found guilty by a packed jury. He was sentenced to twelve months imprisonment, fined £2,000, and bound over for £5,000 to keep the peace for seven years. He died, exhausted, on 17 May 1847, aged seventy-two.

Before his death, O'Connell had been seriously challenged by the Young Ireland Movement, led by John Mitchell and William Smith O'Brien. In July 1846 the Young Irelanders seceded from O'Connell's movement because they could no longer endorse the policy of non-violence. The next three years were witness to frenzied political activity on the part of the Young Irelanders, as they attempted to raise the country against the English. Wild rumours circulated in Dublin, and at times the streets were a mass of red and blue uniforms, as thousands of troops were poured in. The activities of the Young Irelanders came to a head in a rather abortive rebellion at Ballingarry, County Tipperary, in July 1848. Smith O'Brien, John Mitchell and Terence MacManus were sent into exile in Van Diemen's Land. Sadly, the Young Irelanders were not as practical as they were intellectual and they failed to grasp the fact that the Irish people were exhausted by both the famine and the failure of previous rebellions. It would not be until the rise of Charles Stewart Parnell, nearly thirty years later, that Ireland's political history would start moving again.

Such was the history of suspicion and hostility towards the English that was the heritage of Stephen Howard, Ellen Lydon and their fellow Irish, both at home and in enforced exile.

2

Limerick and the Peasant Guerillas

The Howard family lived at the townland of Ballintaw, near Croom, County Limerick. Stephen Howard's father, Patrick, lived in a small hut on a piece of land 1 rood 14 perches (one-third of an acre) in area. The ship's indents, when Stephen was transported, show he had five brothers and two sisters at his native place. However, they must have grown up and left home by 1843, because the petition Stephen put up to the lord lieutenant shows Patrick as being a crippled old man, unable to walk without crutches, and Stephen as the only support of both his father and his three little orphan nieces.

Ballintaw is situated on 449½ acres at the eastern extremity of the parish of Croom. To the west it is bounded by the townlands of Tullovin and Ballyculleen and by the parish of Athlacca. It was owned by an English absentee landlord, Mr St Leger, and was marked by a trigonometrical station on its south boundary and an ancient fort in the centre of the town, thus making a contrast between ancient and modern. During the first half of the nineteenth century the adjoining townlands of Tullovin, Glenbevan, Ballintaw and Ballyculleen were so turbulent with Whiteboy activity that a police station was built in the south Glen Bevan, Ballyculleen area.[1]

Almost in the centre of County Limerick, Croom is eleven miles south-west of the city of Limerick on the banks of the Maigue River. Maigue means river or plain and the Maigue valley is part of the famous Golden Vale of Munster, a fertile tract of land stretching thirty miles from the River Deel to the Tipperary border. Croom village grew up around a Geraldine castle which belonged to the Kildare branch of the famous Fitzgerald family, who always considered Croom as their ancestral home.[2] In the nineteenth century Croom was described as a post town on the road running between Limerick and Cork. The bridge over the Maigue was a fine structure of six arches, and the town was always considered to be prettily situated. In 1841, it had a population of 1,470, while the parish as a whole contained 7,097 people.[3] The town had a police station, where petty sessions were held every

Monday, two churches (Catholic and Protestant), and 213 houses. Fairs were held there four times a year. At Caherass, a few miles downriver from Croom, there was a powerful modern flour mill which complemented the large mill situated at the bridge of Croom. The chief occupations of the town were shopkeeping and agriculture.[4]

In the mid-eighteenth century, Croom became famous as a meeting place of Gaelic poets who gathered regularly in the tavern of Sean O'Tuama. Himself one of the two chief poets of the district, O'Tuama and his associates 'wrote love songs, elegies, drinking songs, songs of farewell and songs of a patriotic nature' and are today spoken of as poets of the Maigue. Sean O'Tuama died in 1775 and his fellow poet, Aindrias McCraith, died in Kilmallock in 1795.[5]

The gentry were fond of hunting and racehorses, and the Maigue valley was and still is wonderful horse-breeding country. The love of horses filtered down to the poor people, but at the time they had little opportunity to take part in any sports associated with them. In mid-nineteenth century Ireland, many landlords had enormous estates: 'the Duke of Leinster had 73,000 acres in Kildare and Meath, the Marquis of Downshire had 115,000 in five counties, and the Duke of Abercorn . . . had 76,000 acres in Donegal and Tyrone'.[6] Over half the country was owned by fewer than a thousand great landlords, and 20 per cent was owned by landlords with estates ranging from 2,000 to 5,000 acres. By contrast, in 1851 over half of the 570,388 tenant farmers had less than fifteen acres each. W. E. Vaughan notes that:

> Even the typical Irish landlord was wealthier than all but the grandest of Prussian junkers; as a class, with a specific definable source of income, they were a formidable group, with a collective income that was more than the public revenue of Ireland, and more than the cost of maintaining the Royal Navy.[7]

Although large estates in the Maigue valley were relatively modest in size, not exceeding two or three thousand acres, they were well wooded and had big houses. Their homes were built in the late eighteenth or early nineteenth century and were surrounded with high stone walls built 'to keep the natives out'. Their proprietors, with few exceptions, belonged to the Protestant Ascendency.[8]

This sort of inequality made for the emergence of the peasant guerillas, later known as Whiteboys, who first appeared in 1711–13, during an outbreak of agrarian crime in Connaught. On one occasion a Galway shepherd watched 'as a group of eight men dressed in white shirts with white linen bands about their heads rode into a park and deliberately killed the sheep'. Such an act was characteristic of later Whiteboy activity. The outbreak died down as suddenly as it began, and nothing was heard for half a century, when an outbreak began in the counties of Tipperary, Cork, Limerick and Waterford. Whiteboy activity then became an ever-recurrent factor on the Munster law-and-order scene until the famine in the late 1840s destroyed the class of impoverished peasants upon which the Whiteboy movement was built.[9]

Two particular grievances of the Irish peasant were pasturage rights in certain wastes and commons, and tithes which were paid to the Protestant clergy. Renewed Whiteboy activities are believed to have begun amongst the Levellers in Tipperary during 1757. Their name is almost certainly derived from their distinctive dress or uniform, which consisted of a white shirt worn over their other clothes. Their oath, which was quite impressive, virtually makes each recruit a soldier in a military organisation:

> I do herby solemnly and sincerely swear, that I will not make known any secret now given to me, or hereafter may be given, to anyone in the world, except to a sworn person belonging to the Society called Whiteboys or otherwise Sive Ultagh's children.
>   Furthermore, I swear, that I will be ready, at an hour's warning . . .
>   Furthermore, I swear, I will not wrong any of the company I belong to . . . nor suffer it to be done to others . . .
>   Furthermore, I swear, I will not make known . . . to any person who does not belong to us, the name or names of any of our fraternity . . .
>   Lastly, I swear, I will not drink of any liquor whatsoever whilst on duty . . .[10]

Whiteboy groups usually elected a captain, who then assumed a sobriquet such as Captain Starlight or Captain Rock. More than anything else, these names were 'the embodiment of a collective identity carrying with them the usual function of anonymity'.[11]

The police classified offences against the person, against property and against the peace as outrages. Whiteboys were usually involved in offences of a destructive nature such as murder, attempted murder, malicious wounding and all forms of assault. Their offences against property included arson, housebreaking, the killing and maiming of livestock, and armed robbery, particularly with firearms. Offences against the peace included threatening letters, attacking houses, administering unlawful oaths and firing into houses. Firing into dwellings after dark was a favourite Whiteboy form of intimidation. According to Michael Beames, these tactics had two main purposes: 'The first was the binding together of the population by persuasion and intimidation . . . The second was the carrying out of punitive measures against those who broke the "laws" thus established.'[12]

The Whiteboys made considerable use of threatening letters, such as the one written to an unpopular landlord's bailiff, Phillip Hourigan, in 1852:

> Take notice Phillip Hourigan you are hereby cautioned to act more liberal with Mr Ross's tenants, lest something might occur to you as there did before, so let this be a caution to you not to be so fond of going to Limerick with eronious pactrents [back rents] to Mr Hunt. So take notice or choose a coffin—signed
>
>   Captain Rock[13]

Hourigan lived on the townland of Ballyculleen, adjoining Ballintaw, and was the bailiff for an absentee landlord called Ross for whom the Mr Hunt referred to in the letter was the land agent. Hourigan's wife and son had already been murdered in 1847, during a raid on Hourigan's house while he was away. Interestingly enough, Mr Hunt was also an insurance agent based in Cecil Street, Limerick.

During the commission of enquiry into the state of the poor in 1836, the Rev.

C. J. McCarthy, the priest of Ballingarry parish which adjoined Croom and then had a population of 8,651, gave the following information about his parish. He estimated the number of labourers in Ballingarry at 800, of whom only two or three had permanent employment. They were maintained while out of employment by their wives and children, who begged or drew turf on their backs, from a bog, for a small profit. The diet consisted of potatoes, with a bit of milk and salt, and an occasional herring. Their clothing was particularly wretched. Labourers received 8d. a day without food, or 6d. a day with it, and they were least employed during the winter. In spring and autumn, women and the bigger children obtained seasonal employment, but McCarthy believed a male labourer's yearly earnings did not exceed £5. He felt the collective earnings of the rest of the family—that is, a wife and four children—would not clear £3 10s. 0d., with the wife earning 5d. per day and each of the children 4d.

McCarthy estimated the yearly expense for food for an able-bodied labourer and his family at £8. Wages for labour could be paid for in money, food or 'con acres' (small holdings), but McCarthy knew of no herds in the parish of Ballingarry. He went on to say that the landlords of cottages were middlemen or farmers. Cabins with land rented for £4 per year, and without land for £2. The cabins were made of mud covered with straw, with home-made beds and very poor furniture. If it was permissible to pay the rent with labour, then the poor cottier felt himself to be well off. In the village of Ballingarry there were numerous instances of two or more families sharing the one cabin, although such a practice was less frequent in the countryside. The population was increasing, and with it poverty, and the area had been the focus of several disturbances in 1822 and 1823. But since then it had been peaceable. McCarthy did not answer questions concerning savings banks, pawnbrokers' shops or public houses in the area, but he said there was no private distillation.

The Rev. Thomas Gibbings, the Protestant minister of Ballingarry, generally agreed with McCarthy, and particularly stressed the wretchedness of the furniture and accommodation. However, Gibbings disagreed with McCarthy concerning the yearly income of a labourer and his family. He believed a labourer might earn £10, and his wife and family about £5, while the cost of food for such a family would only be about £5 per year. In short, Gibbings felt labourers were much better remunerated financially than McCarthy did.

Gibbings also gave much more information in other areas. He said that there was no savings bank in Ballingarry, or pawnbroker's shop, although there were two or three in Rathkeale which were patronised by the poorer classes, particularly those addicted to drink. Amazingly, there were no fewer than 100 public houses in the Ballingarry area, and Gibbings noted that whiskey was so cheap it was not worthwhile carrying on illicit distillation. He said it would be greatly to the advantage of Ireland if the price of whiskey was raised considerably.[14]

At the time of his arrest in 1842, Stephen Howard was working for a large farmer, James Lynch, in the townland of Granagh, which is in the south-east extremity of the parish of Ballingarry. Granagh contains 366 acres of arable land, most of which was owned by the Court of Chancery and leased to Lynch, of Granagh Cottage, who had 208 acres, and Catherine and James Lyons of Granagh House who had 148 acres. At the crossroads at the top of the townland there was a Catholic chapel which was built in 1831 of stone, with a thatched roof.

Granagh Cottage was a typical Golden Vale farmhouse, being painted with yellow ochre which had mellowed over the years to give it a golden appearance. As a concession to the troubled nature of the times it had bars on the windows. The cottage was in fact a large house, 24 paces long and 7 paces wide in its outer dimensions. It had two small bedrooms at one end, a large kitchen with an open hearth, a large dining room, and a master bedroom at the other end. A scullery at the back of the kitchen had a high ceiling. The only upstairs accommodation was a bedroom for the servant. The front door opened on to a courtyard flanked by outbuildings which accommodated carriages and horses belonging to the family. It had two doors, one in the middle of the house and the other at the rear of the kitchen. By far the most impressive parts of the cottage were the walls, which were a yard thick. The roof was thatched.

Granagh nestles at the bottom of the sacred hill of Knockfierna, which is one of the sacred hills of Limerick. Knockfierna is 948 feet high, and the name means simply the hill of truth. The source of much folklore concerning leprechauns and fairies, ancient mythology has it that a mysterious being called Donn Firinne lived there and gave it its name. Donn, who is believed by some scholars to be a Celtic god of death, or of the other world, reputedly exacted grim reparations upon people who tampered with his abode. For example, a deep hole in Knockfierna is supposed to lead to the entrance of Donn's dwelling. A surveyor who tried to fathom it with a plumb line was pulled down and never seen again, while a man who threw a stone down it had it thrown back in his face, breaking his nose. In all, Knockfierna and Donn Firinne accounted for an amazing body of myths in the Ballingarry parish.[15]

Stephen Howard had worked for some years as a labourer on James Lynch's property and had been known to his employer for six or seven years. He lived on the property in the type of one-roomed cabin, known as bothan scoir, inhabited by the labourers of substantial farmers (referred to often as 'strong farmers') in the eighteenth and early nineteenth centuries. The better type of bothan scoir was built of rough stone, mortared with clay, with rough saplings for roof timbers. Externally, they measured about 7 yards by 5 yards, and the walls were about 18 inches thick. A typical bothan scoir only had a small window on either side, with one door, and the roof was thatched with straw and reeds. Although later types of bothan scoir had chimneys, the cabin was still very smoky. There was no ceiling or lining on the roof. Generally, there was little furniture, and most of the family slept on the floor, on bundles of straw or rushes which they shared with any livestock they owned. More affluent labourers may have had a bed, a table, a lamp which was usually placed between the window and the hearth, a holy picture of some sort and some cooking and eating vessels. These vessels were a camp oven, earthenware jars, iron cooking pots, earthenware mugs and plates.[16]

Perhaps it is pertinent here to compare the lifestyle of Stephen Howard with that of a substantial farmer such as James Lynch. According to Gearoid O'Tauthaigh, in the mid-nineteenth century,

> The substantial farmer enjoyed a comfortable standard of living. His house was well built and well furnished. A spacious farmyard, well kept outhouses, and a hunter among his horses might all be taken as reliable indexes of prosperity. He kept a good table . . . He could afford twelve guineas a year for private tuition for his children.[17]

In the wealthier areas such as the Golden Vale the substantial farmers usually occupied the standard Golden Vale Farmhouse, which compared favourably with any of a similar type in Europe:

> The comfortable farmer had well-cut kneebritches, waistcoat, shirt and cravat, tailcoat, warm stockings and sturdy boots, while his wife's ample cloak covered a dainty bodice, 'midi'-skirt and shift. The lower grades had generally the same cut of clothes, but they had to last longer and were consequently more ragged and patched. Few of the labourers had overcoats and their womenfolk and children generally went barefoot. Among the very poorest, clothing was little better than rags.[18]

Despite such a contrast in their lifestyles, Stephen seems to have had a good relationship with Lynch, who spoke favourably of him in court.

The police record of Stephen Howard at the time of his arrest describes him as twenty-seven years of age, 5 feet 7 inches tall, with a pale complexion, oval head, dark brown hair, dark brown whiskers, oval visage, forehead of medium height, dark brown eyebrows, light grey eyes, medium nose, medium mouth and medium chin. He had a scar on his left arm and another on the right side of his nose. By the standards of the time he was considerably above average height, and his photograph as an old man shows him to have had a powerful frame. He would almost certainly have been a good worker, and quite capable of the sustained feats of exertion that had made the Irish sought-after as labourers on big construction projects in Britain and the United States.

Somewhere along the line it appears that Stephen got involved with the Whiteboys, and it was this which led him to becoming involved in the felony at Patrick Hogan's house. Patrick Hogan was a substantial farmer situated near a ruined castle, Rathcannon, in the Parish of Dromin and Athlacca. Rathcannon is two miles from Athlacca, three miles from Bruff and seven and a half miles from Granagh. Patrick Hogan was the great-grandfather of Patrick and Joseph Hogan, who both became well known in Irish racing and hunting circles, and the family has for generations been prominent in breeding hunters. Hogan's house was a large one, with a relatively simple plan. The ground floor was divided into two main sections, with the parlour on the right and the dining room and kitchen on the left. The upstairs section contained three large bedrooms and a harness room. The front door was in the middle of the house, and the rear door to the left, to service the kitchen and dining rooms. There was a laundry and a spare room behind the parlour.

On the morning of Sunday, 14 August 1842, Patrick Hogan and his family attended Mass in Athlacca and only two servants, Ellen Nunan and Deborah Dunsworth, accompanied by a friend Bridget Malone, were at home. At about 11 a.m. the front door was thrown open and six men, armed with a pistol, a pitchfork and a wattle between them, entered. Five came into the kitchen, while the sixth remained at the door. One of the intruders, apparently William Burns, took a gun which was hanging over the fireplace while Timothy Noonan placed the pistol to Bridget Malone's breast and asked her where the firearms were. When she replied she was a stranger and did not know, Noonan turned to Ellen Nunan and asked her the same question, striking her on the chest with the pistol as he did so. Nunan said, she could take her oath, she did not know where they were. Stephen Howard replied that he would not believe her oath, but Burns said he did and added that if any damage were done to the house, he would turn them in himself. Noonan and another man then went upstairs to search for guns. Malone told the intruders that she could see them quite clearly and that she knew them, as none of them was disguised. If they did any harm, they would be sorry, as she said her master had only gone to the end of the farm and would soon be back. After three-quarters of an hour, Noonan and his companion returned downstairs and all six men departed, taking the gun and two shot pouches with them. Four of them went in a southerly direction towards Bruree Castle, and the other two went westwards towards Harding Grove. At first Bridget Malone attempted to follow them, only to have Noonan threaten her with his pistol. After waiting for a while she followed the four until she reached Athlacca, where the Hogan family and their fellow parishioners were coming out of Mass. After they had been alerted, Hogan led the parishioners in a chase afer the fugitives, but to no avail.

Shortly after the robbery, Burns, who seemed to have been a reluctant party to the crime, surrendered to Mr Harding at Harding Grove and showed him where he had thrown the gun into a ditch. It was some time, however, before Burns' accomplices were caught. Presumably they were sheltered by Whiteboy sympathisers, but Stephen Howard was arrested by Constable Sheehan, in a farmer's house convenient to his own, at midnight on 9 December. Noonan was also arrested at night and at a farmer's house, by Head Constable Ward in Charleville on 15 January 1843.

After his arrest, Stephen Howard was taken to Bruff, which had both a resident magistrate and a barracks for the Irish Constabulatory. A description of Bruff at mid-nineteenth century is given by *Slater's Directory*:

> Bruff is a pleasant post village, in the parish of its name, barony of Coshma county of Limerick . . . Seated on the banks of the River Dawn, in a delightful and fertile part of the country . . . The town, which consists of one long street, with several lanes branching from it, was formerly the property of the Hartsonge family, and now forms part of the Limerick estates. The constabulary force have a barrack here. In a neat court house general sessions are held in January and June, and petty sessions every alternate Wednesday . . . The trade of Bruff is mainly of a local and retail character; a corn mill and a good hotel are perhaps, the most prominent branches.[19]

In December 1842 Bruff's resident magistrate was Thomas Cannon, who had only recently been transferred there from Loughrea. Born in Kildare about 1812, Cannon graduated from Trinity College with a BA in 1837 and was appointed resident police magistrate in Loughrea on 16 November 1836.

Robert Carey was sub-inspector in charge of the police at Bruff. Appointed to the force as a head constable on 1 March 1837, Carey was made a third-class sub-inspector four months later and a second-class sub-inspector during May 1841. Shortly afterwards, he had received the testimonial of a grand jury in his favour. In 1842, aged forty-one, he was very much a man on the move.

The Irish Constabulary was formed in 1822 when the lord lieutenant was empowered to appoint a chief constable in each barony. The lord lieutenant was then able, by proclamation, to require the magistrates of each county to appoint a limited number of constables. These then served under a provincial inspector-general and had a special uniform:

> The uniform of this new force was a green frock-coat and trousers, and shako cap for dress with a soft cloth cap, and a short or slop jacket for undress, armed with a short carbine . . . The men were drilled at the headquarters of the provinces . . . and this preparatory training generally occupied a period of about three months.[20]

In 1836 the Constabulary was amalgamated with the Peace Preservation Force. Established by Chief Secretary Sir Robert Peel in 1814 to maintain order in disturbed districts, the Peace Preservation Force was so unpopular with the peasantry that 'the service became one of great danger as well as odium; it was therefore found exceedingly difficult to induce men of good habits to join it'.[21]

The new force was organised under an inspector-general, who had two deputy inspectors-general, four provincial inspectors, and thirty-five county inspectors; with one sub-inspector, two head constables, and sixteen constables for each barony.[22] Limerick had John S. Rich as county inspector, with eight sub-inspectors under him, and Robert Carey was one of them.

The bridewell of Bruff is in Chapel Lane, on the right after you cross the Dawn or Morning Star River to enter the main street. In 1829, during the annual inspection, the building was described as containing two day rooms, four cells and a keeper's apartment, all furnished, clean and in excellent order. The report did not mention the refractory cell—a small, dark windowless room, approximately 5 feet 6 inches long and 6 feet high, with an entrance only 4 feet 6 inches in height.[23]

For Timothy Noonan and Stephen Howard, their first real brush with the law must have been bewildering. Both were virtually illiterate, as the National Board of Education, which administered a centralised system of undenominational schools, was not established until 1831. Prior to that, the only education provided for the poor was by the Christian Brothers and the Poor Clare, Ursuline and Carmelite orders of nuns. These, however, only accounted for a small percentage of Irish children, and the great majority of those who received some smattering of education did so at the hedge schools, under the hedge-school master.

As the name suggests, hedge schools were held in the open air during summer. By the mid-1820s it was estimated that close on half a million children, of whom 80 per cent were Catholics, received their education in such schools.[24] If Stephen Howard or Timothy Noonan ever received any education, it would have been at a hedge school, where they may well have also received their Whiteboy sentiments.

The authorities certainly regarded hedge-school masters with great suspicion, believing them to be anti-British, the writers of threatening letters and the brains and inspiration behind many Whiteboy outrages. Very often hedge-school masters had been students for the priesthood, or teaching or lay brothers, but the schools themselves soon became defunct as the National Board of Education made impressive progress. By 1849 the board's schools were educating nearly half a million children, and the influence of the hedge-school master became a thing of the past.[25]

On 17 August 1842 an abstract report of the outrage on Hogan's house was made out at Bruff. It was noted that William Burns had surrendered, and it proposed the two servant witnesses should be maintained, while the little boy and girl who raised the alarm—who were not mentioned in reports of the trial, and whose role remains a mystery—should be given £2 each. Thirty pounds reward was offered from public funds for the apprehension of the culprits, and a private reward of £10 was also offered, probably by Patrick Hogan. On 20 December the same abstract report noted Stephen Howard had been arrested.

On 14 December 1842, Thomas Cannon wrote to the Chief Secretary's Office in Dublin:

> I have this day committed to the County Gaol at Limerick for trial at next Assizes Stephen Howard fully and satisfactorily identified by two witnesses, as being one of six armed men who on Sunday the 14th day of August last at 10 o'clock in the morning, entered the house of Patrick Hogan of Rathcannon in this district and carried away a gun, and for the apprehension of whom with others concerned Government authorized one at the time to offer a Reward of £30.
>
> Howard to the present has evaded the vigilance of the Police.[26]

The following year, on 8 February, Thomas Cannon wrote a similar letter to the Chief Secretary to report that Noonan had been arrested and committed for trial at the next assizes in Limerick. As there were no railways at that time, the men would have gone by coach to Charleville, via Kilmallock, and from there to Limerick the next day. Cars for Charleville left the Carberry Arms Hotel, which was also the post office for Bruff, daily at 5.30 p.m. Those from Charleville to Limerick left at 7.30 a.m. Normally any prisoners being transferred to the county gaol at Limerick would travel by this means, escorted by constables.

3

Trial of a Whiteboy

Stephen Howard and his police escort arrived at Limerick on 16 December 1842. Upon arrival they proceeded down Military Road to George Street, through the rows of dignified Georgian houses that accommodated many of the nobility, clergy and gentry of the day. Then, nearing the heart of the city, they turned right into William Street, stopped briefly at the police headquarters, and continued on to upper William Street until they reached Mulgrave Street, proceeding past the artillery barracks on the right to the forbidding gates of the county prison.

Immediately Stephen was taken charge of by a turnkey who took him to the reception room, where he had his hair cut and was told to wash himself thoroughly. His private clothing was taken from him and he was issued with a plain-coloured cap, jacket, shirt, waistcoat, trousers and shoes. He was given his classification and, as he was neither a debtor nor a misdemeanant, he was declared an untried felon. He was next shown to his cell, which was furnished with an iron bedstead, a mattress, three single blankets and a bag for extra clothing.[1]

The prison routine, which revolved around bells, would have been explained to him as follows. A bell was rung at dawn each day, or 6 a.m. in the summer, upon which the turnkeys open the cells and every prisoner must rise, dress, wash and comb himself. He must fold his bedding, sweep his cell and open the windows. Half an hour after the first bell, the turnkeys inspect the cells, form the prisoners into ranks and march them to their dayrooms and yards, where they are carefully inspected before being paraded before the governor. Certain prisoners are selected from each class to perform the office of wardsman, whose duty it is to sweep and wash the corridors, staircases and galleries of their class. They are also, under the direction of the turnkeys, to see that the night cells and bedding are properly cleaned and arranged before they are left by the prisoners each morning. It was also the duty of the wardsmen to assist any new prisoners; no mean task when confronted by a bewildered peasant undergoing his first experience of gaol. At seven o'clock a bell rang for work and school. Those who were classified F, or misdemeanants, attended school for two hours, while the prisoners who marched to work went to the tailor's shop, the carpenter's or the shoe-maker's, depending on their skills. Others were employed weaving, stone-breaking, forge and nail-making, flax-dressing, sweeping or picking oakum.[2]

The principles underlying the British penal system also applied in the Limerick county prison. Upon their arrival, all male prisoners were put into six different classes. These were: master debtors; poor debtors, and persons for contempt of court or civil process; felons convicted; felons untried; misdemeanants convicted; and misdemeanants untried, along with persons confined for want of sureties. Female prisoners were graded first class and second class.

The master debtors, who represented the wealthier class of prisoners, provided their own food and necessaries and were placed in a separate part of the prison, where they had private rooms, each with a fireplace. They were not allowed to bring their wives, or any other person, to sleep on the premises, and they were not permitted to bring a servant into the prison during the daytime. They were allowed to work or employ themselves on their own account, at the discretion of the prison authorities. They were expected to keep their rooms tidy and required to attend Divine Service every Sunday. No smoking, gambling, swearing or indecent language was permitted in their quarters. They were permitted to procure for themselves, at stipulated times, food, beer, wine, bedding and other furniture or goods, but under no circumstances were they permitted to use spirituous liquors, more than one pint of wine or a quart of malt liquor or cider in any one day. They did not work with the poorer classes of prisoners, and as they were already educated they did not attend school. The master debtors were required to be punished the same way as anybody else for any offences committed in the prison.[3]

The matron classified the female prisoners according to their conduct, character and degree of criminality rather than the offences they had committed. The first-class females had the best clothing and did lighter and more profitable work. The second class, which usually consisted of vagrant women of immoral character or those who had children in the gaol, were given inferior clothing and worked as laundresses or at other laborious tasks. A special room was kept for the use of chaplains, who gave religious instruction, or for the use of the Ladies' Committee.[4]

At nine o'clock, a fourth bell rang for breakfast, and half an hour later the fifth bell rang for work and school. At the sixth bell, prisoners were to air themselves in the yards until three o'clock, when the seventh bell summoned them for dinner. At half past three the eighth bell went again for work and school, and at six o'clock the ninth and last bell for the day rang to lock up the cells. From 1 March to 1 October this routine was varied and the cells were locked at eight o'clock.

The chief purpose of the schools was to teach poor prisoners how to read and write. Books were provided and the schools were under the immediate superintendence of the chaplains. The schoolmaster was highly qualified, and much good was considered to have come from his work, as the literacy of young prisoners improved greatly. Since Stephen Howard was an untried felon, his class was held between 3 and 5 p.m.[5]

In 1843 the governor was Henry Woodburne; the Catholic chaplain was the Rev. William Burke, a curate attached to St John's Chapel, Limerick; the physician was David O'Callaghan, MD; and the surgeon was James T. Wilkinson, MRIA. The annual report of the inspectors-general of prisons for 1844 observed:

> There is no local inspection in this establishment, and no inconvenience arises from it, as the Governor, Mr Woodburne, is highly qualified, zealous, and intelligent, and justly possesses the full confidence of the Grand Jury and Board, whose support has enabled him to bring this gaol into its present high state of discipline and order. The Chaplains attend to their various duties with regularity and attention, and should be paid larger salaries, if required to attend the separate classes daily. There are ten turnkeys, five of whom are tradesmen, which system works well. The Governor reports some of them to me as good officers; but much difficulty arises in obtaining such sub officers, highly qualified, without a system of training in each gaol, and a certainty of the best succeeding on vacancies . . . The hospital as reported by Dr White last year, is a very inferior one, not easy of access, and not separated from other buildings; the accommodation is small and has no proper airing yards for convalescents. However, Dr O'Callaghan and the surgeon state the general health of the prison to be good, and their zealous attention to the care of the patients, and the economy exercised by purchasing the medicines wholesale and mixing them in the surgery, is very creditable to the Medical officers.[6]

The prisoners only had two meals a day: breakfast at 9 a.m. and dinner at 3 p.m. The diet of the Limerick county gaol was 8 ounces of Indian meal stirabout and a pint of new milk for breakfast, while dinner consisted of a pound of household bread and a pint of sour milk.[7] It would be interesting to compare this economical prison diet, which cost only 2½d. per day, with the normal diet of Stephen Howard and his fellow farm labourers. One suspects that the prison food was more regular and had greater bulk, though it could also have been more monotonous, due to the total absence of meat and fish. The prisoners received their meals on trays in their dayroom, and the trays and utensils of each class were clearly marked.[8]

The prisoners' spiritual and physical welfare were well attended to. Regulations stipulated that all new prisoners had to be inspected by the physician, and Stephen Howard must almost certainly have had the first medical examination in his life when he entered the county prison. The physician was required to visit the prison at least twice each week, to see every sick person, and to inspect both the state of the hospital and the state of the health of any prisoners who were in it. The physician or surgeon was also required to keep a close watch on the mental as well as the physical health of each prisoner. If he thought a man's health was impaired by the prison routine, he was required to report it to the governor.[9]

The nineteenth century was favourable to religion, and the chaplains held great sway within the prisons. They held Mass or Divine Service every Sunday, visited the gaol on two other days of the week and inspected the provisions served to the prisoners every alternate week. They had to attend all condemned prisoners, previous to and at the time of execution, and were required to inspect the schools regularly to see that the school registry was kept. No Roman Catholic prisoner was obliged to attend Protestant services, under any circumstances, unless the approval of the Catholic Chaplain was first obtained. Sufficient Bibles, both Protestant (King James) and Catholic (Douay), were to be supplied for any prisoners who wished to use them. Attendance at chapel on Sundays was compulsory for all prisoners, including the master debtors.[10]

Limerick county gaol was built in 1821 and is still in use as a maximum security prison. In 1843 it was seen as something of a model institution. The female section consisted of a small autonomous wing on the left-hand side of the main gate that sloped towards the main prison at an angle of 45 degrees. Female accommodation was later increased by the addition of a central section, which had the main gate running through the middle, and another flanking wing which also sloped back to the main prison at 45 degrees. The male accommodation consisted of a circular central block containing the governor's house, boardroom and chapel. Around this central block was a large yard bordered by a decagonal, or ten-sided, fence. On every second side of the decagon five large rectangular blocks jutted out like the spoke in a cart wheel. These blocks contained a total of 131 cells, 17 of them heated and prepared for isolation, 5 solitary cells with fireplaces and yards, dayrooms, 9 yards and 4 workrooms, along with a treadwheel, hospital, chapel, kitchen and laundry. At the time of the inspector-general's visit for his report in 1843/44, there were 123 prisoners confined—10 debtors, 90 male criminals and 23 female criminals. The average number for the year was 125 per day.[11]

It could well be argued that most prisoners of peasant origin were better off in gaol than out of it. They had regular medical attention, chaplains were on hand to minister to their spiritual needs and they had regular food, work and lodging with a suit of clothes thrown in for good measure. But unfortunately, this was hardly true. To be brought into a city, probably for the first time in one's life, and shut behind thick walls and iron bars for twenty-four hours a day, under the complete control of the turnkeys in a closely regimented system totally alien to the prisoners' previous lifestyle, could only bring about bewilderment, resentment and terror. Such problems were greatly aggravated by the fact that so many peasants, including Stephen Howard, were illiterate and therefore lacking the means of extended communication enjoyed by literate people.

Limerick City in the 1840s was well summed up by *Slater's Directory*:

This ancient city, eligibly and delightfully situated on the banks of the noble Shannon, is supposed to have been founded by Yuorus, in the year 155, while by some writers, it is said to have been the *Regia* of Ptolemy . . . Saint Patrick is said to have visited it about the middle of the fifth century; but the first authentic records of Limerick notice it as a Danish settlement; by that people it was first plundered in 812 . . . The English took possession of Limerick in the year 1174; and, as a proof of the early importance of the city, in the year 1197, and in the nineth year of the reign of King Richard, he granted a charter to the citizens to elect a mayor, which honour was not obtained by the citizens of London till ten years after that period; nor had Dublin and Cork a mayor till the 13th century . . . This city is now composed of three parts, named Irish Town, English Town (the latter situated on the island formed by the river Shannon), and Newtown-Pery which latter may with propriety be termed the court end, as in this quarter of the town the streets are spacious, uniform and elegant . . . The County Gaol is generally considered to be one of the most complete prisons in Ireland.[12]

The name Limerick very likely comes from Loimeanach, meaning bare marsh.[13] In 1841 the city had an overall population of 57,755, of whom 48,391 were inhabitants of the inner city. Limerick had several excellent public buildings, among them the Customs House, completed in 1769, and large elegant commercial buildings also in Rutland Street; the Chamber of Commerce in George Street, which was the nerve centre of business; the courthouse, built in 1808–10 and described as a noble spacious building; and the Exchange in Nicholas Street, which was a handsome building with a fine council chamber, where people settled their debts. St Mary's Church of Ireland Cathedral in Bridge Street is said to have been built in 1172. The Limerick Institution, founded in 1809 for the promotion of literature and science, had a library of 4,000 volumes. The city also included barracks for cavalry, artillery and infantry, and the police headquarters for Limerick County. It was a large lace manufacturing centre and had a busy port which turned around nearly a thousand vessels a year. It also had two weekly newspapers, the Protestant *Limerick Chronicle* and the Catholic *Limerick Reporter*.[14]

Despite an apparently quiet surface, Limerick was simmering politically. On Wednesday, 7 October 1840, Daniel O'Connell, known throughout Ireland as 'The Liberator', held one of what were known as his 'monster meetings'. A vast multitude from all over the county came to hear him speak on the repeal of the Union of the two parliaments. They came both rich and poor, in carriages or donkey carts, and they were not disappointed. O'Connell was a great orator, and when he came to Limerick he was at his best. On arrival at the city outskirts he was met by a large procession of twenty-three guilds, representing all the trades and categories of labourers in Limerick, who marched five deep, dressed in sashes and carrying wands or banners. They were led by a man called Lucas, who was president of the congregated trades, and the *Limerick Reporter* noted that: 'A large boat, moved along by men, elegantly decorated with flags, colours etc., and in the stern a beautiful Festooned canopy, under which sat one of the Strand fishermen, representing Neptune, formed an object of much notice, and contributed to enhance the grandeur of the procession'.[15]

O'Connell, who was driving in a carriage and four, passed through streets thronged with cheering crowds until he reached the Treaty Stone, on the Clare side of Thomond Bridge. According to tradition, the Treaty of Limerick, which brought to an end two years of warfare in Ireland, was signed on the stone in 1691. The terms of the treaty were dishonoured and an era of bitter persecution of the Catholic Irish followed. Because of this, Limerick became known as 'the city of the violated treaty'.[16]

When O'Connell reached the Treaty stone, Mr Lucas read out 'the address of the congregated trades of Limerick', after which O'Connell stood up on the seat of his carriage and it was reported that:

He received that admirable address with more pride and pleasure than he could possibly announce at present.—It was not his intention to reply to it here, as he meant to do so from the window at Cruise's Hotel. He only came to receive it here, that it might be presented to him in the presence of that stone that attested Ireland's fidelity, and England's treachery (Loud cheering).[17]

Mr Thomas Steele, whom O'Connell had elected as Head Pacificator, then gave an address in which he attacked leading British politicians and called for repeal of the Union, which was to be done by constitutional means, preserving the allegiance to the British Crown.

O'Connell then drove back to Cruise's Royal Hotel, where he stood up in the dicky-seat of his carriage once more and addressed a crowd estimated at between 80,000 and 100,000 people. He began by reminding them of the violated treaty of 1691 and the terrible persecutions and suffering inflicted upon Ireland as a result. Next, he dealt with the Union of the two parliaments, describing how it had been brought about by bribery, and how this alone had cost the country a great deal of money. O'Connell then described the terrible impact the Union had upon Irish industry and concluded his speech by telling the multitude that:

> By sobriety and union, they would carry the Union. By and by the Orangeman that would see it his interest to join them would do so. The concentration of public opinion carried Emancipation, and by it they would in like manner carry repeal (hear, hear.) . . . Mr O'Connell then referred his auditory to some noble traits in the Irish character; of their faithful attachment and defence of their religion, despite every persecution, by which they preserved their admitted morality; their warm acceptance of the pledge of perpetual abstinence, and their calm and patient conduct under persecution and wrong. (hear)[18]

After he had finished his speech, O'Connell left his carriage and retired into the hotel. The people cheered themselves hoarse, and then began to disperse back to the county towns whence they had come. The parishes of Adare, Bruff and Croom were strongly represented, and perhaps Stephen Howard and his crippled father Patrick, riding in their little donkey cart, were numbered among those present.

But O'Connell's power was failing and in 1844, at the age of sixty-nine, he was convicted on a charge of conspiracy against the government by intimidation and demonstrations of great physical force. The conviction was only made possible by a packed jury, but O'Connell, his confidence already shaken by having to call off the greatest monster meeting of all time, at Clontarf, because of Peel's sudden proclamation against it, declined in health. He died in 1847, aged seventy-two. William Smith O'Brien, the member for Limerick who had formerly been a Conservative, threw in his lot with John Mitchell and Charles Gavin Duffy's Young Ireland movement. In Limerick, they were well represented by John M'Clenahan, the editor of the newly established *Limerick Leader* and generally recognised as being 'the ablest of the provincial journalists'. It was within this setting of growing turbulence that the three Whiteboys charged with robbing Patrick Hogan awaited their fate.

When they faced their trial, Howard and Noonan had been held in custody for almost three months, Burns for closer to eight. To travel to the courthouse, the accused were taken down Mulgrave Street to William Street, then turned right at George Street, past Cruise's Royal Hotel in Patrick Street and the Customs House in Rutland Street, until they came to the New Bridge over the Abbey River. The New Bridge had three arches, of which the central one was so much higher than the others that, particularly in frosty weather, passengers often had to get out and push their cart or coach over the steep incline. At the centre of the middle arch were two iron lampposts, facing each other, that had been extensively used by the authorities for hanging rebels during the rebellion of 1798.[19] As it was early in March, it is likely that Stephen, Timothy Noonan and William Burns had to get out and push the carriage that was taking them to the courthouse. The lampposts and the evil legends by then associated with them could only have struck fear into their hearts.

By comparison, the judges' entry into Limerick for the Lenten Assizes was grand to say the least. Judges Nicholas Ball and Joseph Jackson were expected from Ennis, the principal city of County Clare, at 3 p.m. on 2 March, but they were delayed. Judge Ball was the first to arrive, and he was met five miles from the town by the city high sheriff and the under-sheriff, each dressed in brilliant livery. They drove straight to the courthouse in Merchant's Quay, on the banks of the Shannon, where they were met by the Right Worshipful Lord Mayor, in robes of office, attended by the sergeants at mace and bailiffs of the corporation, with their maces and staffs. Ball was conducted to the bench by the mayor, who then sat to the right of the learned judge. Sometime after 7 p.m. the commission was read by William Roche, Clerk of the Crown, and the grand jury was sworn in. Judge Ball then addressed the assemblage in the courtroom, apologising for the late hour of his arrival and noting that his brother judge, Mr Justice Jackson, had also been delayed and would not arrive until a later hour. He then adjourned the assizes till 11 a.m. the next day.

By modern standards, the ceremony was an extraordinary one. The city officials had just been equipped with new livery and were determined to make the most of the occasion:

> The equipage and livery of the City High Sheriff have attracted general notice and admiration. The carriage is completely new, and of the most costly description, drawn by four blood bays, with postillions and outriders. Eight javelin men, dressed in brown and red livery, preceded the carriage to and from court. The reform in this instance is as apparent as it is creditable and excellent.
>
> The Corporation too have provided new and rich suits of livery for their Sergeants-at-Mace, Bailiffs, and Beadles—Indeed, so admirable a 'turn out' could not be seen as that which the City of Limerick exhibits at this moment in Honour of 'the Majesty of the law'.
>
> The County High Sheriff has provided javelin men, dressed in red livery, who occupy the passages to the court.[20]

Whenever the judges were on circuit in Limerick, they stayed at Cruise's Royal Hotel. Built in 1791, the hotel had four owners before it was taken over by the famous hotelier Edward Cruise, who was a personal friend of the Liberator Daniel

O'Connell, who also stayed there several times. It is still one of Limerick's leading hotels.

The two judges on the circuit for the Limerick Lenten assizes were very different in their backgrounds, and as such constituted an interesting comment on mid-nineteenth century Ireland. The senior judge, Nicholas Ball, was born at Galway in 1791 and attended Stoneyhurst Jesuit College in England. He graduated BA at Trinity College in 1812, entered Lincoln's Inn the same year and was called to the Irish Bar in 1814. He practised in equity, was a Roman Catholic by religion, and an emancipist in politics. He became a KC in 1830, was returned as member for Clonmel in the Liberal interest in 1836, became third sergeant at law and attorney-general in 1838, and was appointed a justice of the common pleas in 1839. During the Lenten Assizes he was to be mostly involved with city and civil matters, leaving the county and criminal concerns to Judge Jackson.[21]

Joseph Devonsher Jackson, who tried Stephen Howard, was a vastly different and more controversial man. Born at Petersborough, near Cork, of an old English family in 1783, he graduated BA at Trinity College in 1806, after being funded by Mr Hincks, a leading scholar of the period. He acquired his MA in 1832. Called to the Bar in 1806, Jackson was made a KC in 1827, assistant barrister of Londonderry in 1835, second sergeant and bencher of the Honorable Society of King's Inn Dublin at Easter 1835, solicitor-general in 1842, and a justice of the court of common pleas in 1843. But it was as a politician and a churchman that Jackson was so controversial.

Elected the Tory member for Bandon, County Cork, in 1835, 1837 and 1841, Jackson was always seen to be on the extreme right in Irish politics. Bandon was then considered to be a Protestant stronghold, and is said to have had this inscription on its entrance:

Turk, Jew, or Atheist,
May enter here, but not a Papist[22]

—which was noticed by the celebrated priest, the Rev. Arthur O'Leary, who added pungently:

Who wrote these lines he wrote them well,
For the same are written on the gate of Hell.[23]

Jackson was derided by Daniel O'Connell as a man with 'leathern lungs' because of his long addresses to the jury and his marathon speeches in the House of Commons. In 1837 he made a strong speech in the Commons, during which he opposed the granting of aid to Maynooth Seminary because its graduates were surpliced ruffians of peasant origin who preached murder and mayhem from the pulpit. D. O. Madden recorded that:

For nearly four hours he kept the House of Commons not only awake but amazed at all the tales he told of Protestant lives recklessly taken—of Protestant property destroyed—policemen massacred—magistrates assaulted—attacks—assassinations whose authors were undiscovered through the carelessness, and agitations whose directors were rewarded through the servility of the Irish Government.[24]

Rathcannon House (*Author's collection*)

The bridewall of Bruff (*Author's collection*)

Granagh, looking towards the sacred hill of Knockfierna (*Author's collection*)

Bothan scoir (labourer's cottage)

Golden Vale house (*Author's collection*)

Judge Joseph Devonsher Jackson (*Ryall's Portraits of Modern Conservatives*)

Christopher Copinger (*Courtesy of Lieutenant-Colonel W. M. C. Wall*)

George's Street, Limerick (*National Library of Ireland, Lawrence Collection No. R5286*)

Limerick county prison (*Author's collection*)

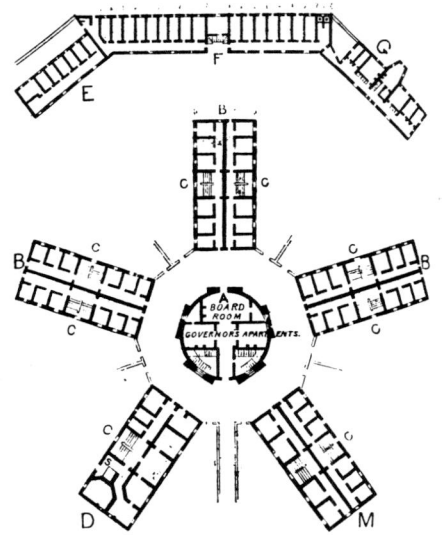

Ground plan of Limerick prison
(*Author's collection*)

The Honourable John Plunkett (*Courtesy
of Lord Plunkett*)

Limerick courthouse (*Author's collection*)

Kilmainham prison (*National Library of Ireland, Lawrence Collection No. R3118*)

Gateway to Kilmainham prison
(*Author's Collection*)

Earl De Grey (*Ryall's Portraits of Modern Conservatives*)

As a churchman, Jackson was a prominent member of the established church, known today as the Church of Ireland, and was described as a prominent Biblical and a zealous propagandist of Scriptural Toryism. For many years he had been secretary of the Kildare Place Society, a government-subsidised organisation for the education of children by Scriptural reading. Although this society at first enjoyed great support, it was soon alleged that many of its members, who were Protestants, were using it for the purpose of proselytising Catholic children. As a result it came to be regarded with odium by Roman Catholics.[25] Jackson was a vice-president of the Royal Dublin Society, dedicated to improving agriculture and other useful arts, and a founding member and master of the rolls of Trinity College Historical Society.

Throughout his career Jackson caused so much controversy that Queen Victoria questioned his appointment as solicitor-general, as she thought he 'belonged to the very violent Orange party in Ireland'. Because of Peel's support for his appointment the Queen withdrew her objections.[26] The powerful Liberal and Catholic elements in the Irish press strongly opposed Jackson's appointment to the court of common pleas on the grounds he was too partisan in his political leanings to be impartial.[27] Now on his first circuit as judge—he had only been appointed the previous autumn—this was the man Stephen Howard and his fellow prisoners had to face in a mid-nineteenth century Irish court of law.

After arriving at the courthouse, the prisoners were taken down to the cells beneath it. Entry into the courtrooms was by a spiral staircase which took the prisoners up into the heart of the courtrooms. The Limerick courthouse was a long, oblong, two-storied building, with two courtrooms on the ground floor and an administrative section above them. The portico was imposing enough by modern standards, being supported by four columns, but it was not comparable with courthouses in the larger towns, such as Cork, whose courthouse had a magnificent domed roof and a huge portico supported by ten columns. Justice was a serious business in nineteenth century Ireland, and the trappings were elaborate to say the least. The courtrooms were well furnished, the walls behind the judges' benches were padded and coloured a deep red, the chairs on which they sat were suitably inscribed with the Victorian Coat of Arms and a large red canopy hung over their heads.

The witness boxes and the witness benches were to the judges' right, the jury benches were on their left, and the prosecution, the accused and his defence sat directly in front. The public galleries were painted light green and their ceilings were an intricate pattern of dark panelled wood.

Whenever the judges went on circuit in nineteenth-century Ireland, a group of senior barristers accompanied them. Most of these were assistant barristers, or county judges, who began their own quarter sessions soon after the assizes circuit was over. Every circuit had its full-time Crown prosecuter, and on the Munster circuit this office was held by George Bennett, QC, who was also the father of the Bar. His assistant was the Hon. John Plunket, QC, son of William Conyngham Plunket, a former lord chancellor and one of Ireland's greatest orators. A big civil case, *Water Bailiff* v. *The Bridge Commissioners* was fought in the city court at the same time Howard and Noonan were tried. George Bennett led the defence in this case, and it therefore seems likely that Plunket was the prosecutor of Howard and Noonan.

In nineteenth-century Ireland, a system of dock briefs existed for prisoners charged with serious crimes. Quite simply, a circuit barrister was assigned to defend the prisoners at assize level. The defence for Stephen Howard was Christopher Copinger, a thirty-eight-year-old barrister who came from a Cork family of great antiquity. He graduated from Trinity College with a BA in 1826, became a barrister at King's Inn in 1829, received his MA in 1832 and was appointed assistant barrister for County Kildare in November 1842.[28] He was the brother-in-law of the Rev. Bartholomew Woodlock, DD, a professor at All Hallows College, Dublin, who was later appointed Roman Catholic Bishop of Ardagh. Nevertheless, in March 1843, Christopher Copinger was under a cloud. Just before his appointment as assistant barrister he had, in company with three other barristers, presided as a revising barrister at the Belfast municipal revision. During the revision some extraordinary decisions had been made, which tended to favour the Tories at the expense of the Liberals. To make things worse, Copinger had voted for the Orange candidates for the City of Dublin during the general election. Despite all this he was generally highly regarded and was probably the best man available to defend prisoners such as Stephen Howard and Timothy Noonan. At his death in 1864, the *Kerry Evening Post* recorded:

> Mr Copinger was a British Roman Catholic—that is to say, an honest supporter of the Constitution under which we live, and was often treated as the type of that patriotic, and we trust, increasing class . . . As a barrister he was able and zealous in the discharge of his duty towards his clients; and his rough and ready eloquence and evident earnestness of purpose were often more effective with juries than the polished periods of more ambitious orators. While presiding at Quarter Sessions he was careful and impartial—the most prominent trait in his character being a stern hatred of oppression or injustice.[29]

Prison regulations allowed legal advisers to be admitted at a certain time in each day, and Copinger would probably have interviewed Stephen Howard and Timothy Noonan soon after his arrival in Limerick. He may well have sympathised with their feelings, but if so he would still have abhorred their methods. A relative of his, Stephen Copinger, was a close associate of O'Connell's and had been heavily involved in the Catholic Emancipation campaign. Christopher Copinger obviously believed in non-violence and in working within the constitution.

The prosecutor, John Plunket, came from a vastly different background. He had graduated from Trinity College with his BA in 1814, and was called to the Irish Bar in 1817, achieved an MA in 1832 and was made assistant barrister for County Meath in 1826.[30] In 1843 he was fifty years of age, but he still walked very much in the shadows of both his great father and his brother, who was shortly to become Protestant Bishop of Tuam, Killala and Achonry. An honest, earnest barrister who was noted for his skill and care in drawing up indictments, his portrait reveals a rather dyspeptic-looking individual.

At 12.30 p.m. on Tuesday, 7 March, the court went into the Crown business and Burns, Howard and Noonan waited their turn in the dock. The first case involved a man named Andrew Lyons who was indicted for bigamy, found guilty and sentenced to seven years transportation. The next defendant, Patrick McCarthy, was indicted for stealing a pig and found guilty, with a recommendation for mercy on the grounds he suffered periodically from mental derangement. A third defendant, William Hickman, charged with feloniously entering a dwelling house for the purpose of robbing it, had been caught in the attempt and had been seriously wounded in the thigh. Judge Jackson gave him a severe lecture and let him off with six months confinement.

It was now the turn of Stephen Howard and his partners in crime, Noonan and Burns. Judge Jackson had spent the weekend at Tervoe House, the beautiful county seat of Mr William Monsell, the future Lord Emly, who was to enjoy a distinguished political career and became a leading Catholic activist. Nonetheless, the judge could only have regarded the trio with concern. The good judge, who lived at 27 Lower Leeson Street, Dublin, owned 180 acres in the townland of Tullovin, which adjoined the townland of Ballintaw, where Patrick Howard lived, and was only three miles away from Patrick Hogan's house at Rathcannon. Nor could much sympathy be expected from the jurymen, three of whom came from the Croom–Ballingarry area. These were Captain John Shelton of Rossmore House, Ballingarry; W. H. de Massy of Glanwilliam, Ballingarry; and John M. Cantillon of Menister House, Croom. To the men in the dock, Judge Jackson must have been an imposing figure. Some years earlier, it had been noted that:

Mr Sergeant Jackson rejoices in a tolerably commanding figure. He is tall and well formed. His countenance has nothing very intellectual about it: but it is sufficiently pleasing. It is of an angular form: his nose is large and prominent, and his forehead is, also, ample. His complexion is fair, and his hair white as snow—not, perhaps in its unsunned state, but after it has been on the ground for some time.[31]

Once Jackson had read the charges, Howard and Noonan pleaded not guilty, while Burns pleaded guilty. The offence was contrary to 9 George IV Cap. 55 section XII which stated:

And be it enacted, That if any Person shall break and enter any Dwelling House, and steal therein any Chattel, Money, or valuable Security to any Value whatever, or shall steal any such Property to any Value whatever in any Dwelling House, any Person therein being put in fear, or shall steal in any Dwelling House any Chattel, Money, or valuable Security to the Value in the whole of Five Pounds or more, every such Offender, being convicted thereof, shall in any of such Cases suffer Death as a Felon.

The following is the account of the trial as given by the *Limerick Chronicle*:

William Burns, Stephen Howard, and Timothy Nunan, were indicted for being of an armed party that burglariously entered the dwelling of Patrick Hogan, of Rathcannon, and forcibly carried away a gun, his property.

William Burns pleaded guilty to the charge.

Bridget Malone sworn—I recollect Sunday the 14th of August last; I know a man of the name of Hogan that lives at Rathcannon; I was in his house that day; Patrick Hogan went to mass; while he was out persons came to the house; it was about eleven o'clock in the day; there was no one in the house but myself, the servant girl (Ellen Nunan) and Deborah Dunworth, who was in charge of the children. When the people came to the house I was sitting in the kitchen with the other girls; the first thing they done was to push in the parlour door, and one of them snapped at a gun belonging to Hogan; which was over the chimney; five came in and one stopped at the door; another of them put a pistol to my breast and asked me to tell where the other arms were; I said I was a stranger, and the man turned to the other girl and gave her a blow of the pistol in the chest (witness identified the prisoner Nunan, as the person); the man who took the gun (not in custody) handed it to Burns; I heard Burns say that if any of them damaged or wrecked the house he would report them himself; when the other girl said she did not know where the arms were Howard said he would not believe her oath—(identified Howard); two men went upstairs; Nunan is one of them; the other man is not here; they remained in the house three quarters of an hour; they were not disguised; the kitchen was light some; I told Howard that if they done the girl any harm I would tell who they were, for I knew them; I said the master was only gone down to the end of the farm, and if they didn't go away with what they had it would be worse for them; they then came down, and on going away took a gun with them belonging to Hogan, and two other things I did not know the name of; they were hanging up over the fireplace; I followed them out, and when they saw me, one of them turned back; and presented a pistol at me, I ran in, but in a short time after I went out a second time and followed them; I was joined by Pat Hogan's nephew, (Paddy Ryan), and pursued them four miles; they went towards the Tower Castle of Bruree; two of them went in the direction of Harding grove; while pursuing them, I was one time in the same field with them, and kept in view of them until the people came out from Athlacca chapel; I told the congregation about it, and several went in pursuit of them; Hogan was one of the congregation; I remained behind when the people went after them; I saw the prisoner Howard first in the bridewell of Bruff; I saw Burns the next day; I never saw any of the prisoners before.

Cross-examined by Mr Copinger—I am from Bruree, about a mile from Hogan's; I lived in Galbally, with my uncle which is 14 miles from Hogan's it was to see my sister who was in service in Hogan's that I went in there; I lived under the care of the police since the prisoners were arrested, and very good company they were (laughter); it was in Head Constable Murray's house I stopped. (The witness was examined at some length with a view of shaking her direct testimony, but it was impossible to do so, as a better witness seldom appeared for the crown in a court of justice.)

Ellen Nunan sworn—I was in the service of Patk. Hogan on the 14th of August; Hogan was at the chapel that day. (Witness then went on to detail the circumstances as related by the first witness.)

Deborah Dunworth also deposed to the above facts.

Constable Sheehan swore that he frequently searched for the prisoners, and on the 19th of Dec. arrested Howard at a farmer's house convenient to his own house; he asked him if he knew what he was taken for, and he replied 'it was for Hogan's business'; searched frequently for Nunan, but could not find him.

Head-Constable Ward examined—I arrested the prisoner, Nunan, in Charleville on the 15th of Jan. last, in a farmer's house at night.

Henry Hardinge, Esq. sworn—Burns surrendered himself to me, and gave me up a gun, which it is supposed was taken from Hogan's; I was not at home when he first went to my house, and my sister being afraid to leave him there, sent him into the orchard, where I saw him; he told me he dropped the gun in his flight, and knew where it was; he brought me to a dyke, and found the gun; the gun was identified by witness as the one he had got from Burns.

Patrick Hogan, (whose house had been attacked) having been called to the table identified the gun surrendered to Mr Hardinge.

The case for the prosecution here closed, and Mr Copinger having addressed the jury for the prisoners the following witnesses were examined on their behalf.

Mr James Lynch sworn—I know Stephen Howard for the last six or seven years, and consider him a man of very good character; I recollect seeing him on the day the outrage was committed at Rathcannon; I met him between twelve or one o'clock, and he was dressed in his Sunday clothes; I mentioned to him by way of news what I had heard myself about the attack at Rathcannon; he did not evince the least surprise or emotion, and he would be the last person I would suspect for being concerned in so disgraceful an outrage; Rathcannon is four miles from my house, and the prisoner lives on my ground, in fact he has been uninterruptedly in my service for the last few years, and always under my eye.

Denis Callaghan proved being at Nunan's house on the 14th of August; I was with him about 8 or 9 o'clock, and remained until after two; he was unwell in bed, and I left him in bed after me.

Mr John Mason sworn—I know Timothy Nunan since he was a boy; his general behaviour is good; he was a ploughman of mine, and exceedingly attentive to his business.

Mr John Lynch sworn—I know Nunan for 20 years; I had many opportunities of forming an opinion of his character; he is a good son and a good brother; exceedingly quiet, and from his peaceable disposition I would not think him inclined to possess himself of firearms; he worked for a long time under my father, and for the last two years under myself as a labourer.

Michael Blake, deposed, that on the Sunday Hogan's house was attacked, he met Howard about nine o'clock; he was dressed in his Sunday clothes, and they remained together until they went to Mass to the chapel of Granagh; in twenty minutes after parting Howard, when mass was over, witness heard of the attack on Hogan's house.

The case here closed, and the Learned Judge proceeded to charge the jury, recapitulating, minutely, the evidence given on both sides. At nine o'clock the jury retired, returning to court, in five minutes, with a verdict of Guilty.

His Lordship sentenced both to be transported for ten years.

The Court then adjourned.[32]

While the *Limerick Chronicle* gives the more complete account of the trial, only the *Limerick Reporter* mentions the men as being armed with a wattle, a pitchfork and a pistol. Also in the *Reporter*, Michael Blake's evidence is reported differently in that he said he went to Mass with Howard and he was in his company from 9 a.m. until after 2 p.m. Finally, the *Reporter* said the case did not terminate until after 7 p.m., when His Lordship delivered his charge. It seems, then, that Jackson must have been in excellent form, as he spent nearly two hours addressing the jury. The jury, on the other hand, only took five minutes to reach a verdict of guilty.

Despite this, the case is not without its questionable aspects as, despite the testimony of the three servant girls, James Lynch testified he met Stephen Howard between twelve and one o'clock and Michael Blake testified as being in his company from 9 a.m. till 2 p.m., while Dennis Callaghan testified to Noonan being unwell and also to being in Noonan's company from eight or nine o'clock until after two. Further to this, Lynch's former property at Granagh is seven and a half miles away from Rathcannon, not four miles as stated by Lynch in his evidence. Unfortunately, however, no court records survive and the newspaper accounts may not be accurate.

After the jury reached its verdict, Judge Jackson sentenced Howard and Noonan to ten years transportation and Burns to seven months imprisonment as he had pleaded guilty to the charge. Amidst the inevitable shrieks and wailings from the female relatives that usually followed the announcement of death sentences or long transportation terms, the prisoners filed back down the spiral staircase and were returned to Limerick county prison.

Just ten weeks later, on 21 July, Patrick Hogan was again in court in an almost identical case. A shoemaker in his service named Richard Cooper had been robbed of a pair of pistols by a man called John Hartigan. Hogan, as an independent witness, was able to identify the pistols as being Cooper's property. He also stated that 'he had been recently attacked by White Boys and was very wary since that'. Judge Jackson once again charged the jury and Hartigan was found guilty.

Of the other three people involved in the offence at Rathcannon, a man called Martin Dillon was committed to the Limerick Assizes at Bruff on 17 March, but there is no further record of him. The other two were never arrested.

4

Overland to Dublin

As Stephen Howard and Timothy Noonan were not sentenced till after 9 p.m., it was close to midnight when they were brought back to Limerick County Gaol. In the meantime, Judge Jackson had returned to Cruise's Royal Hotel with his register, Cardin Terry, who was also a Corkman. When Stephen and Noonan got up the next morning at dawn, they found they had moved up the prison scale, from untried felon to convicted felon. Amongst the convicted felons, they formed a special group, as they were to be transported. They carried on with their usual routine for nearly two months until Tuesday, 25 April, when all prisoners who had been sentenced to transportation were marshalled in the main yard of the prison. They were addressed by the governor, who told them they were being sent to Kilmainham prison in Dublin, and were then loaded into large police omnibuses. Their departure was described by the *Limerick Reporter*:

> Four transport convicts from the City gaol, and twenty from the County gaol, left on Tuesday morning for the convict depot, Kilmainham, escorted by a strong police force, under Sub Inspector Williams.
> The city convicts are—Timothy Callaghan, Denis Ryan, Patrick Sullivan, and Micheal Rea, seven years each. The county convicts are—Timothy Noonan, Stephen Howard, Edward Fitzgerald, T. Hanlon, James O'Brien, Patrick Brown, Denis Sheahan, 10 years each. Martin Murphy, John Collins, Andrew Lyons, Roger O'Donnell, Michael O'Donnell, Patrick Veal, Patrick Lynch, Thomas Benson, John Sullivan, Laurence McMahon, David Browne, and James Neville, 7 years each. They were accompanied by five convicts from Ennis and joined by 21 at Nenagh.[1]

The railway did not reach Limerick until 1848, and in 1843 all journeys to Dublin were made by coach. The trip took only twelve and a half hours by the mail coach that left Cruise's Royal Hotel daily at 3.45 p.m. and 7.45 a.m. The stage between Limerick and Nenagh normally took two hours thirty-three minutes, but a convoy of convicts, heavily escorted by police, would have been much slower.

The convicts finally arrived at 2 p.m. and the *Limerick reporter* made the following comment:

> At two o'clock on Tuesday, 1 female and 29 male convicts reached Nenagh from Limerick en route to Kilmainham.
>
> After refreshments they proceeded on their journey, accompanied by 21 convicts from Nenagh gaol, under an escort of one sub inspector, one head constable, and 52 police.
>
> There are still remaining in Nenagh gaol three convicts, two of them Mary Ryan and Pat Bourke who were too sick for transmission. The third is Pierry Gorman, to whom the clemency of the executive has been extended on condition: that he would marry the prosecutrix, Catherine Meagher, of Lisheiveen, near Lyttleton. The marriage was celebrated in the Nenagh gaol on Saturday.[2]

It would not be very palatable for most people to be married under such circumstances, and it can only be hoped the marriage went well. Just what time the convicts reached Dublin is not known, but they must have arrived well after that morning's mail coach, which normally reached the Hibernian Hotel in Dawson Street at about 8.15 p.m.

Kilmainham prison was in the St James area of Dublin, on Inchicore Road near where it joins the South Circular Road. The oldest buildings date from 1787 and the gaol was ready for occupation in 1792. It was enlarged due to the alarm caused by the French Revolution, and the extended prison was officially opened in August 1796. It had fifty-two cells, and they were immediately reserved for the most important political prisoners and convicts who had previously been accommodated in the hulks moored in the Liffey while they waited for convict ships to take them to Australia.[3] The new prison soon had plenty of business, as the closing years of the eighteenth century proved to be very turbulent. The Irish parliament's Anti-Insurrection Act of 1796 led to the disarming of the rebellious province of Ulster by General Lake, who then went on to quell the rebellion in Wexford and other places. His troops committed brutal excesses wherever they went, and the country's prison system was placed under great stress to accommodate the rebels while they awaited their trials. As these rebels were inevitably hanged, the stress was not prolonged. Kilmainham had held some of the most important of these prisoners, including Thomas Addis Emmet, the Sheares brothers, and later Napper Tandy, Robert Emmet, General Corbet, and for a short time Lord Edward Fitzgerald— a leader of the United Irishmen who spent a few hours within its walls, disguised as a prisoner. It held less celebrated prisoners in the nineteenth century before the Young Irelanders were imprisoned there in 1848, but its gatekeeper and executioner still did brisk business.[4]

As seen from the air, Kilmainham gaol is a long oblong-shaped building, rounded at the eastern end and resembling a blunt-nosed bullet projecting from its cartridge case. Over its gate there is a metal frieze in which the five demons of crime, represented by reptilian creatures with demoniacal heads, are restrained by the chains of law and justice. A plan of the gaol in 1796 shows a rather different prison, oblong and divided into two almost equal sections, with the one on the right being slightly larger,[5] and the Ordnance map of Dublin in 1848 shows it to be the same size and shape. However, the annual report from the inspectors-general of prisons in 1844 had complained strongly about the gaol's limited accommodation, which made it very difficult 'to carry on a sound system of discipline, by minute classification, employment of every prisoner, and moral government in all its details'.[6]

The report noted the situation would soon be relieved, as Smithfield penitentiary was being fitted out to take the male convicts awaiting transportation, thus relieving Kilmainham of a burden it had carried for many years. The report also noted that thirty cells were being added to the female section, while it was hoped to add thirty large new cells to the male side in the not too distant future. The Kilmainham prison population in 1844 totalled 154, of whom 85 were male criminals, 39 were female criminals, 8 debtors, and 22 convicts. The distinction between county criminals and government convicts is quite clear in the report, which also points out that while there were four classes for the male prisoners, limited accommodation allowed for only two classes for the female prisoners.

The four male classes referred to would have been debtors, untried felons, convicted felons and convicts. While the convicts were mainly housed in the yard on the left-hand side of the main gate, one of the other yards was very likely utilised as well. In his 1844 report, the inspector-general, Major James Palmer, reported the prison as having 68 cells, with no solitary cells, 7 day rooms, but no work rooms, 11 yards, 3 baths, a treadwheel, a hospital consisting of only 2 large rooms, a public kitchen, a chapel and a laundry.

The complete plans of Kilmainham as it is today show this to be rather rudimentary. When finally completed, Kilmainham had 177 cells of various sizes, ranging from 9 feet 10 inches by 5 feet 10 inches in the old section, which were approved for one man, to 13 feet 2 inches by 6 feet 9 inches in the newer section, which were approved for two men. It also had several rooms whose use was unstated, but it is assumed these could have accommodated prisoners if necessary. All the cells in the newer section had board floors, and many had vaulted ceilings. The basement contained the workshops, paint shop, coal and wood stores, refractory rooms, mortuary, kitchen and scullery, washrooms, boiler rooms and heating chambers. The central section of the ground floor contained two reception halls, a shop and stores, a visitors' room and the condemned cell. The death chamber was to the rear of the corridor on the left-hand side, immediately over the mortuary. Both wings of the ground floor had nothing apart from the cells, except some drying rooms and baths. The administration block was on the right-hand side of the entrance hall, and contained the guardroom, general office, governor's office and store. The governor's house, which was of two stories, was to the left of the entrance hall. The central section of the first floor contained the Catholic chapel at the front, two condemned cells, a governor's room and another execution chamber directly above the one on the ground floor. The turnkeys had rooms adjacent to the cells, and sleeping quarters on the first floor, next to the governor's house. The only other part of the prison worthy of notice was the Protestant chapel, which was on the central section of the second floor.[7]

The newer section of the prison—consisting of a larger remodelled east wing, additions to the female quarters of the prison on the right-hand rear section, and almost certainly the addition of the whole of the second floor—did not come until after 1844 and were probably added in degrees between then and 1864. As it was a ten-hour journey from Nenagh to Dublin by mail coach, and the prison convoy did not arrive at Nenagh until after 2 p.m., the convicts could not have arrived until after midnight unless they broke the journey at Maryborough or Kildare, stayed overnight, and proceeded on the next day. When the convicts did arrive, they may have found the atmosphere rather sombre. On 18 April, a week earlier, a convict from County Meath called Kellet, who was awaiting transportation, took straw from his bed, twisted it into a rope and hanged himself in his cell. He left a message asking for the forgiveness of God and declaring he had no-one to blame but himself.[8]

After arrival at Kilmainham, the convicts were taken to the transportation yard immediately to the left of the main gate. There they were stripped and carefully searched. As they were already wearing regulation prison clothing and their stay was to be a short one, they were not issued with the new clothes. Straw was supplied to them for bedding and they were told to whitewash their cells twice a week. With accommodation extremely short, many of them were probably lodged in dayrooms or corridors which were specially segregated and reinforced for these purposes. Kilmainham had much the same routine as Limerick county prison, as this was standard throughout the country.

The big difference was the food. In Kilmainham, the convicts received better food than the county prisoners, to prepare them for their journey to Australia. Their bread was white, rather than brown, and the same as that supplied to the prison staff. They also received better quality milk, all at the extra cost of ½d. per loaf and 1d. per gallon of milk. Breakfast consisted of 3½ ounces of oatmeal, as much Indian meal, and a pint of new milk. Dinner consisted of a pound of bread and a pint of new milk.[9] Compared with Limerick, the difference lay in the oatmeal and in the quality of the bread and milk. The chaplain regularly inspected the quality of the bread, which was weighed every day, and it was sent back if it was two ounces light. Nevertheless, there were often complaints that the bread was salty or poorly baked, and that the milk was too thin. The cost of the diet was 5½d. per day for each convict, as a gallon of milk for the convicts cost 8d. and a two-pound loaf cost 4½d.[10]

The prisoners also had a thorough medical examination before embarking on their voyage. Surgeon Roney came twice every day, in the morning and evening. A fire was lit at 6 a.m. in the convicts' dayroom, and kept burning all day. However, the prisoners were very closely supervised. Three warders by the name of John Wright, Patrick Lawler and David Jackson supervised them at their meals; the deputy governor had charge of the main gate; and a man called Nathaniel Beatty, who was a son-in-law of the governor, had charge of the hatch inside the main gate. The turnkeys had a room next to the inner hatch, with a large fire which was kept blazing all day. Nine turnkeys were allocated to the convict side, and those who were engaged in the active supervision of prisoners were relieved every second hour. Only two turnkeys, David Jackson and Patrick Lawler, slept on the premises after the debtors were locked up.

The inspector-general of prisons, Major Palmer, had been appointed in 1820. He had spent nearly twenty years as an army officer, was a committee member of the Hibernian United Service Club, and it was his boast that he had been in the service of his country for over forty years. However, in 1843 he was just emerging from the most trying period of his life. First, he had made himself the laughing stock of Dublin by being confined in his own prison for three or four weeks as a master debtor. Whilst in Kilmainham he had lived with the governor, Mr Dunne, who had special accommodation available in his own apartments for persons of respectability. On 7 September 1842 an enquiry was held into the administration of the convict side of the Kilmainham gaol, following allegations of corruption by two former deputy governors, William Harris and James O'Connor, and several anonymous sources. The complaints seemed to be aimed at Major Palmer, the former governor, Mr Dunne, who died at the end of 1841, and his successor, Mr Edward Allison, who had been Dunne's deputy for a number of years.

The allegations were of gross nepotism within the prison administration, the misuse of vehicle hire in transferring convicts back to County regions, corruption with prison contractors, improper accounting, and of not keeping a proper account book for private work done by convicts within the prison.

Major Palmer's brother-in-law, Mr Nash, was officially the administrative officer, in charge of the convict section on a salary of £60 per year plus rations. He came at 11 or 12 a.m. and remained until 2.00 p.m. The committee of enquiry had great difficulty in establishing what, if anything, Mr Nash did while in the prison. Further to this, Mr Dominick Marques, the keeper of the Richmond female penitentiary, was married to Major Palmer's sister-in-law. However, it was the relatives of Edward Allison who gave most concern. During Mr Dunne's governorship the Allison family had dominated the prison. Edward Allison was deputy governor; his eldest son, Robert, was storekeeper; another son, William, acted as clerk to the convict department until he became deputy governor of Clonmel gaol; and a son-in-law, Mr Beatty, was turnkey. As Mr Dunne was virtually illiterate, the Allison family prepared all the books and accounts, thus making their grip on the Kilmainham administration complete. The governor's salary was worth £700 per year, and there were several emoluments. The deputy governor had £200 per year, plus coals and quarters. At the same time the turnkeys were paid £1 per week, plus a two-pound loaf of bread and a quart of milk per day, two pounds of soap and candles per week, and a ton of coals each quarter. The county turnkeys were considered to be a better class of officer than the convict turnkeys, although they were not paid as much.[11]

Convicts were transferred back to the county regions by cars, whose yearly cost of £33 8s. 3d. was considered to be very heavy. Turnkeys received 5s. per day for transferring county prisoners, and 7s. 6d. per day for transferring convicts as regulated by the governor. This was regarded as a privilege and much discontent was brought about by the fact that it was a privilege Mr Dunne and Mr Allison appeared to monopolise. It was also alleged, in the matter of prison contractors, that Major Palmer and the prison administration were dealing with middlemen instead of buying food, clothing and religious books wholesale. Several contractors were questioned along these lines, without any definite evidence being found to this effect.

It was further claimed that the Treasury was charged for a full day's meals when prisoners came in late from the country, even though they may not have received any food at all. Finally, it was alleged that no proper account books were kept for private work done by convicts within the prison. It was here the committee of enquiry was on very firm ground, as accounting in the prison was either haphazard or non-existent.

The enquiry cleared Major Palmer of the grosser charges, but found many irregularities and recommended that the convict side of Kilmainham should come under the superintendence of an independent official. Although several witnesses gave evidence before the committee of enquiry, by far the most damaging came from Dr Francis White, a fellow of the Royal College of Surgeons and an inspector-general, who made seven strong allegations: the convict department was a mass of confusion, owing a good deal to the want of space; turnkeys were quite incapable of instructing their classes; Robert Allison was untrained in medicine, and was therefore unfit to attend prisoners; Mr Edward Allison was of the old school of gaolers, a rough uncouth man who was fonder of harshness, terror and locking-up as remedies than of seeking reform through kindness; Mr Harris, who was appointed a deputy gaoler, bore a very high character and was a gentleman, but could not live in the situation; there were too many of Mr Allison's family in the gaol; and, last, there was not a worse conducted gaol in Ireland.

Despite Dr White's evidence, Allison managed to survive well enough, and was spoken of quite highly in the inspector-general's report 1844 as being zealous in the discharge of his duties.

When Stephen Howard and his fellow Limerick convicts arrived in April 1843, the Kilmainham administration was on its best behaviour. The prison was about to have substantial additions made to its structure, and the administration was in a state of change as members of the Allison family were being transferred to substantial positions in other prisons. An atmosphere of tension and expectancy also existed at that time, as Major Palmer always made a visit when a convict ship was in.

In the meantime, the relatives and friends of Stephen Howard and Timothy Noonan were not idle. On 10 March 1843, a most impressive petition was put up on Noonan's behalf. The petition, which had eighteen signatories, read as follows:

To His Excellency Earl De Grey Lord Lieutenant General and Governor General of Ireland etc. etc.,
    The humble petition of Timothy Noonan of Granagh near Ballingarry in the County of Limerick, now a convict in the gaol of said county, Most Humbly Sheweth.
    That your excellency's petitioner is of an honest and respectable family no member

of which had ever before been charged even in the worst of times with disaffection, disloyalty or crime and that as to his own conduct he had never before deserved to be a prisoner nor even so much as summoned before a magistrate. That in consequence of a gun having been taken from one Patrick Hogan of Rathcannon in the month of August last year your Excellency's petitioner was tried and found guilty of the offence and sentenced to be transported for the period of ten years.

That your excellency's petitioner is the only support of his mother who is a widow and of two young sisters and that your petitioner has been for some years afflicted with that awful malady called evil [consumption?] of which his father died and which since his confinement [has] been greatly aggravated as will appear from the annexed certificate of the physician of the gaol and therefore he humbly prays that your excellency taking into consideration his youth his character hitherto unblemished and to which on his trial two gentlemen who had known him from his infancy had borne testimony, will be graciously pleased to look upon him with compassion and exercise the Royal perogative of mercy on his behalf—The neighbouring clergyman and gentleman will support his humble prayer and bear testimony to his previous character and for as much mercy in the attribute of Royalty, Petitioner humbly prays your excellency will commute his dreadful sentence to such period of imprisonment as your excellency will be pleased to think proper.

and petitioner will ever pray.

March 10th 1843   Timothy Noonan.[12]

The support for Noonan was very strong, as it came from a large segment of the gentry in the Ballingarry–Granagh area and showed him to be well-liked and popular in the locality. The handwriting of the petition bears strong similarity to that of his employer, John Lynch, who probably put it up on his behalf. Five of the men who signed the petition added their own comments, and there seemed to be a strong doubt as to Noonan's guilt. One of these men spelt out Noonan's disease as scrofula, or tuberculosis of the lymph glands. It is interesting to note that Patrick Hogan of Rathcannon also signed the petition, as did the parish priest to Croom, Archdeacon Michael Fitzgerald. Probably Hogan was influenced by the parish priest, but he may also have been shocked by the severity of the sentence.

By contrast, the petition for Stephen Howard was made out on 16 April, five weeks after Noonan's, and the stamp of the Chief Secretary's Office shows it was received on 17 April, more than a month after Noonan's. Further to this, it had only two signatories, Archdeacon Fitzgerald and Patrick Hogan. One reason for this would have been Stephen's employment, which took him away from his home area for a number of years; another might have been insufficient time to go around and to get all possible signatures.

Surprisingly, James Lynch's signature is not on the petition, even though he had spoken in Stephen's favour at his trial. The handwriting on this petition bears a strong resemblance to Patrick Hogan's signature and suggests that Hogan, having signed the petition put up on behalf of Noonan, decided to also intervene on behalf of Stephen Howard. The petition of Stephen Howard reads as follows:

To His Excellency De Grey, Lord Lieutenant General and General Governor of Ireland.
The Humble Petition of Stephen Howard of Granagh near Ballingarry in the County

of Limerick, but now a Convict in the gaol of said County most humbly showeth,

That Your Excellency's petitioner is a very young man of respectable family, and that neither himself nor any of his family were ever before this any way connected with a breach of the Laws, or that he was ever summoned before a Justice of the Peace.

Further sheweth that a man named Patrick Hogan was deprived of his gun in August last, and that petitioner was tried and convicted with a man named Timothy Nunan for said offence and that both were sentenced to be transported for ten years, that Your Excellency's petitioner is the only support of his aged father who is a cripple, supported by crutches, and of three little orphan nieces.

Your petitioner has heard and believes that said Nunan who was convicted by the *same evidence*, as a petitioner has addressed Your Excellency for the purpose of obtaining the Royal Prerogative of Mercy vested in your most noble Excellency, petitioner begs to say that the petitioner trusts that whatever clemency is shown to said Nunan that petitioner will have an equal share in it, both being convicted as before stated on the same testimony, and your petitioner most humbly begs that his dreadful sentence may be commuted to any penance of imprisonment Your Excellency may deem fit, and your petitioner will forever pray, April 16th, 1843.

We hereby respectfully recommend Stephen Howard as a fit object of Mercy to His Excellency of the Lord Lieutenant and we hereby subscribe to the truth of what has been mentioned in this petition—

> Mick Fitzgerald P.P.
> R.C. Archdeacon.
>
> Patrick Hogan.[13]

Having received these two petitions, the chief secretary wrote to Judge Jackson at the Crown Pleas Chamber on 19 April. Jackson replied two days later:

I have had the honour to receive your letter of the 19th instant desiring that I should acquaint you for the information of the Lord Lieutenant with the particulars of the case of Stephen Howard, and that I should report whether in my opinion there are any mitigating circumstances which would make the prisoner a proper object of mercy.

I have to state for His excellency's information that Stephen Howard, Timothy Noonan and William Burns were indicted for stealing a gun and two shot cannisters from the dwelling of Patrick Hogan a farmer in the County of Limerick and putting two females, Bridget Malone and Ellen Nunan in bodily fear at the time of committing the felony.

William Burns pleaded guilty, and the prisoner Howard and Nunan having pleaded not guilty, they were convicted upon evidence in my opinion, most clear and satisfactory of this very audacious outrage, and I sentenced them to 10 years transportation.

The party were armed and committed the offence in the broad day, during the time of Divine Service, whilst the farmer and his family were at Chapel, and no male in the house. I beg to state further for His Excellency's information, that this crime of robbing houses and individuals of arms, is continuously prevalent throughout the County of Limerick indeed to an alarming extent that there were no mitigating circumstances in this case whatever and that in my humble opinion it is necessary that the law should take its course.

I would add that the conduct of a peasant girl, Bridget Malone, (who was the principal witness for the Crown at the trial), was so heroic and her example altogether so valuable

that the Jury as well as Her Majesty's Council recommended her to the consideration
of His Excellency, and if there be any fund out of which she can be rewarded I would
beg leave to concur in their recommendation.[14]

This uncompromising reply shows that Judge Jackson was particularly concerned
about Whiteboy offences in the Limerick area. Indeed, such a reply would have
allowed a conservative viceroy such as De Grey little scope to show clemency.
Both De Grey and Jackson were hardliners as politicians and churchmen, and as
they were also the same age, they presumably knew each other quite well.

On 8 May a petition was put on behalf of Stephen Howard by his father, Patrick,
who was the only signatory. The Christian name is roughly written, and it seems
as though it was the old man's writing, while the surname was almost certainly
written by the man who wrote the petition, probably Patrick Hogan, as the
handwriting in the second petition is the same as that for the first. The petition
reads as follows:

> To His Excellency Earl De Grey, Lord Lieutenant General and General Governor of
> Ireland.
>
> The Humble Petition of Patrick Howard father to Stephen Howard now a convict
> on board a vessel at Kingstown most humbly shows that petitioner's son said Stephen
> Howard was found guilty at the last Spring assizes of Limerick of having deprived one,
> Patrick Hogan, of a gun and that a man of the name of Timothy Nunan was convicted
> of the same offence and on the same testimony as your petitioner's son. That both
> prisoners were sent from Limerick to Dublin for the purpose of having their sentence
> of transportation for ten years carried into effect, petitioner further begs leave to state
> that said Timothy Nunan has been kept in Kilmainham Gaol in the City of Dublin,
> and that his son Stephen Howard has been put on board the vessel for the purpose
> as it appears of being transported, petitioner most humbly hopes that Your Excellency
> will not allow such an act of injustice to take place, but that you will extend your
> clemency to petitioner's son to the same extent that Your Excellency has humanely
> showed it to Nunan both prisoners as before stated being convicted for the same crime,
> and on the same testimony, petitioner further states that there was a petition sent to
> Your Excellency by both prisoners, and petitioner's son's petition was signed by his parish
> Clergyman and as respectable persons as was signed to Nunan's who are as confused
> at the difference said to be made of one being pardoned, and the other not, petitioner
> begs to refer Your Excellency to the Judge Jackson who tried the case for the purpose
> of ascertaining the truth of this statement, and petitioner trusts that Your Excellency
> will deal out mercy with an even hand to all, and petitioner who is a poor old destitute
> man will forever pray. Petitioner begs further to state that there was no answer to
> the last petition except as related to Nunan, and begs earnestly that Your Excellency
> will order an answer to this petition to be directed to PATRICK HOWARD CROOM,
> COUNTY LIMERICK dated 8th May, 1843.
>
> Patrick Howard.[15]

This petition shows the old man believed Noonan had achieved a last-minute
reprieve in his sentence of transportation, while his son was being sent to Van
Diemen's Land. Both it and the other petitions show how much the nineteenth-
century Irish people dreaded transportation, and also the sheer brutality of the

system. The pathetic thing about Patrick Howard's petition is that it was made out the day before the *Constant* sailed, and as such was too late to be of any use.

Perhaps it was no use anyway. The British administration was entering yet another stormy period, with the Young Ireland Movement getting underway and widespread discontent in rural areas. Earl De Grey had succeeded to the viceroyalty of Ireland in September 1841. A former First Lord of the Admiralty, he was sixty years of age, handsome, wealthy and popular. He was generally understood to belong to the more uncompromising section of the Protestant party, and although not a prominent Conservative, he was not unknown to political life. He was included in *Ryall's Portraits of Eminent Conservatives* and seems to have been a power behind the scenes. When in Dublin, he spent much time entertaining, and his wife, a daughter of the first Earl of Enniskillen, not only made her mark as a hostess, but did much to foster Irish trade and manufacturing. Perhaps the best comment on De Grey, and the period in which he ruled, is made by Charles O'Mahony:

> It was not, of course, the most auspicious time for a genuine attempt to do something practical towards the social salvation of Ireland. Crime was rife; agitation was rampant; patriotism rioting deleriously. Many districts became acquainted with famine, but if food was short orators were plentiful. De Grey had plenty of work to do, and it was he who initiated the proceedings that led to the arrest of Daniel O'Connell and some of his friends in the autumn of 1843. The Government took advantage of a public meeting of the agitators to apprehend them for conspiracy, and eventually O'Connell and his associates were placed on trial, found guilty by a packed jury, and subsequently 'imprisoned' in an old-fashioned country home.[16]

It comes as little surprise, then, that the answer written on the back of the petitions on 24 April 1843 was 'THE LAW MUST TAKE ITS COURSE'.

It is not known exactly when Stephen Howard and Timothy Noonan boarded the *Constant*. Dominick Marques, who gave evidence at the enquiry into corruption at Kilmainham in 1843, said the convicts were sent down to Kingstown at a cost of 5s. per car. He also noted that the expense of sending out each convict, from the day they embarked until they landed in Van Diemen's Land or New South Wales, was £25. Very likely the convicts were sent down to Kingstown in drafts, heavily escorted by police, to be fitted out and organised by Surgeon-Superintendent Hampton on their arrival at the *Constant*.

5

Hobart Bound

For the most part, the military contingents drafted to escort convicts to Australia were drawn from the depots of line regiments already stationed in Australia. Regular marines would have been much more suitable, as they were accustomed to shipboard life, but the government was able to economise by using soldiers already posted to the colonies as guards on the convict ships, even though such economies were sometimes at the expense of efficiency and security. According to Charles Bateson:

> The military detachment occasionally was composed of raw recruits, but generally consisted of veterans, frequently disolute, ill-disciplined and in poor health. It was, of course, the cheapest way to send regiments out to Australia and probably also of getting small drafts of reinforcements to India, but in proportion to their numbers the guards required greater medical attention *en route* and frequently caused much trouble by their drunkenness and unruly conduct. Often they were much more severely punished than the convicts, who probably regarded their own plight, dire though it was, as better than the lot of their gaolers.[1]

The soldiers chosen to guard the convicts aboard the *Constant* were drawn from the 99th Regiment, which had its depot on Chatham, in Kent. The Chatham barracks at the time were overcrowded and many officers were quartered at the Sun Inn, a move that did not improve their reputation for sobriety. Chatham in the 1840s was also the scene of the Rochester balls recorded by Charles Dickens, who also based some of his characters on members of the military establishment at Chatham.

The officers chosen to command the detachment from the 99th Regiment were Lieutenant Lempster R. Elliot and Ensign George Jean De Winton. Elliot had been gazetted an ensign in the 16th Regiment in 1839 and had been promoted to lieutenant with the same regiment at the end of 1841. He transferred to the 99th early in 1843, obviously intent upon foreign service and the prospect of active duty in New Zealand during the Maori wars. His photograph shows him to be a tough-looking character. Indeed, with his large bushy beard and beetle brow he bears some resemblance to the bushranger Ned Kelly. Elliot was an average line officer with no important hereditary status or family connections.

Ensign De Winton was a vastly different man in this sense. A member of the great landed family of De Winton and the son of Captain George De Winton of Heywood Hall, Somerset, he was gazetted as an ensign in July 1841 and had enthusiastically chosen the 99th after having seen them march down Regent Street, London. This began a lifelong association with the regiment which is exuberantly outlined in his memoirs. Indeed De Winton gives a vivid description of Chatham as it was in the 1840s.:

> At the time of the arrival of the 99th, the Chatham Barracks were exceptionally crowded, and for some time the officers' mess was at 'The Sun', the well-known coaching house kept by Winch. Good old 'Sun'; Who of those quartered in Chatham in the 'forties' does not remember the supper laid out for the passengers by the Dover mail; the egg-flip, a speciality of the house; the parting glass of that alluring compound exchanged with the traveller, seen often for the first time and for the last, while the expostulating guard, hardly appeased by the proferred glass, declares that he will never be able to make up the time in the next stage.[2]

From De Winton's memoirs, Chatham in the 1840s certainly appeared to be a soldier's town, very different from the sober well-ordered Chatham of today, and he clearly remembered how well equipped it was to entertain young officers in their off-duty moments:

> Imagine a number of young fellows, just released from the strict discipline of school, suddenly severed from the controlling influences of family associations, and in many instances supplied with money with injudicious liberality, launched amidst the temptations and the demoralising associations of a garrison town, and we can readily realise the result—dissipation, debauchery, and utter ruin of not a few . . . The scenes I have witnessed would, if described in detail, be derided by the novelist. I have known twelve dozen of wine sent after mess to a subaltern's room, and have seen the morning's sun revealing prostrate forms in hopeless intoxication, amidst a wreck of furniture and broken bottles. There were low public-houses which a lax police suffered to be open until all hours, or, what was worse, though nominally closed during the prohibited hours, open to all possessed of the watchword and a golden key, where orgies indescribable were enacted . . . Large indeed must have been the number of young men, the pride of their parents, with bright prospects before them, who succumbed to the horrible fascinations which allured those who desired—ill-omened expression—'to see life'.[3]

At the time De Winton was quartered at Chatham the 99th Regiment included in its ranks several well-known officers, some of whom were to make their mark upon early Australian history. The commandant of the garrison was Sir Thomas Willshire, commonly known as 'Tiger Tom', who was a stickler for high standards of equitation. This did not prove to be a problem for the 99th, as most of their officers were good horsemen, but the marines, many of whom did not dare to gallop their horses, must have found Tiger Tom's term at Chatham a nightmare. Sir John Gaspard Le Marchant, the colonel of the 99th, was so appalled by the idea of service in Australia that he joined another regiment and his place was taken by Lieutenant-Colonel Henry Despard, who was later to command the regiment during the Maori Wars.

In April 1843 the detachment of the 99th chosen to go to Australia aboard the convict ship *Constant* marched out of Chatham. The detachment consisted of forty-nine soldiers and an army boy, William Joseph Wyme, the son of one of the soldiers. The passing-out parade took place at the barracks, near what is now Brompton's Hill, and was presided over by Sir Thomas Willshire, Major Edward Last and RSM James Grime. Major Last was one of the few officers of the 99th left at Chatham, and Gaspard Le Marchant's antipathy to colonial service notwithstanding, the men would not have been unhappy with their posting as there was a well-known army saying: 'I would rather be a private in Sydney than a general in India'. This no doubt was due to the climate, the absence of plagues and the small number of hostile natives.

The detachment, with Lieutenant Elliot and Ensign de Winton at its head, marched down Dock Road and through the streets of Chatham to the tune of 'The Girl I Left Behind Me', which was played by the accompanying military band. Many young women followed them, and a festival air prevailed until they reached the outskirts of Strood, after which both the band and the young women took their leave. The detachment marched on to Gravesend, where it bivouacked for the night. The next day the detachment boarded a hoy, or barge, commanded by a garrulous old salt, and drifted up the river to Deptford, where the *Constant* was waiting to take them on board.

Deptford was an important fitting-out centre for sailing ships in the nineteenth century and the barque *Constant* had only recently completed all her fitting-out and victualling for the long voyage to Australia. The *Constant* had just been built by John Mowbray Gales of Gales Shipyard at Hylton Durham. Gales was the most successful designer and builder of ships in his day and his yard produced 200 vessels between its opening in 1812 and its closure soon after Gales' death in 1857. The *Constant*, which had only just been completed in time for the voyage to Australia, was of 535.3 tons burthen (new measurement). Her description was as follows: two and a poop decks, three masts, length 114.5 feet, breadth midships 25.5 feet, and depth in hold at midship 19.7 feet. She was square-rigged with a standing bowsprit, square sterned, carvel built, with sham galleries and a woman figurehead. She was first registered as number 78, but this was changed to 128 when John Hemery purchased her on 10 April 1843 from Joseph Somes of Ratcliffe Cross, Middlesex. Finally, the *Constant* was armed with six guns to guard against pirates.

John Hemery was a scion of a Huguenot family that had fled to Jersey from France after the revocation of the Edict of Nantes in 1598. Like many other families in Jersey in the eighteenth century, the Hemerys traded with Newfoundland and also owned both privateers and merchant ships. As time went on, the family took on a position of considerable wealth and standing on Jersey. John Hemery's father, Clement, was the colonel of the St Helier town regiment and purchased Columbier House, a mansion in Hemery Row. At the time he was preparing the *Constant* for her voyage to Hobart, John Hemery was twenty-seven years of age. However, let De Winton describe Hemery and the surgeon-superintendent in his own words:

> The 'Constant' was a barque of about 500 tons, owned and commanded by John Hemery, a Jersey man, about thirty years of age, every inch a sailor and a gentleman, and engaged to be married to a cousin of one of our officers, a beautiful girl, to judge from the portrait which hung in the captain's cabin. The surgeon-superintendent was John Stephen Hampton, R.N., later chief of the Convict Department in Van Diemen's Land (now Tasmania), and afterwards Governor of Western Australia. He had made many voyages as surgeon-superintendent, and stood high in esteem in the service.[4]

Despite Hemery's youth, he was well qualified for his command of the *Constant* in terms of his experience. He had purchased his first ship, the *Bengal Merchant*, in September 1839. Built in India in 1812, the *Bengal Merchant* was 503 tons burthen and had previously made several voyages as a convict transport, although Hemery used her as a cargo vessel between England and India or England, Australia and New Zealand. Alexander Marjoribanks wrote of Hemery's captaincy on a voyage to New Zealand in 1839–40:

> The commanding officer of our ship, Captain John Hemery, from the Island of Jersey, was a handsome young man of good address, and though said to be opulent, preferring a sea life to any other—a singular choice I must admit. He had some faults, and who has not; but he was an excellent seaman; very sober and attentive to the duties of the ship, and a strict disciplinarian. He was disposed to be somewhat haughty in his deportment—keeping very much aloof from us all; but this, I am inclined to think, arose, in a great measure, from the situation in which he found himself placed; and really, when we consider his youth, and the difficult part which he had to act, amidst the jarrings and quarrels that invariably occur in emigrant ships, I cannot help thinking that this feeling was highly commendable.[5]

Before he bought the *Bengal Merchant*, Hemery had been a ship's officer on the *Lord Hungerford*, a large ship of over 700 tons. It has not been possible to establish whether he had any experience on convict ships before the *Constant*'s voyage.

As has been already seen by De Winton's statement, the surgeon-superintendent John Stephen Hampton was on the verge of what was to be an outstanding although controversial career. Hampton obtained his surgeon's diploma at Edinburgh in 1828 and joined the navy as an assistant surgeon in January the following year. Although the aftermath of the Napoleonic wars was not a good period for ambitious naval officers, Hampton lost little time distinguishing himself. He obtained his surgeon's certificate at Edinburgh in 1832, in which year he was also highly commended for his services during the cholera plague at the Plymouth dockyard. In December 1834 he was promoted, on merit, and in 1835 his superior officers aboard the *Portland* commented very favourably on his 'talent and attention'. In 1839 he was commended by the physician general of the navy, Sir William Burnett, for his 'talent and industry' after submitting a paper on the diseases of the West Indies, and in 1840 he was further commended for the 'zeal, intelligence, and attention' with which he performed his duties aboard the emigrant ship *Florest*. In 1841 he had sailed to Hobart as surgeon-superintendent aboard the female convict ship *Mexborough*, 376 tons burthen, with 145 convicts. He only lost two of these convicts through death, and upon his return to England he submitted a plan for improving the ventilation aboard the smaller female transports such as the *Mexborough*. Now aged thirty-three, he was about to embark upon his second voyage as surgeon-superintendent aboard a convict ship.[6]

The *Constant* sailed from Deptford on her maiden voyage on 14 April, *en route* to Kingstown, Ireland, where she was scheduled to pick up 204 male convicts who were about to embark upon the most terrifying period of their lives. Fifty-one were skilled workers, the other 153 were unskilled. Since only three were sailors, the remaining 201 landlubbers, most of whom were peasants, faced a personal maiden voyage of nearly four months duration aboard a small 500-ton barque. The *Constant* waited a week at Kingstown before the convicts arrived, and the time was spent entertaining the many people who came on board to inspect the facilities for the prisoners, and also enjoying the reciprocal hospitality of the Irish.

When Stephen Howard and his fellow convicts set foot on the *Constant*, most of them would have been boarding a ship for the first time. A brand new ship, it had spent two weeks at Deptford being specially fitted out for them. Some idea of the type of accommodation provided for the convicts can be gained from accounts of other convict transports. The first is by Peter Cunningham and dates from the 1820s:

> Two rows of sleeping-berths, one above the other, extend on each side of the between-decks, each berth being 6 feet square, and calculated to hold four convicts, every one thus possessing 18 inches of space to sleep in—and ample space, too! The hospital is in the fore-part of the ship, with a bulkhead across, separating it from the prison, having two doors with locks to keep out intruders; while a separate prison is built for the boys, to cut off all intercourse between them and the men. Strong wooden stanchions, thickly studded with nails, are fixed round the fore and main hatchways, between decks, in each of which is a door with three padlocks, to let the convicts out and in, and secure them at night. The convicts by these means have no access to the hold through the prison, a ladder being placed in each hatchway for them to go up and down by, which is pulled on deck at night.[7]

In December 1839, Commodore Charles Wilkes of the United States Navy called at Sydney and was shown over a convict ship. His description showed that little had changed from Cunningham's time:

> Between decks a strong grated barricade, spiked with iron, is built across the ship at the steerage bulkhead. This gives the officers a free view of all that goes on among the prisoners. Bunks for sleeping are placed one each side all the way to the bows. Each of these will accommodate five persons. There is no outlet but through a door in the steerage bulkhead, and this is always guarded by a sentry. Light and air are admitted through the hatches, which are strongly grated . . . The quarter-deck is barricaded near the mainmast, abaft which the arms of the guard are kept.[8]

The wooden stanchions used to separate the convicts from the rest of the ship were between 5½ and 6 inches wide, with only half that much space between each of them. In 1817, the Navy Board experimented with the use of iron railings in place of the stanchions, but the design was not retained, even though surgeons constantly recommended it. Iron bars allowed the convicts better light and ventilation, but stanchions were still in use as late as 1850. Some ships even possessed barriers on deck, as can be seen by John Boyle O'Reilly's description of the *Hougoumont*, the last transport to sail for Western Australia in 1868:

> She was fitted in the usual way of convict ships. Her main deck and her lower deck were divided into separate compartments, the dividing walls below being heavy and strong bulkheads, while those on deck were wooden barriers about nine feet high, with side doors, for the passage of the sailors while working the ship. At each of these doors, during the entire voyage, stood two soldiers, with fixed bayonets on their loaded rifles.
> 　　The hatch coverings opening to the lower deck, where the convicts were confined, were removed; and around each hatchway, reaching from the upper deck, or roof of the convicts' room, to the lower deck or floor, was one immense grating, formed of strong iron bars. This arrangement gave plenty of air and a good deal of light, the only obstruction being the bars.[9]

It is not known whether the *Constant* was fitted with barricades on the main deck, but it is almost certain she would not have been as well ventilated or as well lit as the 875-ton *Hougoumont*, which was built nearly ten years later, at a time when the design of sailing ships was improving rapidly. Nevertheless, the convicts would be thankful that the *Constant* was a new ship on her maiden voyage, characterised by the smells of newly sawn timber and fresh pitch rather than the hideous odours that contemporaries described as pervading the older ships:

> The smells were, of course, among the most notable feature of life on board. The combination of animal and human excrement, foul water from the bottom of the ship below pump wells which never came out, the remains of old cargoes and the perpetually rotting wooden structure of the vessel herself must between them have produced a dreadful stench, unrelieved by any kind of ventilation system in the ship. People were accustomed to this ashore in towns and villages which stank like an Oriental slum today.[10]

So much for the *Constant*, which was engaged by public tender at £5 per ton, the agents or brokers being T. Haviside of 69 Cornhill, Westminster. But what of the crew who were to guide her on a 13,000-mile voyage to Van Diemen's Land? The schedule A crew agreement shows that the *Constant* had a crew of thirty-five when she left Deptford, and that eight more were engaged at Kingstown. The final complement was three mates, a boatswain, a carpenter, a cuddy servant, a steward, a cook, fifteen able seamen, fourteen ordinary seamen, a butcher, three apprentices, and two ship's boys. Hemery seems to have been able to attract some loyalty as a ship's master, as nine of the crew had previously served under him on the *Bengal Merchant*. These were William Rowe the first mate, the carpenter, the cuddy servant, three able seamen and the three apprentices. The crew signed on to go to Ireland, then to Hobart, and thence anywhere else at the captain's discretion for a period not exceeding two years. Spirits were not allowed as rations, but were entirely at the option of the captain. When signing on, the boatswain, officers and the whole of the crew engaged to inflict corporal and other punishment on the convicts when required to do so by the surgeon-superintendent. The pay scale of the crew varied from £7 per month for the first mate to 15s. per month for the ship's boys. Five ordinary seamen are shown to be paid only 1s. per month. As four of these men were previously from the one ship, the *Landsman*, there seems to have been some special agreement in force. Probably they were going to Australia to join a ship, and received rations and token pay in exchange for light duties. Crew members were paid in relation to their skills. The carpenter received £5 per month, the steward £3 10s. 0d. and the cook £3 3s. 0d. Able seamen received £2 per month, while ordinary seamen received only £1 10s. 0d. The second mate received £4 4s. 0d. and the third mate £2 10s. 0d.

On their arrival from Kilmainham, the convicts were immediately given numbers from 9,785 to 9,988. Stephen Howard's number was 9,871, and Timothy Noonan's was 9,987. They were then split into two divisions, with the odd numbers in the first division and the even numbers in the second. After that they were divided into messes of eight convicts. Only half the men in each mess belonged to the same division, so that when one division was admitted on deck, the crowd in the prison was lessened equally throughout all the messes. A man was appointed head of each mess and given charge of the mess utensils and rations: because of this responsibility, he was not a member of the cleaning party, and he had his berth and mess utensils cleaned for him by the other men. Each of the remaining seven men had a day appointed to him as a member of the cleaning party, which consisted of twenty-five men each day, or one-eighth of the convict numbers. At daylight the party was admitted on deck and cleaned the forecastle, water closets and main deck. The ship's company cleaned the after part of the ship.

Before embarking, the convicts had been washed and fitted out with the regulation dress for the voyage, which consisted of jackets and waistcoats of blue cloth or kersey, duck trousers, check or coarse linen shirts, yarn stockings and woollen caps. Peter Cunningham summed up the clothing and food provided for the convicts as follows:

> Each is allowed a pair of shoes, three shirts, two pairs of trowsers, and other warm clothing on his embarkation, besides a bed, pillow, and blanket—while Bibles, Testaments, prayer-books, and psalters are distributed among the messes.
>
> The rations are both good and abundant, three-quarters of a pound of biscuit being the daily allowance of bread, while each day the convict sits down to dinner off either beef, pork, or plum-pudding, having pea-soup four times a week, and a pot of gruel every morning, with sugar or butter in it. Vinegar is issued to the messes weekly; and as soon as the ship has been three weeks at sea, each man is served with one ounce of lime juice and the same of sugar daily, to guard against scurvy: while two gallons of good Spanish red wine, and one hundred and forty gallons of water are put on board for issuing to each likewise—three to four gills of wine weekly, and three quarts of water daily, being the general allowance.[11]

Generally speaking, there were few complaints about the rations, except for the salt meat, which often shrank when boiled, and the preserved meat which sometimes went bad. The clothing was an entirely different matter. As the navy tended to consider woollen clothes unhygienic, believing they harboured germs, the clothing issued was too light for the colder latitudes. As well, there were no replacements available for clothes that were lost, damaged or worn out. Despite frequent complaints from the surgeons-superintendent, little seemed to have been done to improve the convicts' clothing issue.

Hampton's day began as soon as the upper deck was dried down, generally about 6.00 or 6.15 a.m. All the boys, thirty-five in all, were admitted on deck to be washed and inspected. One of the divisions was admitted on deck for inspection, followed by the other division if time and weather permitted. At 7 a.m. the sick were visited, and breakfast was at 8 a.m. At 9 a.m. the prison was cleaned, the method depending upon the weather. Dinner was at 1 p.m. and supper at 5 p.m. At 5.30 p.m. the sick were again visited, while at sunset the whole lot were mustered below and the prison was secured for the night. By day the convicts were kept on deck as much as circumstances allowed. In fine weather at least half of them were always on deck; all of them when it was deemed prudent and practicable. The bedding was shaken at least once a week, swinging stoves were frequently used in the prison, and the hold was often fumigated and aired. Washing days were Mondays and Fridays, and the convicts were inspected in their divisions on Sundays and Mondays, to see each had on a clean shirt, was shaved and was otherwise clean.

Soon after leaving Kingstown, Hampton appointed the more competent and well-behaved convicts to responsible positions for the rest of the voyage. Five were appointed to the watering party, their duty being to ensure the water cisterns were filled each day. Two schoolmasters, one of them a forger and the other a thief, were appointed; an army deserter was put in charge of the boys; a former divinity student transported for bigamy was given charge of the hospital stores; and a jaunting-car thief was made cook. A head tailor was appointed, and two thieves like himself were appointed as his assistants. Two thieves were appointed head constable and constable and another two were appointed assistant schoolmasters, while a convict transported for malicious assault was appointed barber. Hampton summed up as follows:

> Divine Service was regularly performed. Schools established, and every practicable means used to give employment both to the bodies and the minds of the convicts, and after a passage of 112 days from Ireland the 'Constant' arrived at Hobart Town not only without a convict on the sick list, but with all of them in a much better state of health than they were on embarkation at Kingstown, although the ship did not call at any port during the voyage.[12]

Only three convicts died on the voyage.

Two of the most experienced and successful surgeon-superindendents of the convict era were Peter Cunningham, who made five voyages to Australia between 1819 and 1828, and Colin Arrott Browning, who made eight voyages between 1831 and 1849. The two men had markedly different styles of superintendence.

Cunningham was very strict about having everything marked. As soon as he embarked his convicts, he made them mark their bedding, clothing and eating utensils. This he found stopped the convicts from stealing one another's articles. He allowed the convicts to choose their own mess mates, six to a mess, and he then chose from among them six captains of the deck, four of whom officiated in prison and two upon deck. His next step was to appoint mess captains who were entrusted with the cleanliness and rations of each mess, and who were also responsible for the good conduct of the other five mess members. He appointed two convicts to the watering party, two to serve as hospital assistants and four to teach school.

Apart from this, Cunningham's methods were novel to say the least. First, he chose the most incorrigible thieves on board as his captains. His argument was simply that these men were the most experienced and—in their own way—the most enlightened of the convicts. Even more important, since they enjoyed great status and respect among their fellow convicts, they were able to lead them accordingly. Cunningham paid his captains with a double issue of wine and gave them two pounds of tobacco for the voyage; an unusual luxury. He encouraged singing and dancing, but made sure that the convicts were kept occupied at all times. He issued three written codes governing every phase of conduct and activity, and made sure the convicts knew them.

Cunningham might have seemed unorthodox in some ways, but his methods were so successful that he lost only three convicts in five voyages. He did not particularly go out of his way to encourage religion, as he had observed it was not important to the English convicts, although many of the Irish convicts were quite devout.[13]

Browning was very different to Cunningham in his approach to convict discipline aboard the transports. From the first, he organised his convicts into what was probably the most structured system of the whole transportation era. He appointed a first and a second captain, three captains of divisions, four captains of upper deck, two captains of the forecastle, four captains of the main ward and three captains of the boys' ward. He then appointed three cooks, three barbers, one headman to each mess, two delegates of the day, one clerk and one librarian. Browning chose his schoolteachers from amongst the educated convicts with great care, according to scholarship, virtue and good humour. The schools for illiterate convicts consisted of nine or ten pupils only, and those for the partially educated fifteen pupils.

Unfortunately Browning was also a religious zealot, who tended to go to extremes in the service of his religious beliefs. When the convicts were being taken aboard the *Earl Grey* in 1842, one of the petty officers was playing the violin, and this he stopped as highly indecorous. The only music he allowed was psalm singing, and music for marching around the deck. He chose his captains carefully, according to his own observations and to the character he received from the hulks and the prisons. Cunningham's selection methods and means of rewarding good behaviour would have horrified Browning, whose schools seemed to function to teach Scripture reading more than anything else, and whose addresses to the convicts were strange mixtures of religious exhortation and convict regulations.[14] Certainly, chaplains such as the Rev. Robert Downing (*Pestonjee Bomajee*, 1849) and the Rev. R. W. Gibbs (*Cadet*, 1849) made poor comparison to Dr Browning when it came to religious enthusiasm. Derided by many people, Browning nevertheless had a strong following and some thought that he, rather than Hampton, should have been appointed comptroller-general of convicts for Van Diemen's Land in 1846.

In relation to Browning and Cunningham, Hampton seems to have steered a middle course. He appointed head men to each mess, schoolmasters, barbers, constables, tailors and a storeman for his hospital, but he seems to have avoided appointing captains of the deck, the forecastle or the prison. Further to this, there is little mention of religion, as Hampton did not seem to be a religious man.

In his capacity as surgeon-superintendent, Hampton was responsible for the health of the soldiers and crew, as well as the convicts. All-told, he treated thirty soldiers, sixteen convicts and two ship's boys. It is interesting to note that the convicts were much healthier than the soldiers, and the figures also bear out the statement in Hampton's journal that the crew were extremely healthy. The complaints treated by Hampton (and their incidence) were as follows: syphilis (3), rheumatism (6), apoplexia (1), constipation (5), diarrhoea (4), catarrh (9), colica (1), consumption (2), bubo (1), ulcers (1), fever febris (2), vulnus wound (1), pneumonia (5) and 'psora ich' (7).

The three convicts who died did so well into the second half of the journey. John Stewart, who was only nineteen years of age, died of consumption on 27 July, when the *Constant* was seventy-nine days out of port. Hampton first treated him on 2 July, but he developed chest pains and fever, which were greatly aggravated by the exceedingly squally weather. He also had secondary syphilis, and according to Hampton his constitution had been badly undermined by a course of vicious living in the lowest haunts of debauchery.

Stephen Howard's partner in crime Timothy Noonan became ill with pneumonia on 7 August, when the *Constant* was only three weeks from Hobart. Already a sick man on embarkation, he apparently got wet through in a heavy sea and remained on deck too long afterwards. He also developed chest pains and fever, and died four days later.

James Wallace was an eighteen-year-old from a respectable family background who was obviously consumptive when he came on board. He had an irritating cough, and also pains and tightness across the chest which made breathing very difficult. He died after a massive haemorrhage on 21 August.

All three patients experienced respiratory difficulties, which were relieved in each case by venesection (bleeding). Hampton also seems to have used the same medication for each patient. The most prominent of these were magnesium sulphate, 'cerat cetace' (chalk), potassium tartrate, potassium nitrate, tincture digitalis, mucillage acaccia and 'aqua menthol'. One can't help feeling that some of Hampton's treatments were more dangerous than beneficial. Timothy Noonan died suddenly, soon after venesection, and James Wallace was obviously greatly debilitated by it.

Hampton had been appointed an assistant surgeon in 1829, at the age of nineteen, and it is interesting to note the sort of training he would have undergone. In *Medicine and the Navy, 1200-1900*, C. Lloyd and J. L. S. Coulter state that after 1824 the formula in the regulations governing the entry of surgeons ran thus:

> Surgeons shall be appointed by warrant from the Commissioners of Victualling [after 1831 from the Board of Admiralty, according to the Order in Council of Feb. 23. 1831], but no person shall be so warranted as surgeon who shall not have passed such examinations as the Lords Commissioners of the Admiralty may direct . . . No person shall be admitted as Assistant Surgeon in the Royal Navy who shall not produce certificates from one of the Royal Colleges of Surgeons of England, Edinburgh or Dublin, or from the Faculty of Physicians and Surgeons of Glasgow, of his fitness for that office . . . and in every case the candidate producing such certificate shall also undergo a further examination touching his qualifications in all the necessary branches of Medicine and Surgery for each of the steps in the Navy Medical Service.[15]

Lloyd and Coulter further note that:

> No candidate could sit for such further examination until he had served three years as Assistant Surgeon. In addition, every candidate, who must be between the ages of 20 and 26, must produce certificates of morality from a clergyman or magistrate, together with proof that he has held a pharmaceutical post for at least six months and had spent eighteen months in a hospital, where he had experience of operations.
>
> Such requirements implied that before he joined the service a man must have studied anatomy, surgery, materia medica and military surgery, in addition to attending lectures on chemistry, botany and even midwifery. If he lacked these specific qualifications, concessions were allowed for those possessing a medical degree from Oxford, Cambridge, London or Aberdeen, or who had specialised in any one branch of surgery.[16]

Up until 1866, promotional examinations were occasionally held in London at Somerset House, although sometimes with ludicrous results. When a man named Turnbull was asked to give the origin and insertion of the rectus abdominus muscle he replied: 'That I do not know it; that I will not guess it; and I don't think it of much importance . . . I was asked in the end to withdraw, but I passed.'[17]

The regulations governing the training of naval surgeons and their entry into the navy were standardised and overhauled in 1838, and again in 1868.

Hampton's and De Winton's accounts of the voyage—written fifty-five years apart—differ in at least two important aspects. According to Hampton, one of the ships's boys fell from the top gallant mast and so severely fractured his cranium that he died almost instantly. Hampton did not give the boy's name or the date, and the only death recorded in the crew musters is that of John Stephens, a young seaman who died on the return voyage. The seamen's records contain no mention of any of the boys being killed, and De Winton records no such an accident in his account of the voyage.

Hampton also states that the voyage was without incidents: 'A strict and unremittency personal superintendence on deck from daylight until after sunset secured the enforcement of the following regulations, and with the pleasing result of rendering the ship healthy and comfortable for all on board, and that without inflicting corporal punishment on any of the convicts'.[18] However, De Winton alleges that there was an attempted mutiny and that the ring-leaders were severely punished:

> Contrary winds drove us out of our course, and we sighted the island of Fernando de Noronha, the Brazilian convict settlement, which has been described as the convicts' Eden. Whether it was that the fame of this settlement had reached the ears of our convicts, and a desire had seized them to put it to practical test, I know not, but at this time we discovered a plot to take the ship, the plan of which, to put it mildly, did not include the landing of the officers and guard on the terrestrial paradise then in view. The ring-leaders of the plot were flogged, isolated, and put in heavy irons; but, needless to say, our vigilance was thenceforth redoubled. I have often thought that with systematic combination the taking of a ship by convicts might, in those days, have been achieved without very much difficulty; the old flint muskets were to the last degree unreliable, and as for the cutlasses with which the sentries were armed, they were little better than pieces of hoop-iron.[19]

The shipping indents submitted by Hampton show the convicts to have been remarkably well-behaved during the voyage. Only seven merited adverse comments, and these were of a minor nature. In fact the two accounts conflict so sharply that it must be asked: who was the officer and gentleman, and who the liar? Was Hampton, with a big future ahead of him, covering up, or was De Winton exaggerating to give his recollections more incident and colour?

For his part, Hemery had been tested by serious trouble from his crew aboard the *Bengal Merchant* in late 1839. William Webster reported in his journal:

> Some of the sailors were intoxicated today and one who was worse than the rest and unfit for duty was put in irons. Several of the sailors came to the captain and wished their comrade released, but they were dismissed. In a short time they came again on the same errand, but they were again ordered off. Their conduct being rude, the captain put on his sword and the mates had their cutlasses and loaded pistols and the men were informed that the first who came up to the captain without orders or did not attend to duty would be shot or have a yard of steel thrust through him. After this, there was no more disturbance.

But a fortnight later Webster had this to say:

> this morning, the sailors had got a quantity of spirits and were so drunk that only three or four of them were fit for duty. One who had been drunk for three days in succession, was put in irons, in solitary confinement. Another who was very drunk and riotous, was ordered to be flogged. He was tied hand and foot to the side of the vessel and his woollen shirt cut off his back. The Captain got on his sword and ordered every sailor to be present. He warned them against further drunkennness. He pardoned the one who was to be flogged and ordered them to take him away and tie him in his hammock. Several more of the men who were unable to come forward were next brought from the forecastle and tied to the guns and side of the vessel until they got sober . . . one of the fellows got very noisy and a marlinspike was tied to his mouth to try and cure him. The next subject was an enquiry where the fellows could have got the spirits.[20]

If trouble did occur on the *Constant*, it would be interesting to know both how it was handled and who had the final say concerning punishment meted out to the convicts.

De Winton's account also mentions how during a 'Buster' in the Bay of Biscay he, Hampton and Elliot were taking a glass of grog in the cabin when the cuddy table came loose and broke all the glass windows, with the result they were nearly washed overboard when the *Constant* suddenly shipped the heavy seas. He also described how the pilot boat came to meet them at Storm Bay, Van Diemen's Land, and brought them a sack of fresh potatoes.

When the *Constant* arrived in Hobart on 29 August 1843, the weather was cold, with snow and sleet falling everywhere, causing a convict to fall so ill he had to be sent to hospital rather than to one of the probation stations. The new Convict Department was very busy, as the *Gilmore* had arrived with 249 convicts only ten days earlier. The *Constant* was the first ship to arrive from Ireland under the new probation system, and thirty-three of her convicts were chosen to go to the probation gang at Salt Water River on the government brig *Isabella*. It was Stephen Howard's fate to be one of them.

6

The Assignment System

The Vagrancy Act of 1597 first gave the courts the power of transportation, and this power was further reinforced by the legal system which operated under Charles II. Usually, certain criminals were not formally transported, but were given the choice of exile or death.[1]

By 1718, the problem of disposing of the criminal population of Britain had become so serious that contractors were employed to transport shiploads of convicts to the British colonies in America. As a result, a new form of slavery prevailed, since the contractor was given the rights to the criminals' labour for a specific term. On arrival at the New World, the contractors simply held an auction and sold them off to the highest bidder. As the law-and-order situation worsened during the eighteenth century, due to lack of a professional police force in Britain, heavy penalties were seen as the main deterrent and transportation was prescribed for an increasing number of crimes. In addition, the death penalty was often commuted to transportation. This offered the contractors an increase in an already profitable trade, as they received a bounty of £5 for each convict and could then auction his services for between £10 and £20, depending upon his marketability. By the time the American War of Independence stopped transportation to the American colonies in 1775, 40,000 men and women had been transported.[2]

To replace the lost American colonies as a dumping ground for unwanted criminals, large naval vessels which were out of commission were converted into prison hulks, while the convicts they accommodated were often employed upon public works. This system worked well for a while, until the hulks became overcrowded and their burgeoning population became a matter of great concern and embarrassment for the civil authorities. In March 1786, a serious uprising occurred on a prison hulk at Plymouth, which resulted in eight convicts being shot dead and another thirty-six wounded. Lord Sydney, the Home Office secretary, decided to establish a colony at Botany Bay in the newly discovered continent of Australia.

A fleet was fitted out by the Admiralty to sail to Australia under the command of Captain Arthur Phillip, who had established a good record for himself both as a navigator and a disciplinarian. The fleet consisted of two warships, three supply ships, and six convict transports which carried 568 male and 191 female convicts. It sailed from Spithead on 13 May 1787 and arrived at Botany Bay on 20 January 1788, after accomplishing a voyage of 15,063 miles without serious loss. Charles Bateson describes the voyage as being 'a magnificent piece of navigation and seamanship'.[3] Botany Bay was found to be unsuitable and the fleet moved to Port Jackson, to found what was to become the city of Sydney.

Between 1787 and 1800, forty-three transports, carrying 6,634 prisoners, arrived in Australia. The first transport to arrive in Hobart was the *Indefatigable* in 1812. After a gap of some years, transportation to Hobart really got under way with the arrival of the *Minerva* and *Lady Castlereagh* in June 1818, and the *Lord Melville* in December.

Transportation to New South Wales ceased in 1840, but 151 transports sailed to Hobart between 1841 and 1853.[4] During the early years of New South Wales, officers, settlers and freed men (ex-convicts) were all allowed to choose their servants from amongst the convicts, the number they were allowed being in accordance with their resources. At no time were convicts auctioned in New South Wales, after the American system, but in 1804 Governor King formalised the assignment system. An assignment board was created and those wishing to be allocated convicts had to apply, giving full details of land under cultivation and convicts in their present employ. The convicts were accommodated on the farms in rough slab and bark huts, with shingled or thatched roofs, that usually accommodated four convicts whose weekly allowance 'was a peck of wheat, seven pounds of beef, or four and a half of pork, two ounces of tea, two ounces of tobacco, and a pound of sugar'.[5] Two full suits of clothes were provided each year by the master or mistress, and a convict was also issued with a blanket, a bed tick, a tin pot and a knife. Each mess or hut had an iron pot and a frying pan. Convicts formed a large percentage of the population in the early years of Australian settlement: in New South Wales in 1791 it was nearly 82 per cent, and in Van Diemen's Land in 1820 it was nearly 73 per cent (2,956 people), although by 1848 the figure for Van Diemen's Land had dropped to 38 per cent (28,459).[6]

The arrangements concerning the disposal of the convicts under the assignment system were very thorough. As soon as a transport arrived, it signalled the port officer that it had male or female convicts on board. The port officer then went down the river or out to sea to meet the transport and to examine the state of the prisoners and of the ship. He also left printed instructions which forbade any communication with the ship until permission was given from the shore. When the port officer returned, the colonial secretary and the colonial surgeon went off to meet the transport. The prisoners were then drawn up on deck to be inspected by the colonial secretary, who also inspected the state of the ship. The inspection completed, the colonial secretary asked the convicts, the master of the vessel, the commander of the guard (if applicable) and the surgeon-superintendent if there were any complaints. If everything was in order, the colonial secretary reported accordingly to the governor.

The surgeon-superintendent, who at this stage was the only one allowed to leave the vessel, went on shore and reported to the governor, taking the despatches with him. He also presented a comprehensive set of returns regarding the convicts, which gave their criminal records, personal histories and details of their behaviour on the voyage. In addition to these returns, he presented a despatch from the secretary of state for the colonies which included the indent, or nominal list, of all the prisoners on board, along with their criminal records. The colonial secretary sent copies of these documents to the muster master, who was a member of the Police Department and had charge of all the convict records. The muster master immediately prepared two large summaries from the returns, and on the third day the vessel was in port he boarded the transport, accompanied by the principal superintendent of prisoners, and they interviewed each prisoner, questioning him about his past, his qualifications and his aptitudes. This task occupied up to two days, and the interviewing team usually managed to form an accurate picture of each convict. They then reported to the governor and the assignment board assembled next day to assign the prisoners, being largely guided by the muster master's returns.

The assignment board was composed of the chief police magistrate, the treasurer, and the principal superintendent of prisoners. Later it was found desirable to abolish the office of clerk and to appoint an administrative officer as a working member of the board.[7] The assignment board then considered the settlers' applications for servants, and also those from the civil engineer, who usually needed men for the public works of the colony. The more dangerous or intractable prisoners were sent to road gangs or to penal settlements such as Macquarie Harbour or, after 1833, to Port Arthur or the Coal Mines. Boys were sent to Point Puer. The board inevitably had problems concerning supply and demand, as there were always demands for good farm labourers and mechanics (skilled tradesmen) while there were not so many demands for pickpockets, although it was said London pickpockets made excellent domestic servants.

The assignment system had many critics, who believed it was either too corrupt in its leniency or too cruel in its severity. In 1837 the House of Commons appointed Sir William Molesworth chairman of a select committee of enquiry into transportation. Twenty-three gentlemen were examined as to the efficacy of the system both in New South Wales and Van Diemen's Land, and there were some interesting revelations. The assignment system was found to function very much like a lottery, in that much depended upon chance. Generally, a convict was well off if he fell into the hands of a good master. If he was a labourer, he was well clothed and better fed than the soldiers or the poor in Britain. As convict servants on farms were not often trusted they were usually lodged in outhouses, well away from the family. Many of them took advantage of this to go on sheep-stealing forays on other properties. The stolen sheep were usually disposed of to settlers of a respectable character. Apart from this, there was great concern about the influence convict servants had upon the 'rising generation'.

John Russell, the founder of Port Arthur, said in evidence given before the select committee that he felt the convict servants were a corrupting influence, as it was natural for the younger generation to associate with the convict servants about the houses. Russell gave as an example three convict servants who were hanged for the rape of the five-year-old daughter of one of the most respectable settlers in the colony. Within a week of this he examined two children in Launceston, in his position as surgeon at the civil hospital. One had allegedly been raped by her convict schoolmaster.

If anything, Russell believed the female servants were worse than the men. They tended to get rather close to the daughters of the family to which they were assigned, and unfortunately some mothers trusted these women too much. Instances were given by Russell of daughters of the household used as spies by the female convicts, to assist them with their paramours. In some cases girls received their sex education by witnessing the convict servant maids having intercourse with their lovers. Not surprisingly, the girls themselves were often soon pregnant. In fact the conduct of the convict women was so bad the ladies of Hobart Town often preferred male servants. The convict women, when corrected, would make use of the vilest language because they knew their mistresses could not repeat it in court before a magistrate. Russell felt the situation was rather general, regarding the corrupting influence of female convicts, and when he was asked to give his opinion on the effect of the assignment system on the character of the master he was utterly pessimistic. He thought it blunted the master's feelings, as he looked upon his convict servant almost as a slave, and he agreed with his examiner that this frequently made the masters tyrannical and despotic. Russell also made the interesting point that the free male servants were not much better than the convicts, as they were frequently overpaid but also demoralised by the convicts. On the other hand, he felt that the free female servants were of a much higher order than their convict counterparts, particularly when they worked in well-regulated households which segregated them from the convicts.[8]

When he was examined, Governor Arthur gave it as his opinion that a convict's situation was superior to that of a labourer in England so far as food and clothing went. But he pointed out a convict had no freedom, and he did not think a free-born citizen would ever want to change places with a convict. Arthur also felt a convict could not be ill-treated, as he could always complain to a police station. Curiously enough, Arthur thought it was possible for a good master to treat his convicts in a better fashion than was intended by the government, but when asked about the punishments available for assigned servants, he revealed the hard side of the penal system. Convicts who misconducted themselves and were habitually negligent were taken before a magistrate, who could have them whipped or sent to a road gang, in or out of chains. They could be punished the same way for having an insolent expression. Arthur admitted that, in this sense, convicts were completely at the mercy of the family to which they were assigned and that their lot was often no better than that of a slave.[9] At the beginning of his evidence, Arthur made the point there were seven classes of convicts:

The first and most desirable class is that class of convicts who are holding tickets of leave; then convicts who are in assigned service; convicts who are on the public works; convicts who are in road parties out of chains; convicts who are in road parties in chains; convicts who are ordered to the penal settlements; and those who are in the penal settlements in chains.[10]

The situation of the ticket-of-leave prisoners was similar to that of the modern offender who is on probation. Exempted from serving a portion of his sentence, provided his conduct was good, he attended a muster at least once a month, and Divine Service every Sunday. If a man was sent out for seven years, he became eligible for his ticket-of-leave after four. He was allowed to work for his own benefit, but could not move from one district to another without permission.

Upon the arrival of a transport, as many prisoners as possible were assigned to private people. Usually, however, the government finished up with a quarter of the prisoners. Several who could be trusted were sent to the Commissariat. Some particularly skilled tradesmen were sent to the Engineer's Department, and some to the Miscellaneous Department. Those who were considered able to endure a good deal of fatigue finished up in the Survey Department. Skilled tradesmen were usually assigned to the engineer's department or to the loan gangs, so they could be loaned out to settlers. During his evidence before the select committee, Governor Arthur denied any knowledge of a distinction being made between those assigned for private service and those assigned to the government. He pointed out that allocation was left to the assignment board, who received applications from both the government departments and private employers. However, Arthur believed that the worst of the convicts would be detained in the government service, and would not be assigned.

Those convicts awaiting assignment who could not be absorbed by the government departments usually finished up in the road gangs, out of chains. The largest of these gangs numbered 120 or 130 men. No convicts were sent direct from the transports to the chain gangs, which were regarded as a severe punishment reserved for convicts who had committed colonial offences. The gangs out of chains were usually supervised by a superintendent who was a free man, and by convicts who were sub-overseers. The gangs in chains, the largest of which consisted of nearly 300 men, were guarded by a sergeant and twelve soldiers.

In 1821 Macquarie Harbour was founded as a prison for the more intractable convicts. Deep inside a landlocked harbour, set in the middle of Van Diemen's Land's grim and forbidding west coast, it was described as nothing less than a 'Hell on Earth'. The men worked all day in the damp wet forests, felling huge logs which were then dragged to the water's edge. Food was poor, discipline rigid, punishment harsh and accommodation primitive. The more fortunate were employed in the shipbuilding industry, which thrived under the guidance of a master craftsman. There were never more than 300 convicts at Macquarie Harbour at any time before the settlement was abandoned in 1834. In September 1830 John Russell, an assistant surgeon of the 63rd Regiment, founded a new penal settlement at Port Arthur, on Tasman Peninsula, which was connected to the main island by a narrow strip of land called Eagle Hawk Neck. Port Arthur made good progress. By 1834 all the residue from Macquarie

Harbour and the shorter lived penal settlement of Maria Island had been absorbed, and the convict population had risen to 300 by the year's end. In 1834, a special establishment for boys was began at Point Puer, just across the bay from Port Arthur, and the Coal Mines were opened. The work at the mines was so heavy and dangerous it was actually used as a punishment centre for Port Arthur.

By 1835 there were 1,000 prisoners at Port Arthur, guarded by 100 constables and some superintendent overseers. That same year the settlement was exporting boots and shoes, sawn timber, boat spars, charcoal, cartwheel spokes, lathes and coal. It was also becoming a shipbuilding centre. Nevertheless, it was a severe punishment centre, and the main instrument of punishment was the carrying gang. In this gang, huge baulks of timber were carried on the shoulders of perhaps thirty labourers, who resembled a huge centipede as they staggered under the weight. Brutal floggings, often in excess of 100 lashes, were used to keep the rest of the convicts in order. The guard at Port Arthur in 1833 consisted of two officers, two sergeants, and seventy-three rank and file. That of Eagle Hawk Neck consisted of one officer, a sergeant and twenty rank and file, plus a line of eleven savage dogs across the narrowest sections of Eagle Hawk Neck. There were no females at Port Arthur, except the wives of senior officers and their servants. No convict was sent there for less than two years, and some became so weary of life they murdered other convicts in order to be hanged. Less than 10 per cent of the convict population finished up at Port Arthur.

During the early days of transportation, educated convicts were given favourable treatment. Classed as gentlemen convicts, in keeping with their former social status, they were usually assigned to positions within the Commissariat or to professional citizens. During the 1830s a determined effort was made to avoid this duality, and they were given the same type of work as the rest. But given the great shortage of educated people in the colony, they were usually spared the most laborious work, and once more found their way into responsible positions.

At the time of the select committee, there were 3,000 female convicts in Van Diemen's Land, most of them based at the female house for correction in Hobart or its counterpart in Launceston. While at the correction centres waiting to be assigned, or serving sentences for offences committed in the colony, the women spent the time spinning and picking wool. The female house of correction, or 'factory', was situated at the Cascades in Hobart, and many of the women were utterly intractable, as the following comment from the Colonial Times indicates:

> There is a class of persons in this colony, the management of which produces more trouble to the prison disciplinarians than that of any other class. We refer to the female prisoners of the Crown, whose tricks, manoeuvres and misconduct have baffled the exertions of every person appointed to control and correct them. We have ascertained that there is what is called a 'mob' always in the Factory, and that this mob has assumed the title of 'The Flash Mob'.[11]

Women were never assigned to publicans, or to single persons. Governor Arthur thought marriage was the best way of reforming them.

One problem which was to dog the administration during the convict era was the need for an efficient police force. Most of the governors found it necessary to employ convicts as policemen, and when Governor Arthur tried to employ ex-soldiers and free emigrants as policemen he found them worse than the convicts. The former soldiers proved to be drunkards, and the free emigrants were also unsuitable. He was therefore forced to select men from each transport 'with the best characters, active, and intelligent' as policemen. Inevitably there were serious failures, and selecting convicts as constables was in itself an abuse of procedure. But such was Arthur's shortage of funds and of suitable manpower, there was nothing else he could do.

This type of problem was endemic to the colony. Many of the first free women who were sent out were reputedly prostitutes from Fleet Street, who readily resumed their trade on their arrival. Nevertheless, there were also quite a few respectable servants, and these found ready employment in good households which preferred them to convicts. The settlers as a whole were heavily dependent upon convict labour. As John Russell told the select committee: 'The generality of settlers, putting morality out of the question, while they can obtain convict labour so cheap, will not pay the enormous price they must now to obtain free labour; they can keep a convict for £25 a year'.[12]

Overall, there seemed to be little doubt in the minds of the witnesses that the assignment system did more harm than good. Surgeon Russell felt it corrupted both bond and free and said of its effects on the convicts: 'I think it hardens them exceedingly, and makes them dead to all sense of honest shame, and careless of trifling punishments'.[13]

Governor Arthur felt no less than one-quarter of all convicts were 'irreclaimable', that there could not be such a large class of persons resident in any community 'without the most polluting consequences', and that the continuation of the system of transportation would only demoralise the community in Van Diemen's Land. As such, its continuation could only be justified in terms of its importance to the mother country.

The committee made the following recommendations, as recorded by the Rev. John West in his *History of Tasmania*:

> that transportation to New South Wales, and the settled districts of Van Diemen's Land, should be discontinued: that (penal) establishments abroad should be limited to places where no free settlers were allowed to enter; that the abridgment of a sentence should be determined by fixed rules; that at its close, encouragement should be offered, to such as might merit the favour, to go to some country where support could be more easily obtained, and character recovered; and, finally, that no convict should be permitted to remain at the place of his punishment after its termination.[14]

The way was now open for the probation system, the architect of which was Lord Stanley, who was secretary of state in 1842.

7

Probation at Salt Water River

Before the convicts on the *Constant* went ashore, they had to be sorted out by the muster master. On the third day in port, after all the preliminaries with the port officer and the colonial secretary had been completed, the muster master and the principal superintendent of convicts boarded the *Constant*. The muster master was John Price, a tall, powerfully built Cornish man, aged thirty-five, who had distinguished himself against bushrangers and who viewed the world about him through a monocle in his right eye. Three years later he was appointed commandant of the penal station at Norfolk Island, where the severity of his seven-year regime was to make him a notorious figure in early Australian history. Married to a niece of the outgoing governor, Sir John Franklin, he had already gained a reputation as an inflexible disciplinarian as police magistrate of Hobart. The principal superintendent of convicts was a tall, solemn man named William Gunn, who had also encountered bushrangers and lost an arm in an encounter with Matthew Brady.

Many of the convicts on board the *Constant* must have been amazed at the knowledge Price showed of their backgrounds. Since less than half of them were fully literate, they may not have understood that their police records had come out in the *Constant* with them. Furthermore, Price had an astonishing knowledge of the artifices of convicts. He knew all the jargon or 'flash language' used by criminals of the time and spoke to them in that vernacular, presumably to help him obtain more accurate information. They were asked about their ages, trades and previous convictions, and if they gave an evasive or incorrect answer they were quickly corrected from the record. De Winton remarked upon the demand for mechanics: 'An instance—Trade?' "Well, sir, I've worked a bit in a brickfield." "Build a house?" "Oh no, sir." "Build a wall?" and before an answer could come— "Put him down a bricklayer. Next," became a saying.'[1]

After having gone through the hands of the muster master, Stephen Howard and his fellow convicts were marched to the prisoners barracks in Campbell Street, which occupied a whole block between Melville and Bathurst Streets, where they awaited assignment to their probation gang. According to the report submitted in the first half of 1846, there was not room for more than 816 prisoners in all.[2] On their arrival they were assembled in the yard before the lieutenant-governor, Sir John Eardley-Wilmot, who had only taken up his appointment on 21 August. Also present were John Hemery, master of the *Constant*, and Lempster Elliot, in his capacity as commander of the guard. The colonial surgeon made a final examination of the convicts, while a number of respectable citizens looked on as a novelty. The principal superintendent then called each convict by name and told him the probation station to which he had been assigned. After he had finished, Eardley-Wilmot, dressed in full uniform, stepped forward and addressed them. He told the prisoners that they had been sent out to Van Diemen's Land for their crimes, that they had brought their punishment on themselves, and that they stood in a most degraded situation. Nevertheless, the governor told them, they also had it in their power to redeem themselves. He explained that they would serve an allotted period at the probation station, the time depending upon their original sentence, after which, given good conduct, they would become eligible for a probation pass. This would allow them to engage in any private service for wages. He also reminded them that the government in its humanity would see they had sufficient food, clothing and medical treatment, before reading out the clauses of the Quarter Sessions Act which imposed very hevy penalties on the convicts if ever they offended in the colonies.

How did the convicts from the *Constant* feel as they listened to the sixty-year-old lieutenant-governor? As they were mainly of peasant origin, some idea may be gained from Arthur's observations, concerning the agricultural convicts who came out in the *Eliza* in 1831. When asked if he believed that the agricultural population feared transportation much more than the London thieves, he replied: 'I was very much struck with the replies of the men who came out in the "Eliza"; they were very much affected, and I never saw men who appeared to suffer more than they did; and a great many of them were very dejected, and I am sorry to say a great many of them died'.[3] However, the *Eliza* had carried English convicts, transported for riots and smashing machines, and the Irish convicts were somewhat different, as Peter Cunningham pointed out:

> The Irish convicts are more happy and contented with their situation on board than the English, although more loth to leave their country, even improved as the situation of the great body of them is by being thus removed, numbers telling me they had never been half so well off in their lives before. It was most amusing to read the letters they sent to their friends on being fairly settled on board (all such going through the surgeon's hands) none ever failing to give a most circumstantial account of what the breakfast, dinner, and supper, consisted of; a minute list of the clothes supplied, and generally laying particular emphasis on the important fact of having a blanket and bed to 'my own self entirely', which seemed to be somewhat of a novelty by their many circumlocutions about it.[4]

Cunningham wrote this in 1827, but conditions in Ireland had deteriorated if anything in the following fifteen years.

Several days later the principal superintendent, William Gunn, marshalled those convicts who were to go to the Salt Water River probation station and marched them down to the waterfront, where the government brig *Isabella* was waiting. In addition to the thirty-three convicts from the *Constant*, there were twenty-five from the *Gilmore*, which had arrived on 19 August, ten from the *Cressy*, berthed on 20 August, and another convict, an old hand who had arrived on the third voyage of the *Moffat* on 1 April 1838. The convicts from the *Cressy* and the *Constant* were unique in that they were the first convicts from England and Ireland to come under the system introduced on the formation of the Convict Department in 1843.

After the select committee of enquiry into transportation, there was a general dissatisfaction within the British government concerning the assignment system. In 1841 Lord Edward George Stanley became colonial secretary in Peel's administration. Stanley had already had a very mixed political career. He left the Whigs in 1833, was an independent for a while, and then drifted towards the Tories. In 1838 he emerged as one of Peel's chief lieutenants, and when he became colonial secretary he immediately decided to replace assignment with the probation system.

The probation system consisted of five stages, of which the first was detention at Norfolk Island, which was reserved for those sentenced to transportation for life or for terms not less than fifteen years. Norfolk Island was regarded exclusively as a place of confinement, and no-one was permitted to live there except the convicts, the penal officials and the military detachment which supervised the convicts. While there the convicts were employed in hard labour for two to four years, depending upon their sentences and their behaviour while on the island.

The next stage of probation was the probation gang. These gangs consisted of convicts who had already passed through the period of detention at Norfolk Island, those serving terms of ten or seven years, plus those who were indicated by the secretary of state as being suitable for this class. These gangs were also to be employed in hard labour, though it would vary according to their behaviour. Lord Stanley estimated the average probation gang as consisting of 250 to 300 men. The terms to be spent in the probation gang depended upon the original sentence according to the following scale: 7 to 10 years transportation, 2 years probation; 10 to 14 years, 2½ years probation; 14 to 20 years, 3 years probation; 20 years or more, 3 years probation; transportation for life, 4 years probation. The gangs were later increased to 300 or 400 in number.

Once convicts had passed through the probation gang, they proceeded to the third stage of punishment, during which they became eligible for a probation pass which enabled them to engage in private service for wages. To obtain a probation pass, convicts had to obtain both a certificate of good conduct from the comptroller-general of convicts and to complete the original term of gang probation. The holders of probation passes were divided into three classes. Members of the first or lowest class had to obtain the consent of the governor before they could engage in any service, while those in the second and third classes did not have to go through this formality. The members of the first class could only receive half their wages from their employers, and the members of the second class two-thirds of their wages, the balance in each case being paid by the employer into a savings bank account. The members of the third class were allowed to receive the whole of their wages from their employers. If the holders of probation passes were unable to obtain employment, they were to return to the service of the government, to be employed without wages, merely receiving rations of food and clothing. If they were living off rations, they were usually employed in making or repairing roads, or as members of jobbing parties hired out to perform agricultural labour for private people. They had to be inspected by a magistrate once a month.

The fourth stage of probation was that of tickets-of-leave. Convicts did not become eligible for their ticket-of-leave until they had served at least half their sentence of transportation. Ticket-of-leave holders were required to remain in a particular district, within which they could hire themselves out for wages. They had to obtain permission from a magistrate before leaving this district, and they had to register their new address. They were subject to a strict curfew, and had to be at home from 10 p.m. until break of day. They had to report regularly to the police station in the district and, if they offended, they could be treated summarily for some classes of offences. Their ticket-of-leave could be revoked for misconduct, and they could be subjected to severe penal labour at Port Arthur.

The fifth and last stage of the probation system was that of a pardon, either conditional or absolute. Pardons could be granted 'either by the Queen directly or by the Governor in the exercise of the Royal Prerogative delegated to him for that purpose'. No convict could be considered for a pardon until he at least reached the third stage of ticket-of-leave.[5]

Although ideal in its concept, the system did not have a chance. The probation camps were usually dedicated to roadmaking and timber-getting, and only a few were in good agricultural country. As well, they were not ready to accommodate large numbers of convicts. Despite this, no fewer than 127 convict transports arrived in Van Diemen's Land in the 1840s, as against eighty-six in the previous decade. From 1841 to 1845 there arrived 18,929 convicts, of whom 3,383 were females, and in 1849 no fewer than twenty ships arrived from the various parts of the Empire carrying 1,860 convicts in all. During the period 1841–44, the colony was in the grip of a severe economic recession and it was difficult for those holding probation passes to find work. Nor could the government afford to employ the convicts on the terms originally laid down by Stanley.

The *Isabella* left the Hobart waterfront with her human cargo on 9 September 1843. A 150-ton brig, the *Isabella* was built at Macquarie Harbour in 1830 by a convict shipwright, John Rider. In addition to the master she carried a crew of thirteen, including three convicts.[6] Given good conditions, it was only a four or five hour run from Hobart to Salt Water River.

Salt Water River was one of four probation stations on the Tasman Peninsula,

John Hemery, c. 1845 (*Courtesy of Mr P. Hemery*)

John Stephen Hampton (*J. S. Battye Library of Western Australian History*)

Captain Lempster Elliot, 1859 (*National Army Museum, London*)

Captain G. J. De Winton, c. 1857 (*Wiltshire Regimental Museum*)

Salt Water River convict station (*Archives Office of Tasmania*)

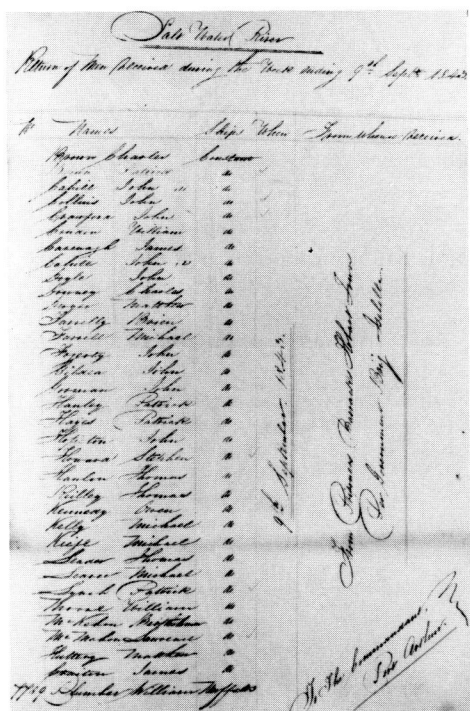

Return of men from *Constant* received at Salt Water River probation station per *Isabella*, 9 September 1843 (*Archives Office of Tasmania*)

General Alexander Thomson (*Courtesy of Mrs R. Willoughby*)

the others being Impression Bay, the Cascades, and the Coal Mines. Under the assignment system, Port Arthur ranked only second to Norfolk Island in terms of the severity of its discipline. The Cascades and the Coal Mines were reserved for convicts guilty of offences in the colony, while Impression Bay was mainly used for invalids and had good accommodation for that purpose. Salt Water River was the principal agricultural station for the peninsula, and in 1846 had 270 acres under cultivation.

The report of the comptroller general on 31 December 1846 describes Salt Water River station as having mainly brick buildings, with the exception of the stores and the hospital. No partitions existed in the dormitory, thus making for easy supervision. The store was a bad and insecure building, and the hospital was nothing more than two wretched huts. Good land was under cultivation, and a dam had been constructed to prevent salt water from mixing with the fresh. The station had good roads linking it to the other penal stations, and it was regularly visited by a magistrate and a medical officer. The number of prisoners had reached 499, with fifty men at any given time employed in fencing and putting up huts. Sheep husbandry was also being developed. Most interesting, however, was the superintendent's method of classification and segregation within the settlement. Three yards, three messes, and presumably three sets of dormitories, had been built for three distinct classes of prisoners. In addition, there were a number of boys at Salt Water River, all of whom were in the third class and were kept segregated from the men.[7]

When Stephen Howard disembarked from the Isabella he had reached the end of an incredible odyssey. Since his arrest on 14 December 1842 he had been through a chain of prisons which had reached from one side of the Earth to the other— the bridewell of Bruff, then Limerick county gaol, Kilmainham convict prison, the convict transport Constant, a brief period at Campbell Street prisoners barracks in Hobart, and now Salt Water River probation station 13,000 miles from home. For nearly nine months this Irish peasant, who was used to unrestricted movement in his employment as an agricultural labourer, had been confined behind massive walls and strong, heavy doors. The usual noises of bleating sheep, barking dogs and lowing cattle had been replaced by the clank of manacles, the ring of iron bars when struck by other metallic objects, and most of all the ever-continuing sounds of huge keys being turned in great locks. Now as he stood in the centre of the probation station with his fellow convicts, listening to superintendent Pringle, he must have hoped that he had reached his final destination. The convicts from the Constant had been sent to nineteen different probation stations, although Salt Water River had received more than twice as many as any other. Presumably the intention was to further develop Salt Water River as an agricultural station. Compared with the trip aboard the Constant, the run down from Hobart on the Isabella was a pleasant little interlude, and Stephen had four other Limerick convicts with him.

The entire camp turned out to greet the convicts. The staff consisted of superintendent James Jones Pringle, the catechist Robert Crooke, three assistant superintendents, a medical orderly, a storeman and three overseers. The military detachment consisted of fifteen men. Only one of the civilian staff members was married, but five of the soldiers were, and they boasted thirteen children between them. Pringle repeated in a simpler fashion what Eardley-Wilmot had already told them and then spoke of the segregation which existed at Salt Water River. He warned them they would all start in the lowest class, and would only proceed to the second and third class on the basis of good behaviour. As the probation system had only just got under way, they were warned there was much work to be done. A lot of land had to be cleared and put under cultivation, and many buildings had to be erected, all of which offered these poor bemused convicts from the far side of the Earth a splendid opportunity to redeem themselves by hard constructive toil. Pringle did all he could to drive home the principle of the whole scheme of convict discipline as 'that of a very formidable punishment at the commencement, gradually relaxing in severity with the lapse of time: each successive mitigation being expedited by good conduct, or retarded by ill behaviour'.[8]

As Pringle explained the routine, Stephen and his fellow prisoners would have soon realised it was similar to that of the other prisons they had been in. They were up at daybreak, the hour depending upon the season; they had two meals a day, breakfast and dinner, with an hour being allowed for each; and they were locked up at five or six in the evening, again depending upon the season. Their daily rations consisted of 1½ pounds of flour (12 per cent protein content), half a pound of vegetables, 1 pound of fresh meat or of salt beef or 10 ounces of salt pork, and half an ounce each of salt and soap. Their clothing allowance was two cloth jackets, two pairs of cloth trousers, three striped cotton shirts, four pairs of shoes or two pairs of ankle boots in lieu of three pairs of shoes, and two leather caps. For bedding, each prisoner was supplied with a rug, a blanket and a palliasse.[9] According to Robert Crooke, the prison dress consisted of a coarse grey jacket and trousers, with a black leather cap.

James Jones Pringle was twenty-nine years of age when Stephen and his fellow convicts arrived from Hobart. He had arrived in Van Diemen's Land in December 1833 and had worked in the office of the colonial treasurer as a volunteer until August 1834, when he received a permanent appointment as a junior clerk in the Treasury. In 1836 he was appointed to the Colonial Secretary's Department, where he was employed in the lieutenant-governor's private office. Upon the introduction of the probation system, Pringle accepted a posting as superintendent of convicts at Salt Water River on 4 April 1841, although it was a move he was greatly to regret. A highly strung young man who turned to excessive drinking to soothe his nerves, his career took a serious downturn in 1846 when he was drunk during a visit by Governor Sir William Denison. However, at the time Stephen arrived at Salt Water River Pringle's troubles, including the tragic death of his young wife only sixteen months after their marriage, were all in the future.

In fact, all the early reports on Salt Water River probation station were highly favourable. Major Cumberland of the 96th Regiment, who was the visiting magistrate, gave the station an excellent report in December 1842, and Major Frederick

Mainwaring of the 51st Light Infantry, who succeeded Cumberland, gave it a series of equally complimentary reports throughout 1843. He congratulated Pringle for the order, discipline and cleanliness of the station, despite the presence of a great many bad characters who committed numerous offences and were often before the magistrate. Mainwaring's remarks all relate to Pringle's ability to keep up the 'spit and polish' side of the station, but as later events were to confirm, Pringle was failing in the fundamental tasks of development and reform. Nevertheless, in his report on the station in November 1843, nearly three months after Stephen Howard's arrival, Mainwaring is loud in his praise of the superintendent:

> I now turn with pleasure to Salt Water River where the Superintendent's mild, firm, zealous and gentleman like manner of carrying on his duties leaves me nothing to censure— the men were clean and well clothed, and the station in nice order, the crops look well, and more land is rapidly clearing, the school is well conducted, and the Catechist attentive to his duties.[10]

Captain Mathew Forster, the comptroller general of convicts and a nephew of the able and authoritarian Arthur, visited the station at least three times while Stephen Howard was serving his period of gang probation, and he was pleased with every aspect of the station. In August 1844 he found the 'men healthy' and he noted that Pringle was working hard on the farming side of things. In January 1845 he praised Pringle for his management and noted 'crime very small in amount'. In December 1845 Forster noted that he had less trouble with this station than any other.[11]

The Salt Water River correspondence book of 1843 is mostly concerned with routine matters, such as requisitions for crockery and cutlery, the transfers of storekeepers, a dispute concerning the conveyance of mailbags and queries concerning pay and rations. The Brilliant (Sun-Grazing) Comet of 1843, with its huge tail, caused great excitement at the station. In his report to the observatory of 17 March 1843, Pringle described it as an 'extraordinary visitor' with a position 'west south west' to the station. An uproar also ensued at the neighbouring station of Impression Bay when a private vessel called the *Sophia* landed goods and people in violation of the regulations. The master was fortunate his vessel was not seized.[12]

But was Salt Water River in as good a state as it seemed? Robert Crooke was the settlement's catechist, and the authorities gave great weight to religious instruction. They believed a moral change could only be brought about by the untiring exertions and exhortations of the religious instructor. Crooke, who was later ordained a minister in the Anglican church and became one of its most controversial figures, gives us the other side of the picture. It was the policy of the government to make no distinction for educated convicts until they had finished their gang probation, and during Crooke's term at Salt Water River there were several educated convicts undergoing their probation. Crooke contrasts the lot of the educated convicts with that of those who came from the labouring classes:

> To the English, or more especially the Irish labourer, it is a question whether transportation was in reality, a punishment at all. His food and clothing were better than at home,

his hours of labour less, and his opportunities of improving his condition far greater than he would, under any other circumstances, have met with. But all the convicts were not of this class. Clergymen, lawyers, doctors, stockbrokers and gentlemen were transported as well as labourers and mechanics and their sufferings were worse than death. Let the reader imagine a well-educated gentleman who has had the necessaries and some of the luxuries of life at home, accustomed to cleanliness, the decencies of a well-ordered home and tolerably good society, imagine, I say, such a man placed in the same shed or hut with some 40 or 50 burglars, thieves, ravishers, murderers, Sodomites and pick pockets, and he will be enabled to form some faint idea of the Hell upon earth in which such men were placed.[13]

Crooke described the plight of a well-known convict called Beaumont Smith, who had been convicted for forging exchequer bills and was located at the Impression Bay probation station a few miles from Salt Water River. Smith, who had mixed with the best society in England, was forced to perform the most menial tasks such as cleaning wards, emptying urine tubs, cutting wood and drawing water.

All this he doubtless deserved, and could have borne, but when night came, and he was led to his sleeping place, and found himself in the same room with some 30 ruffians of the darkest dye, and heard their oaths, execrations and obscenities, and witnessed their brutal and unnatural beastialities, he was shocked beyond measure and felt like Cain, that his punishment was more than he could bear.[14]

Poor Beaumont Smith approached the superintendent, telling him that as a criminal he was prepared to undergo whatever punishment they choose to inflict. His one request was for a private sleeping place, no matter how humble:

The superintendent refused his request with a brutal sneer, and night after night was this unfortunate wretched man compelled to board with veritable demons. Sodomy and onanism were openly practised in his sleeping barrack, and had he dared to state openly what took place, his life, he well knew, would have been the forfeit.[15]

Finding the nightly scene more than he could bear, Beaumont Smith approached the comptroller-general, Mathew Forster, during one of his periodical visits to the station, and repeated his plea for a private sleeping place. He was told by Forster that his request could not be complied with. As an educated man he had 'not the temptation of want and ignorance', and if anything he deserved more than those who were uneducated. Crooke was fascinated by the spectacle of gentlemen convicts in these circumstances and notes that, with a few exceptions, they mostly lost 'caste' and sank to a depravity equal to that of the lower social orders.[16]

Crooke seems to feel the educated convicts were the only ones who could be credited with any sensibility, and that labourers who had plenty of food and clothing would not be concerned with the dormitory situations. But Stephen Howard was one amongst many young men who had lived close to nature, in a sexually conservative society, where sexual continence was highly regarded. For such prisoners to be placed in a dormitory with twenty or thirty men, many of whom were brazen and even predatory in their sexual activities, would have shaken the sensibilities of many of them, educated or otherwise.

According to Crooke, a convict's life at Salt Water River was extremely monotonous. They rose at 4.30 a.m. in the summer, dressed and washed, and then paraded for prayers, which lasted for five minutes. After breakfast they went to work, except for those who reported sick to the doctor. Schools were held in the evening, under the management of the religious instructor, for those it was thought would benefit from them, and books, slates, pens and ink were provided for this purpose. Surprisingly, all convicts were forced to attend Divine Service in the Anglican ritual, regardless of their creed, although this seems to be in contradiction to regulation 44 which forbade convicts from any dealings with a religious instructor outside their own creed.

The probation stations were tightly organised and came under the direct control of the comptroller-general. The commandant at Port Arthur was expected to visit the probation camps on the Tasman Peninsula regularly, and to keep them under surveillance, but he was not allowed to interfere in their organisation and discipline. The senior officers were expected to supervise the prisoners closely, as were the assistant supervisor and the overseer for each class, and daily inspections were held. The visiting magistrate was required to make regular visits to each camp under his jurisdiction, and to report its state of discipline to the comptroller-general of convicts.

Bakers, cooks, watchmen, hospital orderlies, store labourers and servants were selected from men who had gone through two-thirds of their terms of probation with uninterrupted good conduct. Bakers were appointed in the proportion of one to 150 convicts, as were cooks, while washermen were appointed one to every ninety convicts and were to be changed monthly. Six of the best conducted men of the gang, who had completed two-thirds of their probation, were selected as watchmen.[17] Whether Stephen or any of the other prisoners from the *Constant* were promoted to this exalted status is not known. As Salt Water River was a large agricultural station, Pringle very likely decided they would be more useful as farm labourers, particularly as this was his most vulnerable area. The thirty-three convicts sent to Salt Water River from the *Constant* fared remarkably well, and only two gave real trouble. A fifteen-year-old boy from Monaghan finished up in the chain gang, and was later flogged, while a thirty-one-year-old convict from Leitrim was sent to a chain gang and later to Norfolk Island. A twenty-five-year-old convict from Mayo died after only nineteen months at Salt Water River, but the remaining thirty completed their gang probation without serious trouble.

Despite the good behaviour of the Irish convicts from the *Constant*, Salt Water River was not without its disciplinary problems. During 1845, 267 prisoners were brought before the magistrate, tried and convicted, two for felony and larceny and the remainder for breaches of discipline. The average number of convicts at the station during the year was 481. From 1 July 1845 to 30 June 1846, twenty-seven men were flogged, receiving 1,299 lashes, or an average of forty-eight each. A weekly progress report was kept for each convict, with nine headings to cover the favourable aspects of his behaviour and eleven headings to cover the unfavourable ones.

The returns for early September 1843 showed there were 272 probationary convicts at Salt Water River, while the sixty-nine from the *Constant*, the *Gilmore* and the *Cressy* were on their way. By 29 June 1844 the strength had built up to 421, while returns submitted for 30 June 1846 showed the numbers had risen to 587.

At the same time, the administration began to run into stormy weather. James Jones Pringle was apparently very drunk during a visit by the governor in 1846. In May 1846 John Stephen Hampton, formerly surgeon-superintendent of the *Constant*, was appointed comptroller-general of convicts, but did not arrive in the colony until October. One of the early acts of his administration was to enquire into Pringle's conduct. He obtained a certificate from Dr Black of the Coal Mines, stating Pringle had twice been indisposed for long periods in 1846 because of severe attacks of delerium tremens brought about by an excessive indulgence in spirituous liquors. An enquiry into the state of agriculture of Salt Water River by the deputy commissary general again brought about an adverse report. It was found that progress in clearing land was very slow, and only 270 acres had been placed under cultivation, whereas no fewer than 500 acres should have been. The station produced vegetables and wheat, and had a piggery and a small herd of cattle, but the wheat was insufficient in quantity and exceedingly foul in quality. The report concluded by pointing out that the station should be self-sufficient, and to this end it recommended the appointment of a more energetic and competent superintendent, to be assisted by people who had some knowledge of farming. Poor Pringle was sent to the less important Cascades probation station on 5 February 1847, and was dismissed from the service in August of the following year.[18]

One gets the feeling that Pringle knew very little about agriculture and concentrated his energies upon the station area, as a result of which he received excellent reports for order and cleanliness while the all-important farming side languished. If results mean anything, Stephen and his fellow convicts from the *Constant* must have had a reasonably easy time of it, and they presumably should have been worked much harder. As many of them were experienced farm hands, they would have had the advantage of their overseers, who apparently knew less of agriculture than their charges did. Stephen would not have been worried about Pringle, as on 26 August 1845 he emerged from the gang to become a probation pass holder:

TABULAR STATEMENT of Offences in Van Diemen's Land, committed by 295 Convicts from England per 'Cressy' and 200 from Ireland per 'Constant', the first ships from England and Ireland respectively which arrived at Van Diemen's Land under the System introduced on the formation of the Convict Department in 1843. The period embraced in this statement from 20 August, 1843, to 30 September, 1848, is Five Years and One Month, during which none of the Convicts had become free: 20 had died.

Offences of Men per 'Cressy' from England and 'Constant' from Ireland	In first stage of probation in gang	In subsequent stages of probation	Total
Suspicion of Unnatural Crime	2	1	3
Sheepstealing	1	—	1
Burglary	6	—	6
Housebreaking	—	2	2
Highway Robbery	3	1	4
Receiving stolen goods	1	3	4
Obtaining goods	—	2	2
Larceny	29	27	56
Uttering forged orders	—	1	1
Insubordination	10	11	21
Absconding	92	29	121
Absent without leave	118	123	241
Assault	16	12	28
Drunkenness	2	158	160
Disobedience	107	57	164
Other Minor breaches of discipline	506	488	994
Total	893	915	1808

Number of men without offence in gang   150
Ditto without offence after emergence from gang   157
Ditto without offence on record   101

Total number of men by the two ships, 495.
Total number of offences during the period stated above 1,808.[19]

The table gives an idea how the men from the *Constant* and the *Cressy* fared during their first five years in Van Diemen's Land. Most of the offences, such as absence without leave, drunkenness, disobedience and other minor breaches of discipline, were rather trivial. On the other hand, offences such as absconding, larceny and assault were considered to be serious.

After leaving Salt Water River, Stephen Howard and others who had qualified for their probation pass returned to the prisoner's barracks in Hobart Town.

8

Ellen Lydon of North Galway

Ellen Lydon, the future wife of Stephen Howard, was the daughter of Martin Lydon, a widower of Galway. She had two brothers, Patrick and John, and a sister, Sarah. The records show Ellen to be 5 feet 2 inches in height, with a fair complexion, dark hair, eyes and eyebrows, a high forehead with a round visage, and a medium nose, mouth and chin. Her trade was given as country servant. At the time she was sentenced to transportation in 1849—as were her brother John and cousin Michael, convicted of the same crime—she was twenty-four years old.

It has not been possible to trace any modern descendants of Martin Lydon in Ireland, nor has it been possible to establish exactly where he lived in 1848. The Griffith Valuation of 1851 shows that a Martin Lydon held 101 acres at Finnish Island in the Carna area of south Connemara. The signature of a Martin Lydon also appears on a petition put up at Renvyle, west Connemara, in 1842, requesting that the police station at Renvyle be retained, instead of being moved to Letterfrack. Renvyle must have been a much larger town than it is today, as the petition reckons the population of the district, including the Killaries, as being 3,800 souls. It also credited Renvyle with having two licensed houses, a chapel, a courthouse and a resident magistrate. Renvyle also held four fairs a year and had a patent for a weekly market. At the time of her arrest Ellen Lydon was in service with General Alexander Thomson, who lived in Salrock House, on the property of Salrock, at the head of Little Killary Bay. Thomson had an estate of eleven townlands and an island in the east of the parish, 8,149 acres in all. He had twenty-one smallholders, with an average of 7.1 acres each, and five large tenants in holdings ranging from 60 to 2,201 acres.[1] In April 1897 a large part of this estate in the Carna area, comprising 1,319 acres, was sold for £1,250.[2] The Thomson family papers contain an interesting letter from a Martin Lydon of Carna to Captain Colin Thomson in 1884, concerning prices for cattle and other livestock. It is the writer's opinion that Ellen Lydon was recruited from Carna, for service in the Thomson household.

Of the 200 female convicts who were transported to Van Diemen's Land on the *Australasia* in 1849, twenty-six came from Galway. Only Cork had a greater representation, with twenty-seven female convicts on board. By comparison, only two male convicts from Galway were sent to Australia on the *Constant* in 1843. Certainly the famine of 1846–48 would have had a big effect on criminal activity, although the figures taken from the *Australasia* and the *Constant* are too small a sample from which to draw any hard conclusions. Nevertheless, it is instructive to examine Galway and Connemara as they were in the 1840s. A description of County Galway in 1846 is provided by the *Dublin Almanac*:

A large maritime county in the province of Connaught, bounded on the north by the county of Mayo, on the north-east by the county of Roscommon, from which it is for the most part separated by the river Suck, on the east by portions of Westmeath, the King's county, and Tipperary, on the south by Clare, and on the west by the Atlantic Ocean. Greatest length east and west, 164 miles; greatest breath north and south, 52 miles; comprising an area of 2,447 square miles, or 1,566,354 acres; of which 742,805 are arable, 708,000 uncultivated, 23,718 in plantations, 1,801 in towns, and 90,030 under water. Lough Corrib divides the county into the E. and W. districts; Lough Derg is an expansion of the Shannon, which forms part of the eastern boundary of the county. A branch of the Grand Canal extends from Shannon Harbour to Ballinasloe. The county is divided into 18 baronies—Aran, Athenrie, Ballymoe, Ballynahinch, Clare, Clonmacnowen, Dunkellin, Dunmore, Galway, Kilconnell, Killian, Kiltartan, Leitrim, Longford, Loughrea, Moycullen, Ross, and Tiaquin: the part of the county of the town of Galway, outside the municipal boundary, has been made the new barony of Galway. These are sub-divided into 120 parishes. The county comprehends the whole Kilmacduagh diocese, and parts of Tuam, Clonfert, Elphin, and Killaloe. The Assizes for the county are held in Galway town, and Quarter sessions in E. Galway at Ballinasloe, Eyrecourt, and Loughrea; and W. Galway at Galway town, Tuam, Oughterard, Gort, and Clifden. Petty Sessions in 34 places. The population in 1841 was 422,923; 403,746 in the rural, and 19,177 in the civic district, exclusive of Galway town. The county returns 4 members to Parliament; 2 for the county at large, constituency, 2,113; and 2 for Galway town, 2,084.[3]

Given the fearful conditions that prevailed in Connemara in the period from 1846 to 1855, and the desperation of the people, it is safe to say that the fledgling nation of Australia would have gained many settlers from there via the convict ships. Connemara is the western section of Galway, bounded by Lough Corrib and Lough Mask on the east, the Atlantic Ocean on the west, Killery Harbour to the north and Galway Bay to the south. During his journey through Ireland in 1842, the novelist William Thackeray described it as 'one of the most wild, and beautiful districts, that it is ever the fortune of a traveller to examine'.[4] The Halls, who toured Ireland in 1840, were also generous in their praise for Connemara and had this to say about north Connemara:

to Leenane is about twenty miles, but the tourist must make it thirty, for he will sacrifice the better half of his enjoyment if he does not verge to the right, to first visit the graceful shores of Renville, and the rugged passes of Salruc . . . Continuing onwards:

between Tully and Leenane a rare treat awaits the tourist, for he will walk or drive through the beautiful and magnificent pass of Kylemore. This gap in the mountains extends for about three miles and forms a deep dell through which runs a rapid river, which makes its passage into the lake near its eastern entrance.

Some two or three miles beyond this—the chief beauty of the district—the roads turn off to the north and lead beside lakes which lie at the foot of the mountains to Salruc. The pass of Salruc is said to derive its name from a certain saint—St Roc or Ruc—who is said to have resided in a cell at the foot of the mountains.

And so we pass on, by the side of, yet high above, Killary Bay. As we near Leenane we obtain another magnificent view of its whole extent. Descending from this point of view, we arrive at Leenane, and here a humble but pleasant inn greets the wayfarer, which is situated just as the head of the bay.[5]

It was in the midst of the rugged grandeur of Salruc that General Thomson had his estate. Today the house and the remaining fragments of his estate are called Salruc, while the surrounding townland is called Salrock.

The largest town in Connemara was Clifden, a relatively new town and the administrative centre for north Connemara. In 1846, at the height of the great famine, Clifden was described in *Slater's Directory* as

a sea-port and market town, in the parish of Omey, barony of Ballynahinch, county of Galway, 178 miles w. from Dublin, and 50 w. by n. from Galway, situated on an eminence, on the shore of a winding estuary, that empties itself into Ardbear, or Clifden harbour, on the western coast. It is of modern origin, having contained in 1815 only one house, at which time the late John D'Arcy, Esq. settled here, through whose exertions more than three hundred dwellings have since been erected. It is inhabited principally by intelligent shop-keepers and traders, and there are two excellent hotels, Carr's and Hart's, the former of which has recently undergone great improvement, and both are admirably arranged either for the comfort of families or commercial gentlemen . . . The government of the town is vested in the magistrates, who hold a petty session once a fortnight, and general sessions of the peace for the district twice a year.

The places of worship are a church of the establishment, a beautiful building, and a commodious Roman Catholic chapel, also a monastery of the order of Saint Francis. The other public buildings and institutions are a handsome new stone court-house, a bridewell, the union workhouse, a good building on an extensive scale, a constabulary barrack, a dispensary, a national school, and a loan fund . . . The parish of Omey contained, in 1841, 7,953 inhabitants, and the town of Clifden 1,509 of that number.[6]

Although the *Directory* gives further information about the scenery, and the gentry of the district, no mention is made of the famine or of the terrible scenes that were enacted daily by a starving and desperate people. But having seen western Connemara through the eyes of travellers in the 1840s, it is relevant to examine the living conditions of the people of the parish of Ballynakill, which covered the Renvyle, Tully Cross and Salrock area.

In 1835 a commission of enquiry was held into the state of the poor and Henry Blake of Renvyle House, the largest landlord in the area, gave evidence about the condition of the people of the parish of Ballynakill. The picture he presented was that of a self-employed community of small farmers who were also involved in the herring fishery. The people's diet consisted of potatoes and fish and they were reasonably clad, although the children were rather ragged during the summer. Labourers' wages were 6d. to 8d. per day, or £4 per annum with food and lodging, and they were least employed during the summer. The women were employed knitting stockings, making flannel yarn and fishing nets, and manuring the farm. Task work was not general in the neighbourhood, as the people tended to avoid it due to poor payment from the contractors. An average labourer occupying two acres of ground could within half a year produce ten tons of potatoes and twenty-five hundredweight of oats, valued at £21. He would have £17 to himself after paying his rent and taxes. Blake was convinced that productivity could be increased by a third if the people worked more steadily. The yearly expense for food to an average labourer would be something under £5. Wages for labour were usually paid for in provisions, or by conacre: 'The owner of conacre ground manured the soil and prepared it for the reception of seed; the hirer provided the seed, planted it, and performed all subsequent operations'.[7] In the Ballynakill parish, herds were usually hired by the provision of one or two acres of tillage land and the grass necessary to feed from one to five herd of cattle.

According to Blake, few cottages were let without land, and the rent of the cottages was seldom, if ever, considered in the letting of the land. The cabins were generally built of stone, with a thatched roof, and an increasing number had chimneys. Many had beds with feather mattresses, with some other furniture. However, Blake was quick to add that 'a general state of comfort is no where to be found'. Apart from rent there were seldom any conditions attached to the holding of grounds, except the keeping-up or making of fences. There were many instances of two or more families resident in the same cabin. Blake noted that the condition of the poorer classes was improving steadily, and they would have been affluent, except for Mr Peel's Bill which had robbed them of their acquired capital thrice since 1815. Blake concluded by saying that the parish had been peaceable since 1815, there was no savings bank in the area, nor pawnbrokers or usurers, but that the classes above the poor sometimes lend money at high interest rates. There were only one or two licensed houses, and innumerable shebeens. Illicit distillation was becoming a problem due to the total neglect of the Excise Department.

The Rev. Anthony Thomas of the Ballynakill Union generally agreed with Blake. However, he made the point that a day labourer could earn £10 per year. He also pointed out there were not many middlemen in the area, and that cabins rented from 10s. to 26s. per annum, having cost £2 to £4 to build. He too felt that the condition of the poorer classes had improved since 1815, and then waxed eloquent about the problem of drink. He pointed out that at one time there were twenty-three licensed public houses in the town of Clifden, although the number had been reduced of late. He also observed that illicit distillation prevailed in the Ballynakill parish to 'a lamentable and truly destructive extent'.

The Rev. Peter Fitzmaurice, the parish priest of Omey and Ballindoon, who was based in Clifden from 1832 to 1852, would not say whether or not the state of the parish had improved since 1815, as he had only been there for three years.

In general agreement with Blake and Thomas about the state of the area, he was particularly concerned about the large number of unlicensed public houses in Clifden and the demoralising effect they had on the people. He also pointed out that cottiers paid dearly for land, at the rate of 6d. to 8d. per day. Fitzmaurice was virtually the first parish priest of Clifden, as his predecessor, Myles Prendergast, had only stayed a year.[8]

It must be agreed, then, that conditions during 1835 were quite good. But the famine of 1846 changed all that. By 1849 whole parts of Ireland were devastated, particularly in the south-west and the west, and the population, which had been given as 8,175,124 in the 1841 census, dropped to 6,552,385 in the 1851 census. The census commissioners calculated that, at the normal rate of increase, the population would have been 9,018,799, suggesting that a loss of 2.5 million (or 22.5 per cent) had taken place. The decline in population varied throughout Ireland, with losses apportioned as follows between the four provinces: Leinster, 15.5 per cent; Ulster, 16 per cent; Munster, 23.5 per cent; and Connaught 28.6 per cent. Among the hardest hit was Connemara, which was a central focus of the famine in Connaught after the failure of the potato crop.[9]

Tradition credits Sir Walter Raleigh with introducing the potato into Ireland in the sixteenth century, although it is also asserted that Sir John Hawkins brought the potato to Ireland in 1565. The most commonly accepted date for its introduction is 1586. However, the potato does not seem to have been extensively cultivated as a rotation crop until the early eighteenth century.[10] The potato had an outstanding advantage in that it lent itself to simple spade husbandry, a method which suited the Irish as it did not require ploughing, and the surplus could also be used as food for animals. But above all, the potato in a given area supplied about four times as much food as any other crop. This was of course a great advantage in a situation where the population was expanding rapidly but arable land was limited.

Unfortunately the potato also had serious disadvantages. It would not keep and could not be stored from one season to the next. It was also very much prone to failure, which led to famine and also to outbreaks of typhus. Three serious famines occurred during the years 1725–28 and 1739–41 and twenty-four failures of the potato crop were listed by the Census of Ireland Commissioners of 1851. Ireland soon became known as the land of famines, and the annals of Ireland during the eighteenth century and the early nineteenth century are full of horror stories from travellers and writers who were amazed that such scenes of starvation, disease and depredation could take place in a Christian country. Despite this the Irish population, which increased by 172 per cent between 1779 and 1841, was becoming even more dependent upon the potato. It became increasingly obvious that a major calamity was inevitable.[11]

Potato blight is caused by a fungus, *Phytophthora infestans*, whose spore containers, which grow at the end of the fungus tubes, firstly destroy the leaves of the potato and then descend to attack the tuber itself. They both choke and devour the potato, leaving nothing but a blackened pulp in their wake. The fungus lies dormant in slightly diseased potatoes, waiting for the right weather conditions to multiply and spread throughout the entire crop. Given warm and moist circumstances, the fungus can spread with astonishing rapidity, and the climatic conditions in Ireland in 1846 favoured it to a degree that has not been known before or since. The early signs of the disease began to appear in February 1846, and by August the disaster was universal, with the whole crop wiped out throughout Ireland.[12]

The famine which occurred in Ireland during the 1846–48 was a compound disaster, as the winter in 1846–47 was also the worst in living memory. As Cecil Woodham Smith noted: 'Snow fell early in November; frost was continuous; icy gales blew "perfect hurricanes of snow, hail and sleet," with a force unknown since the famous great wind of 1839; roads were impassable and transport was brought to a standstill'.[13]

As if famine and an unusually cold winter were not enough, the Irish people also had to face a devastating epidemic of typhus and relapsing fever. Early reports of outbreaks of fever started coming in from Galway as early as April 1846, from Carrick on Shannon in June, from Waterford in October and from Cork in November. By March 1847 there was no doubt an epidemic was raging. The British government brought in shiploads of Indian corn from North America, funded public works projects to give some relief, set up dispensaries and hospitals for the sick and dying, and set up soup kitchens, but these proved to be only palliative measures. Hundreds of thousands of disease-ridden Irish fled their country to England, the United States and Canada, bringing with them the typhus epidemic, which caused wholesale death wherever they went. In the meantime, shiploads of grain and cereals left Ireland for export, even though the country was undergoing the greatest famine in European history.

Ellen Lydon was employed as a house servant by General Alexander Thomson during the years 1846–48, and this may well account for her survival in an area that endured a particularly high mortality rate during the famine. Servants would have had adequate food, shelter and clothing, and would above all have been segregated from the disease-ridden populace at large.

General Thomson was born in 1783 and in 1815 married the widow of the original owner of the estate of Cushkillary, whose first husband died during the Peninsular War. After his marriage Thomson, who had distinguished himself as an engineer in the Peninsular War, found himself engaged in a lengthy legal battle over the marriage settlement. His wife died before settlement and Thomson accepted the Cushkillary estate, totalling 8,099 acres, as settlement for his claim. A good description of the Cushkillary estate is given in a 'TO BE SOLD' notice of 16 January 1832:

> The Atlantic Ocean sweeps the shores of this rising and extensive property, adjoining which there are two lakes (having a salmon fishery) discharging themselves into the sea. There are also a small lake and river in the centre of this estate, which discharge themselves into the Killaries, famous for their fisheries. There is one of the best harbours on the west coast, the little Killary Bay, and the great new Government Road around Connemara is marked out, and now in progress through the property.[14]

The exact date at which Alexander Thomson came into full possession of the property is not known, but there is no doubt the former army engineer worked hard to improve his property. He reclaimed land, encouraged fishing and established schools. Between 1840 and his death in 1856 he was active in pushing through public works of all kinds. His distinguished military career had been similarly active and innovative, and *Hart's Army List* of 1854 recorded it in some detail:

> Lieutenant General Thomson accompanied the 74th to the Peninsular, landing at Lisbon in January 1810, and was present at the battle of Busaco, retreat to the lines of Torres Vedras, advance of the army on Messina's retreat there from, action at Foz d'Aronce (wounded), battle of Fuentes d'Onor, siege and capture of Ciudad Rodrigo, where he served as Assistant Engineer, and for his services was promoted to the rank of Brevet-Major: siege and capture of Badajoz, where he served as assistant engineer, and was slightly wounded when leading about 300 men of the party that stormed and took the Raveline of St Roque to reinforce the 3rd division of the army which had taken the castle; siege and capture of the forts of Salamanca where he served as Assistant Engineer and was slightly wounded; siege of Burgos and retreat there from—served as Assistant Engineer and had the blowing up of the bridge at Villa Morel and the bridge at Caheson entrusted to him; battle of Vittoria as second in command of the 74th; siege of San Sebastian where he served as Assistant Engineer, and for his conduct was promoted to the brevet rank of Lieutenant Colonel; battles of the Nivelle and the Nive, passage of the Bidassoa, and battle of Orthes, besides several skirmishes with his regiment at Alfayate, Villa de Pastores Albidous and other places. He has received the gold medal for San Sebastian, and the silver medal with 9 clasps for the other battles and sieges.
>
> Promoted to Major General 23/11/1841. Promoted Lieutenant General 11/11/1851.[15]

His military record notwithstanding, there is no doubt that Thomson, now in his sixties and the third-largest landlord in the area, fought his greatest battle during the famine when he emerged as the most active and resourceful landlord in the Ballynakill parish. He was a leading member of the Ballynakill Relief Committee, set up during 1846, and when the government was lamentably tardy in coming to the relief of the poor at Salrock he set up his own store, where he sold twenty-four tons of meal during the last quarter of 1846. He sent his *Hooker*, a boat of 15 tons burthen, to Westport in order to obtain further supplies, with the following results:

> All was shipped on board my Hooker . . . and on Sunday 3rd inst. she left the quay of Westport to come home but the day having come to blow and wind being against her after getting on their way as far as Runa Point near Clare Island they had to run for *Achill Sound* where they purposed to remain till the weather should prove favourable. About 10 o'clock at night on the same evening they were boarded with a boat and a number of men, and on challenging the people—the men on the Hooker three in number were beaten, pelted with stones, and forced under the hatch in the forecastle till they plundered the Hooker of everything on board.[16]

As four tons of Spanish flour at £17 per ton, and one ton of Indian meal at £20 per ton, had been plundered, Thomson wrote to Dublin Castle asking that he be given some compensation for the loss.

Thomson was particularly concerned at the manner in which he felt the more active and humane landlords were imposed upon by both the government and the less active landlords. It is clear from his correspondence that he felt landlords should have received tax concessions in proportion to the number of poor they relieved on their estates. He also felt every landlord should be responsible for the support of his own poor. He was also concerned about his neighbouring landlord, Henry Blake of Renvyle House, who had become very despondent and was in danger of ruining his health through worry. General Thomson felt if Blake were to survive, he first had to make his property viable, and the only way he could do this was to get quit of a half or two-thirds of his present pauper tenancy as soon as possible. Blake could then divide his property into viable farms, which he would let to farmers of sound capital, who would employ the remaining poor on his estate. This might seem to be a very ruthless plan, but Thomson did not say Blake had to get quit of his poor immediately, on top of which his thinking is quite in keeping with a soldier's mentality.[17]

In a letter to John Galway, a solicitor of Dublin, General Thomson put the case for the more active and enlightened of the landlords:

> We are in a most wretched state of destitution . . . and I fear shall be worse . . . some of my tenants have made a partial sowing of oats and barley . . . but speaking of the district generally two-thirds of the ground is still without anything in it, and that in a district where if all the land was well cultivated and cropped it would not support one-third of the population. Many of my tenants have thrown up their holdings not being able to sow them but they are keeping still possession of their houses and what to do with them I know not—I am giving employment to such of them as are not on the public works as yet, putting down my own crops, but what way I can manage after my crops are down I know not for tho' in my debt for rent I am obliged to pay them weekly in cash which will not last always . . . as for paying rent there is not a thought about it, and this outdoor Relief Bill with all the rates to be levied to carry it out will make the proprietors as bad as the poorest man on their estates for they will not be able to pay it.[18]

The blight which destroyed the potato crop in 1846 did not reappear in 1847, and the potatoes were of excellent quality. But since the people had eaten their seed potatoes the previous year, the crop was inadequate. In 1848 the crop again failed badly, and soon famine and typhus were raging as they had in 1846. It was at this time that General Thomson began to encounter trouble with his tenants and his letter to John Dopping, the resident police magistrate in Clifden, expresses his concern forcefully:

> Salrock 8th February, 1848.
>
> My Dear Dopping,
>   What is to be done to stop the increasing sheep stealing that is going on in this neighbourhood it is frightful—they throw the skins and heads into the sea or into bogholes and sometimes burn them and tho' you find the mutton in their house or even in their pots boiling they cannot be convicted tho' there cannot be a shadow of doubt that they came by it dishonestly—having no means whatever of getting it otherwise.

Would it not be right to represent this fact to Government—Let me know your opinion on the subject.

Yours Very Truly,
Alexander Thomson[19]

It is quite obvious from this letter, and a subsequent one written in March, that in company with most other landlords in Ireland, Thomson was angered by the repeal of a law (28 Geo. 3.7), which placed the 'onus probandi' upon an accused man caught with a large supply of mutton, fat or skins to prove he came by it lawfully. The repeal of this law meant a pauper could have as much mutton in his house as he liked, and it was up to the police and landlords to prove it was stolen. Unless they were able to find a skin with a brand on it, this was an almost impossible task.

On 2 March 1848 Thomson forwarded another letter to Dopping, in which he said he was sending in four people, two men and two women. Although he does not name the culprits, there is little doubt they were Ellen Lydon, her brother John, her cousin Michael and his wife Mary.

> I send four prisoners that were detected last night in killing one of my sheep they have been suspected this long time of killing sheep but no evidence could be had that would convict them. Well now, I hope from the evidence now against them that they will be sent across the water—the county is getting into a dreadful state of disorganisation, they will leave neither sheep or cattle in the country and shortly neither life or property will be safe fifty sheep have been stolen from Robert Fair within the last six weeks. Then Mr Eastwood had 20 sheep stolen from him a few nights ago. I have nothing but complaints from every quarter . . . I beg to remark that the prisoners were in no want. The two men were employed by me breaking stones and last Saturday got half a hundred weight of meal . . . The women were employed by Mrs Thomson spinning wool, and were paid 5/- for spinning one stone on Monday last.[20]

Thomson appears to be both puzzled and outraged that four servants who he had treated so well could have taken advantage of his good nature. But while Thomson was entitled to his anger, it has to be remembered that the Irish family is very close—reputedly the closest in Europe—and as Lydon is a very common name in Galway and west Connemara, the four Lydons would have had many starving relations and must have been under enormous pressure to help them in some way. Killing a sheep and stealing the carcass appears to have been their answer to the problem.

John Dopping, who had only recently been appointed resident police magistrate at Clifden, was born in 1800, a member of a senior Protestant Ascendancy family which had its seat at Derrycassin Granard, County Longford. He graduated BA from Trinity College during the Easter term of 1821, and in 1823 he was high-sheriff for the County of Longford. On 22 May 1838 he was appointed resident police magistrate for Rathangan, County Kildare. He became resident magistrate of Clifden in 1847, and was also a captain in the Longford militia.

The distress in the west Connemara area at this time was fearful. As early as September 1846, reports had come from coast guard officers making tours of

John Dopping, c. 1850 (*Courtesy of Mr L. A. C. Dopping-Hepenstal*)

Assistant barrister William Deane Freeman, c. 1844 (*The Illustrated London News Picture Library*)

Daniel O'Connell, c. 1844 (*The Illustrated London News Picture Library*)

The Earl of Clarendon (*Ryall's Portraits of Modern Conservatives*)

Clifden courthouse (*Author's collection*)

Clifden courtroom (*Author's collection*)

Salrock in winter (*Author's collection*)

Salrock House (*Author's collection*)

Market day in Clifden (*National Library of Ireland, Lawrence Collection No. R5345*)

inspection in north-west Connemara that people in the Killaries, Clifden and Ballynakill areas were dying of hunger. Mr Parker, the commissariat clerk in charge of the food depot at Clifden, was under frightful pressure from two opposed forces. On one hand Sir Randolph Routh, the commissary general, pressed him to make the people live off their own resources. On the other hand, Parker knew well that the people in the Killaries and the other wild areas had no resources left, that they were suffering fearful distress, and that they needed as much assistance as possible. In October 1846 Parker sent two angry letters outlining the people's distress, and also stating that relief must be sent. In January 1847 a respected Quaker minister from Norwich, Mr William Forster, visited Clifden and was surrounded by starving mobs who by their emaciated appearance and agonised cries of hunger appeared more like starving dogs than human beings. As the famine drew to a close in 1848, nine-tenths of the people in Clifden were receiving relief, the dead were burned, though where it was possible they were buried under the cabin floor before its roof was pulled down by the surviving members of the family, who then fled. 'Throughout Ireland the Irish people starved and died in one world and the Irish land-owning classes inhabited another.'[21] James Hack Tuke wrote:

> I have visited the wasted remnants of the once noble Red Man, on his reservation grounds in North America, and explored the 'negroquarter' of the degraded and enslaved African, but never have I seen misery so intense, or *physical* degradation so complete, as among the dwellers in the bogholes of Erris.[22]

Such was the area John Dopping came to serve as resident magistrate at the height of the famine.

Dopping found his bailiffs were being attacked when they tried to distrain cattle or other livestock in lieu of poor rates. At first he sent his bailiffs about their duties unescorted by police, as he thought the duties of the police in the Clifden area so arduous he was unwilling to further impose upon them. However, after a poor rate collector was threatened with sticks and stones, and another by a hatchet, he felt he had no other alternative but to send a heavy police escort with the bailiffs whenever they discharged their duties. On 17 January 1848 Dopping was so alarmed at the state of affairs in Clifden he wrote to the undersecretary at Dublin Castle requesting a company of infantry as a precautionary measure:

> I think it highly expedient that a company of Infantry should be quartered in the town of Clifden, as it is the depot for provisions which supply a considerable portion of the county . . . at the present crisis when a feeling of reckless desperation has manifested itself amongst the portion of the people nearly in a state of starvation, and when instances are not wanting of depraved persons taking advantage of such a state of things, and wantonly plundering their neighbours, I am of the opinion that a military force has become necessary as a precautionary measure.[23]

After being sent to Clifden from Salrock, Ellen Lydon and her co-accused were incarcerated in the Clifden regional bridewell. They were later joined by John and Patrick Hyland and Michael Kyne who were charged with the same offence. The bridewell was yet another of Dopping's major concerns, and on 14 January 1848 he wrote again to the undersecretary, pointing out how widespread criminal activity had become: 'Poverty, destitution and crime are still on the increase . . . so desperate and daring have the people become that they not infrequently enter dwelling houses through the roof, and steal what ever they can find, whilst the inhabitants are asleep'.[24]

Because of the large number of people appearing before the magistrate, and the inevitable remands or prison sentences that followed, the Clifden bridewell was hopelessly overcrowded. Dopping pointed out that the current prison population in Galway county gaol was 564, no fewer than 100 of whom came from the west Connemara area. He also observed that the poor were so desperate they were anxious to be committed, because they regarded the prison as an asylum. To support his complaint about the overcrowded routine of the Galway bridewell, Dopping forwarded a letter from the keeper, Dominic Kerrigan, who quite succinctly summed up the general state within the bridewell:

> Clifden Bridewell 14 Jan 1848
>
> Sir,
>   In reply to your enquiry I have the honour to inform you, that there are at present in this Bridewell 69 prisoners. In reply to your other query. That my Bridewell was only intended for 18, having only 6 cells and a refractory Cell for Misdemeanants, the most I could put in each cell of six is three in each bed, having no further accommodation. Remaining your humble servant,
>
> Dominick Kerrigan. Keeper.[25]

Kerrigan, however, neglected to mention the numerous deaths which occurred daily at the bridewell.

At the end of March, Ellen Lydon and the other three members of her family appeared before the court of petty sessions in the relatively new courthouse at Clifden. In the grey rectangular courthouse, the interior of which still retains a Dickensian appearance and atmosphere, the four defendants were remanded to the court of quarter sessions at Galway.

About the same time, probably during the same sessions, the particularly distressing case of *Queen* v. *John Connelly* was tried. A humane man, John Dopping intervened on behalf of Connelly, who was charged with sheep stealing, and described to the court how the family were starving so much the mother ate the legs and feet of one of her dead children. He had carried out an exhumation of the dead child's body, and had found it true as described.[26]

The court wept and the prisoner was discharged.

9

Trial of a Peasant Girl

On Sunday, 17 September 1843, Clifden had been the venue for one of Daniel O'Connell's monster meetings, and the young town had reverberated with the political zeal only O'Connell could engender. The meeting was held in a small valley, slightly to the west of the town, and the reporter from the *Galway Vindicator* estimated the crowd to be more than 100,000. As was usual for such meetings, there was a procession consisting of 200 representatives of the various trade guilds from Galway, with banners and temperance bands from Galway at the front and the rear. The procession met O'Connell when he arrived in the town at midday, and during a burst of sunlight led him to the meeting place amidst the cheering thousands who had come from as far as Westport, the Killaries, Renvyle, Oughterard, Galway, Ballinahinch and the numerous islands along the coast. Carried away by the grandeur of the occasion, the reporter caught the spirit of it all in his report:

> And now the wild spirit of the west has been aroused. Connemara has spoken—its mountains have echoed the sounds of nationality, and its hardy inhabitants have gathered to their leader to be guided by his counsels, and to adopt the course he recommends them to pursue.—Connaught ought to be proud of its efforts in the cause . . . the thousands upon thousands defiling along the gorges and the roads on horseback and on foot— the banners trembling to the breeze—the rich strains of music that echoed away amidst the caverns or reverberated along the hills, and the pealing cheers of the multitude, all formed a spectacle not merely of grandeur or magnificence, but of sublimity and beauty, and filled the heart with inexpressible pleasure . . . And when the liberator ascended the platform, there could not have been present less than ONE HUNDRED THOUSAND made up from every district along the coast, the interior, Outerard, Galway, and other places—His presence was again cheered with the wildest enthusiasm.[1]

Hyacinth D'Arcy, a senior magistrate and the son of the founder of Clifden, opposed the meeting, and was probably sulking in Clifden Castle when it took place. Lacking the insight and leadership qualities of his father, Hyacinth became a target for O'Connell in his speech in favour of repeal. The speech itself disappointed nobody present, as it both flattered the listeners and appealed to their deepest patriotic instincts.

However, by the time Ellen Lydon, her brother and her two cousins were incarcerated in the Clifden bridewell, in its picturesque situation overlookng the Owenglin River, circumstances in Clifden had changed greatly. A horrendous situation existed, both inside and outside the bridewell, and Dominic Kerrigan would want to get the prisoners under his care to Galway as soon as possible. Normally he would order cars for the purpose, and the prisoners would be escorted by police, but the records show that in 1848 the constabulary were stretched to the limit. The police were then commanded by second-class sub-inspector James Ireland, a married Protestant from Roscommon. Ireland, who was then forty-five, had twenty-four years service with the police, of which fifteen had been spent in the eastern districts of Galway and the remainder in the west. His police were under such enormous pressure that he had refused escort duty for prisoners being transferred to Galway County Prison in March 1847. Hyacinth D'Arcy had then approached the lieutenant commanding a detachment of the 49th Regiment stationed at Clifden, only to meet with a firm refusal for the same reasons. The officer wrote to his headquarters at Athlone, pointing out he had only two subalterns, six NCOs, fifty-two privates and a drummer under his command. Of these, one NCO and five privates were confined, on suspicion of plundering the stores; two NCOs and five privates were already away on escort duty at Galway; while another NCO and seven privates were sick. He also pointed out the distance from Clifden to Oughterard was thirty-three and three-quarter miles, he did not believe the soldiers could complete the round trip in one day, and there was no place between Clifden and Oughterard where the prisoners could halt for the night.[2]

As there is no evidence of the army receiving reinforcements, it is almost certain that police were somehow found to continue the duty of escorting prisoners, and that Ellen Lydon and her family must have been taken to Galway under escort. Clifden was only fifty-one miles from Galway, on a road that had been completed in the 1820s, and it should have been an easy day's journey for mounted police and the horse-drawn vehicles carrying convicts.

In 1846 *Slater's Directory* described Galway as:

A sea port, a borough (both corporate and parliamentary), an ancient market town, and a county of itself . . . Galway, so early as 1728, was a place of note, for we find in the town records, that about this time, the inhabitants began to fortify themselves, and to build walls, towers, and bastions . . . The exports are now very considerable, consisting of corn, butter, and provisions, for the English and Scotch markets, and a large quantity of limestone has of late been sent to St John's, Newfoundland, for building Roman Catholic chapels . . . There are two extensive distilleries, several corn mills, one for the manufacture of paper, a tannery, an iron foundry, and three principal hotels . . . Two newspapers are published every week—the 'Galway Mercury' on Friday, and the 'Galway Vindicator' on Wednesday and Saturday. The shops of Galway are abundantly stored with all those articles which taste and fashion may demand, or necessity require . . .

The neighbourhood of Galway is the residence of numerous respectable families and many of the mansions are delightfully situated, particularly those on the Salt Hill or Connemara side . . . The population of the county of the Town of Galway (including the borough of civic portion), according to the parliamentary returns in 1841, was 32,511, and that of the town, at the same period, 12,275 of that number.[3]

The county prison at Nun's Island, at the western end of town, was opened for the reception of prisoners in June 1811. It was in the shape of a huge horseshoe, with the governor's house and main gate in the centre of the open ends. The horseshoe was divided into eight cell blocks, each of which contained yards which radiated like large spokes from the governor's house. The female section was directly on the right-hand side of the entrance and contained a cell block with a yard and a second block containing a large ward which abutted directly onto the side of the governor's house. The governor's house consisted of a basement, a ground floor and a first floor. The basement contained a kitchen, a scullery, and accommodation for servants and turnkeys; the ground floor contained a study, a drawing room and a dining room; the first floor contained six bedrooms, with the main bedroom over the drawing room. No doubt selected women who were long-term prisoners worked in the governor's house.[4] The wards were opposite the debtors' quarters.

In the late 1840s there was no classification of female prisoners at Galway County Prison and women who were generally innocent and unsophisticated were placed with the most depraved.[5] It is not known exactly when the Lydon family reached Galway, but they were almost certainly the four prisoners referred to in General Thomson's letter to John Dopping of 2 March 1848. A close check of the records has failed to reveal any other possibility. Given the desperate state of Clifden, Dopping would certainly have remanded them to Galway as soon as possible. But, judging by the correspondence of General Thomson, and the memorial of Edward Purcell, a stonemason who appeared at the trial as a witness, there seems to have been some problem with the evidence, as a consequence of which Ellen and Mary, who had an infant son Bartholomew, seem to have been in captivity for twelve months before being brought to trial.

In 1848 Galway county prison was in a state of serious disorganisation, and complaints came from all quarters. The inspector, the Rev. John D'Arcy, a senior minister of the established church in Galway, reported several irregularities. This led to an investigation into the management and discipline of the prison. The final report of the gaol investigation committee, published in the *Galway Mercury* on 31 March 1849, found a large number of disturbing irregularities:

No proper accounting system for the receipt and consumption of coal and turf existed, as a consequence of which a very great latitude for fraud and irregularity prevailed.

No proper accounting system existed for the purchase and consumption of groceries and chandlery. As the hospital attendants had been consuming wine and spirits intended for the patients, it was recommended these be placed under the control of the governor, instead of the matron.

No proper inventory of bed clothing and furniture had been made in the gaol for several years.

The committee of enquiry found it impossible to balance the gaol accounts.

The work department, an important element in prison discipline, had almost ceased operations since 1846, and had only just been recommenced.

The functions of the clerk of works and the governor had become so interchanged and entangled that each was often performing duties normally the exclusive preserve of the other.

The sewerage system was defective.

There were no washhouses in the female ward, and cleanliness was therefore impossible.

The committee found the complaints of the Roman Catholic chaplain, the Rev. George Cummins, to be fully substantiated. These complaints concerned the lack of proper classification of female prisoners and the Committee made the following remarks:

> We know nothing more conducive to the propagation of the worst immorality than the contact of young girls convicted of wilful tresspass, theft of food, or any very venial offence, with the worst and most abandoned of their sex. They return in many instances at the expiration of their sentence to their houses thoroughly corrupted and spreading that corruption, or else at once betake themselves to a life of infamy.[6]

The committee recommended that the Roman Catholic chaplain, the governor and local inspector should confer to see how this great evil might be remedied. It also recommended that a wall should be constructed through the middle of the female ward, thus making proper classification possible.

The governor of the prison, Thomas Ryan, was let off lightly, due to his illness with fever caught in the course of his normal duties. However, two senior members of the staff were treated more harshly. The head turnkey, Patrick Kerrigan, was dismissed for keeping improper hours; he was often out drinking until the early hours of the morning and was frequently late on duty as a result. In addition to this, he was held responsible for a printing press which had disappeared from the prison. A nurse, Peggy Thornton, was dismissed for improper association with a wardsman at the hospital.

Such was the state of Galway county prison when it welcomed the Lydon family some time in 1848. For many years the Catholic chaplain was the Very Rev. Lawrence O'Donnell, the vicar-general. When he became bishop of Galway, George Cummins, the parish priest of St Nicholas West, became chaplain of Galway regional prison. During the enquiry the vigilant Cummins stated that the prison hospital at one stage had forty-six prisoners but only sixteen beds. He also revealed that requisitions for clothing, blankets and bedding submitted by the inspector for clothing, and later by the inspector-general, had been ignored. As a result the unfortunate prisoners were lying in filth and rags, despite the fact many of them were suffering from dysentery.

The report of the inspectors-general of prisons for 1849 shows the prison was visited on 29 October 1849 by an inspector-general, James Galway, who reported the sewerage as being in bad order and complained of a most offensive smell permeating parts of the prison. Galway also noted some improvements. The female prison had been divided into two sections, with a wall across the yard, and he described the matron as efficient and anxious to perform her duties. He went on to say there were several female prisoners employed in carding, sewing, knitting and needlework in fourteen small separate sheds. They were all tolerably well clad, and appeared healthy. The number of prisoners confined at the time of the inspection was 361 males and 97 females. The male prisoners were employed at breaking stones, tailoring or cobbling. The report spoke warmly of the frequent visits of 'those excellent and philantropic ladies, the Sisters of Mercy'. The female diet consisted of seven ounces of meal in stirabout and half a pint of new milk. Dinner consisted of twelve ounces of bread and three-quarters of a pint of new milk. Finally the governor, Thomas Ryan, was described as an excellent man, most humane and attentive to the prisoners and to the duties of his office.[7] This profile contrasts strongly with the state in which his prison had languished in the previous year.

The county courthouse is a large rectangular building, situated across the Salmon Weir Bridge, on the banks of the Corrib. The front door opens onto St Francis Street, and it was the venue for the quarter sessions and the assizes courts for the County of Galway.

The Lydon family, together with John Hyland, Pat Hyland and Michael Kyne or Coyne, appeared before the assistant barrister at the Galway quarter sessions court on Thursday, 4 January 1849. The assistant barrister was virtually a county judge and the Law Directory of Ireland noted that: 'The statute establishing the office of Assistant Barrister constituted him a magistrate of the county to which he should be appointed, virtute officii, but left it optional in the magistrates to appoint him chairman of their county or not; but few instances have occurred in which he has not been so chosen'.[8]

The assistant barrister for Galway was William Deane Freeman, who was then aged fifty-six. Born in 1793, he was the fifth son of the late Edward Deane Freeman, Esq., of Castlecor Buttevant in the County of Cork. William Deane Freeman obtained his BA at Trinity College in 1814 and an MA in November 1832. He was called to the Bar in 1817 and was made a Queen's Council in 1841. He had been assistant barrister for Galway since 1837. Although a major Protestant Ascendancy family, the Deane Freemans had a good name with their Catholic neighbours. During the Penal days, some Catholic families transferred their properties to the Freemans, 'who, thus became quasi proprietors, and held the land in trust for their Catholic neighbours'.[9]

William Deane Freeman was extremely handsome, with a dignified aristocratic bearing. He had a large practice on the Munster circuit, but his main source of income came from defending prisoners, Whiteboys in particular, and he was especially skilled in dealing with those who had betrayed their accomplices. He had an extraordinary courtroom manner, shouting his questions at witnesses in a 'peremptory and dictatorial' manner and roaring his speeches to juries. Not surprisingly, he was too arrogant to be popular.[10] After Freeman became assistant barrister for Galway, Constantine Panormo, who was master of the school for sculpture at the Royal Dublin Society, executed his bust, which was exhibited at the Royal Hibernian Academy in 1838 and at the Dublin Exhibition of 1853. No doubt Freeman was chosen by Panormo for his unusual good looks.

Previous to the quarter sessions court in Galway, Freeman had been at Loughrea, which was twenty-three miles inland, staying with Henry Dolphin, who was a solicitor of the Queen's bench and a commissioner of affidavits. A well-known personality in the area, Dolphin lived at Summer Hill, a long, single-storey stone bungalow fronting out to Cross Street, Mount Pleasant. On the day of the Lydons' trial Freeman had a narrow escape which was described in the *Galway Vindicator*:

> On Thursday morning at 10 o'clock W. D. Freeman esquire; got into his carriage for the purpose of going to Galway, he ordered the postillion to drive down the street and turn at Main Street. The unfortunate fellow was very tipsy, and set off at rapid a rate; attempting to turn at Pigott's house he ran the horses right up against the parapart wall at Mr Cloran's. Both horses fell and one of them is so seriously injured we do suppose he will never again be harnessed. Had not the horses come tilt against the wall, or had they passed twelve inches to the left of the parapet, there is not the least doubt the carriage would have been dashed to pieces, and thus in all probability, the life of an upright honourable gentleman be sacrificed.[11]

Spared but doubtless shaken, Freeman must have promptly requisitioned another carriage, as he still managed a very full day's work.

The Galway solicitor's Bar was a hive of stormy petrels in the late 1840s, led by the father of the Bar, Anthony Donelan, and Columbus Rochfort who was its secretary. Donelan and Rochfort were both leading Catholics who took it upon themselves to defend illiterate peasants who were likely to face transportation. The Crown solicitor or prosecutor was Henry O'Loughlin of Merton House, Dunmore, who was a well-known and colourful figure in the Dunmore-Tuam area.

In 1838 a serious libel action took place in the Galway assizes court. The plaintiff was Mr John Kirwan of Hillsbrook, who was also a magistrate, and the defendant was Richard Kelly, a young journalist and editor of the *Tuam Herald*. Henry O'Loughlin was instructing the defending barristers, and he caused a sensation in the court by accusing James Blakeney, the solicitor instructing the plaintiff's barristers, with having divulged the contents of a private conversation, thus committing a gross breach of professional conduct. A duel was arranged, and the parties met at Corofin on the morning of 9 August 1839. At the last minute Blakeney withdrew the challenge and apologised. They then shook hands and retired.[12] In January 1849 O'Loughlin was sixty-one years of age and had been the Crown prosecutor for the Galway quarter sessions court for over fourteen years. He was a genial man, whose natural unaffected manner made him popular with his professional colleagues. In the course of his duties he had won a reputation for being 'strict, just, and punctual', with the ability to blend 'considerable sympathy with official firmness'.[13] In this way he had won a reputation for justice, both from the executive and from the traverser.

People appearing before the assistant barrister in the quarter sessions courts were not covered by any form of legal aid, such as dock briefs. This meant that many people who were sentenced to transportation at the quarter sessions—possibly even the majority—were not defended. Local solicitors, who were able to act as barristers at the quarter sessions level, often appeared on behalf of these defenceless people. As Catholics with progressive political views, Donelan and Rochfort made a point of doing so, but it was still an unequal business. The prisoners were usually illiterate, spoke only Gaelic, and were both bewildered and unable to express themselves. Further to this, the desperate nature of Ireland because of the famine and the severity of the law left little room for legal manoeuvring. Generally, lawyers like Donelan and Rochfort did what they could, but in cases where the plea was guilty and the police had prepared the evidence well in advance, there was little point in intervening. Donelan and Rochfort only did so when they thought they had a fighting chance of influencing the outcome.

In 1849 Anthony Donelan was in his early or middle sixties. The father of the Galway solicitors' Bar, he was also chairman of the Guardians of the Galway Union Workhouse. He lived in May Street, Galway, and like most professionals of the day, he also had a residence in Dublin. He was a refined, eloquent man whose honour and integrity were of the highest order.

In 1849 Columbus Rochfort was thirty five years of age, secretary of the Galway solicitors' Bar and chairman of the Committee of Ratepayers for the County of the Town of Galway. On 19 July 1848 he had called a meeting of the Galway solicitors' Bar to allow the members to consider the propriety of expressing their opinions concerning the conduct of Attorney-General James Henry Monahan at the trial of John Mitchell. Shortly afterwards he was sentenced to three months imprisonment under the Habeas Corpus Suspension Act of 1796. He was released a few days later, on a bail of £100 for his peaceable demeanour.[14] A colourful and flamboyant lawyer, he was also a powerful orator, and as such he was much sought after as a speaker at public meetings. He always stressed Ireland for the Irish, but also stressed the need for the Irish people to rely on their own efforts if they wanted a better way of life. He attacked the landlords as being either absentee or alien, and pointed out Galway as being a 'great mine of riches' due to Nature's generosity. His involvement with Galway's lively press was also notable. To the *Galway Mercury* he was a lion, while to Robert Allen, the editor of the *Warden of Galway*, he was a bear baiter. The two Protestant organs, the *Galway Express* and the *Limerick Chronicle*, sneeringly labelled him as 'Defender of the Faith'. The *Galway Vindicator* was content to give him strong, but more restrained, support. If Ireland had Daniel O'Connell as its spokesman, Galway had Columbus Rochfort.

Rarely has one man caused as much tension among his professional colleagues as Rochfort did in the years 1845–55, and his clashes with William Deane Freeman were legendary. In October 1846, when Freeman refused to rehear a case Rochfort was pressing, the two clashed so heatedly that Freeman suspended Rochfort for three months. This act threw the Galway solicitors' Bar into such an uproar that Freeman was forced to rescind the order for suspension.[15] The clashes between

Rochfort and Freeman continued, reaching a peak in 1851–52, when Freeman was the defendant in a major constitutional case over a pig valued at £2 10s. 0d. This began in a civil case over a pig but when Freeman refused to allow an appeal by Ward, who was represented by Rochfort and who had lost the case, Ward took the case to the Court of the Exchequer Chamber, on the grounds that Freeman had acted unconstitutionally. On 26 May 1852 the court decided seven to three against Freeman, who took the case to the House of Lords, only to die suddenly before a decision could be made. As a result a *venire de novo* (a writ vacating the verdict and calling for a new trial) was declared.[16]

As if Rochfort's problems with Freeman were not enough, a duel was pending between Rochfort and another Galway solicitor, James Blake Concannon, who had defended people who were ejected from their properties free of charge. The pragmatic Rochfort stated that while it was ethical to defend poor peasants who were being tried for criminal cases without fee, it was blackguardly behaviour to so defend civil ejectment cases.[17] After all, the landlords who had often not received rent for many years also had to be taken into consideration. The duel, which was scheduled to take place at Lake Lavelly, was aborted by the police, who bound both parties over to keep the peace. Clearly, the Lydons were to be tried in a legal environment that was extremely volatile.

The Lydons and the other prisoners held at Galway had to cross the Salmon Weir Bridge to reach the courthouse. After passing through the prison gate, which was manned by the porter, Clancy, whose evidence was to be so damaging during the committee of enquiry into the gaol, they were taken to the courthouse's underground cells and ascended into court by a spiral staircase. The courtroom was not as spacious or as grand in its appointments as the Limerick courthouse. Rather, it was similar to the Dickensian Clifden courthouse, only larger. An ornate metal canopy in the shape of half a cupola overhung the judge's seat. There were the usual places for the witnesses, jury, solicitors and press, and substantial seating in the body of the courtroom, supplemented by a balcony which ran down the room from the judge's left-hand side. The plastered ceiling was unpretentious, its plainness being relieved only by raised bands decorated with rosettes, and large skylights which ran along the walls.

If Rochfort's flamboyant zeal caused problems once a case was being heard, Freeman's personality did little to ease the tension. Not only was he arrogant, but his health was in a serious state of decline for some years before his death. On 3 June 1846 the *Galway Vindicator* reported him as having been suddenly afflicted with paralysis. The paper went on to comment that Freeman, although 'a little unwinning in manner was regarded as an impartial and upright judge', but in July 1849 the *Vindicator* complained about Freeman's 'extreme irritability of temper, and the fact that he was in a vast hurry' . . . 'As this gave the plaintiffs a walkover the defence it was felt there was no fair play, and that Justice was not being done'. On 8 June 1850 the *Galway Mercury* reported 'that W. Deane Freeman had recovered from his serious illness, and would be available for the next quarter sessions'. In short, it seems that Freeman was suffering from bad nerves and hypertension.

The grand jury for 3, 4 and 6 January 1849 consisted of Martin Morris, Walter Joyce, John B. Kernon, John Dopping, Thomas Brereton and Lieutenant General Thomson. It was hardly a representative jury as we know them today. Morris and Joyce were both landlords, while Kernon, Brereton and Dopping were the police magistrates for Galway, Portumna and Clifden. As no fewer than eight of the prisoners were faced with serious charges relating to the thefts of livestock from his property, it is odd that Thomson was allowed to sit in judgment of them, even by nineteenth-century standards. Thomson was also an enthusiastic supporter of Protestant evangelists, who were trying to get a foothold in the strongly Catholic area of Connemara. Inevitably, these evangelists, known as jumpers, finished up in the petty sessions court in Clifden, because of clashes with Catholics. General Thomson usually sat on the bench as a magistrate, and his clashes with Rochfort, who defended the Catholics, made good fare for the press.

As soon as the jury was sworn and settled in, Freeman began his opening speech, which was mainly concerned with the theft of turnips, which he said should have been dealt with summarily by the magistrates in the court of petty sessions. He was also concerned with the larcenies in workhouses, which he said were due to the neglect of well-paid officers, and the complaint against a certain poor-rate collector which he felt should be a civil action. His previous speech to the grand jury at Galway during the quarter sessions in October 1848 had been something of a legal milestone, and its implications could well have spelled trouble for the Lydon family, as there could have been some difficulty in obtaining enough evidence against them, which would account for the long period between their arrest, and the date of trial.

Freeman's speech to the Grand Jury in October 1848 was reported thus:

Gentlemen of the Grand Jury—I am happy to find upon looking over the calender that, although it is a very heavy one in as much as it presents upwards of 80 cases, there does not appear on it many of a serious kind; and I am particularly gratified to observe the absence of those disgraceful cases of larceny, and stealing and killing of cattle which were so numerous at the last, and previous sessions, and which rendered property in this county during the last winter, of scarcely any value to the owners. This circumstance gentlemen, is a matter of sincere congratulation, for although I am aware that many of these offences were committed under the influence of poverty and distress, I have reason to know that a great proportion were the result of an evil disposition in the parties committing them. On the cases which will come before you on this occasion it will not be necessary for me to remark, with the exception of one—a case of abduction— which I do not think it the right of magistrates to have sent to this court. If they proceed in this way we will shortly be requested to try cases of murder, or perhaps High Treason (laughter). By sending cases of this sort before us they are putting the prosecutor to inconvenience instead of giving him the satisfaction they intended. I shall send this case of abduction to the Assizes, and as that will be putting the country to double expense, I trust the magistrates will avoid a repetition of this mode of proceeding, and adopt that which I recommend, and which is recommended by every criminal court of this sort in the kingdom. At the last session of Parliament the law had been altered in some respects. In criminal cases the offender was frequently enabled to evade the law in consequence of its not being competant for the crown to include a count for the receiving in the indictment for the stealing of property. The law relating to that has been lately altered, and a party is now triable for guilty knowledge, concealment etc., in the same indictment which charges him with the actual theft. That is a very great improvement, as previously the crown was bound to select which charge it would go upon. There is another alteration in the law regarding the prosecution of an accessory before or after the fact, without the principal. That was also a change much required, as in my opinion the person who instigates as to a crime or conceals the party committing it is as fully culperable as him whom he thus puts forward. These variations obviate considerably the embarrassment under which the Crown Prosecutor frequently laboured in cases of trial of this nature. I have hitherto endeavoured by the infliction of heavy punishments to repress the plundering of property in this county. I hope I have in some measure succeeded, and if the law, vigorously and consistently administered be sufficient for that purpose I hope to repress it effectively. His worship then referred in the usual terms to the duties of the grand jury, and concluded by assuring them of his assistance on any question of difficulty that should happen to arise. The learned gentleman having concluded, the grand jury retired, and the trial of civil bills was resumed.[18]

Only a few of the defendants would have been at the scene of the crime. Under the new laws they were all triable, largely because of guilty knowledge or concealment. None of the prisoners tried on 4 and 5 January was mentioned in the press, which means the trial of the Lydon family was not reported. But those who were tried on the following Monday and Tuesday were all reported, and the pattern of sentencing seems clear. Those who pleaded guilty and made things easy were sentenced to six months imprisonment. Those who were difficult in some way usually received seven or ten years transportation. Donelan and Rochfort intervened only when they felt it was worthwhile, but given the type of men sitting on the grand jury, the helplessness of the peasants who appeared before them and the carefully collated evidence of the police, it is clear Ellen Lydon and her co-defendants never had a chance.

The Lydon family were fourth on the court list, together with the Hyland brothers and Michael Coyne. To the bewildered and illiterate young peasants from the wilds of north-west Connemara, Freeman must have seemed like an angry god. None of the prisoners spoke English, and the charge—killing a sheep with intent to steal the same, contrary to 2 & 3 William IV CLXII—would have been read to them by an interpreter. The unfamiliar scene of the courtroom, with the handsome aristocratic Freeman shouting at the interpreter and roaring at the Crown prosecutor and the defence, could only have been terrifying for these powerless, lonely young peasants and they were doubtless easy prey for the urbane Henry O'Loughlin, who nevertheless must have had many a quirk of conscience over scenes such as this. It is quite clear the decisive evidence was presented by Edward Purcell, a stonemason of Lecknavarna who testified against the Hyland brothers and Michael Coyne.

General Thomson surely received his satisfaction during the quarter sessions, as not only were the seven prisoners sentenced to seven years transportation each, but a man called Patrick Salmon later received ten years for stealing two of Thomson's bullocks. Another convict, Anne Nevin of Athenry, who was sentenced to seven years transportation for stealing tablecloths, sheets and other articles, thanked the court and said that she never in her life was better pleased.[19] Given the terrible state of Galway at the time, and the overpowering courtroom experience, she could well have summed up the feelings of all of them. Ellen and the other Lydons were returned to prison to await transportation to Dublin. In four days work, Freeman sentenced forty-eight prisoners to 360 years transportation.

On 20 January 1849 the *Galway Vindicator* published a letter from the Parish Priest of Clifden, Fr Peter Fitzmaurice:

> The gloomy and dispiriting anticipations of my last letter are already fearfully realised. It cannot be denied by the government officials here that there are no parishes in the south west of Ireland that surpass in misery, and the destitution that of Clifden and Ballindoon . . . The work house is filled to suffocation—there are 800 in a house, built for the accommodation of 300. There is also an auxiliary one, where there are 300 females huddled together, for the most part without beds of any sort; and as a substitute for a warm fireside, they are driven out in squalls on the road to exercise to guard against the benumbing effects of the cold they endure. Cold and comfortless are these abodes of misery yet every day hundreds are crawling to them enfeebled and emaciated, carrying their almost naked skeletons of children on their backs, craving admission, and denied it, until other receptacles are prepared, and in the meantime no food given to them! Of the nine thousand receiving the outdoor relief last August in these parishes, there are only three thousand three hundred at present on the lists . . . Let the starving applicants be relieved until the auxiliary houses are prepared for their reception. Let the children from nine to fifteen years receive more than that pitiful pittance of half a pound of Indian meal per day. Let not the poor parents be obliged to return to their cheerless homes from the depots with a three days instead of seven days supply of food, as was the case frequently during the last month. Let the poor cottiers, still holding land, be supplied with seed and food whilst tilling the land in the ensuing spring; otherwise the remnant of our once populous, industrious, and peaceable people will be exterminated.
>
> I have the honour to remain, Sir, your obedient humble servant . . .

In another letter, printed in the *Galway Mercury* on 19 May, Fr Fitzmaurice made the following four points:

First, the Clifden Union was twice as poor as any other union as a rate of £1 1s. 4½d. in the pound of all property was needed to support its poor, whereas only 14s. in the pound on property was needed elsewhere.

Second, in 1845 the population of the parishes of Omey and Ballindoon (or Clifden) amounted to 18,000; it now scarcely exceeds 10,000 souls.

Third, since 22 April there have been about 400 cases of cholera, not confined to Clifden as in 1832, but reaching every village.

Fourth, terrible though the situation of cholera was, it was welcomed by the poor as an end to their sufferings.

As cholera broke out in Galway during April, Ellen Lydon and her fellow convicts could well have looked forward to the long sea voyage to Van Diemen's Land as the lesser evil.

10

The Richmond Female Penitentiary[1]

After their conviction, Ellen and Mary Lydon were returned to the county gaol on Nun's Island, and there they languished until early April, when arrangements were made to convey them to the Richmond female penitentiary in Dublin. It was the custom for all female convicts to spend three months there in preparation for the long voyage to Australia. The *Galway Mercury* of 7 April duly reported: 'On Wednesday last, 13 prisoners under the rules of transportation were sent off from our County Gaol in one of Bianconi's cars under an escort of police, for Dublin, and on yesterday 13 more in a similar manner. There are in all 150 under sentence of transportation.'[1]

There is little doubt that these two drafts were the twenty-six female convicts from Galway who were to sail for Hobart on the *Australasia* in three months time. The police escort, dressed in their green frock coats, white trousers, green forage caps, black leather belts and boots, complete with swords and pistols, made a startling contrast with the sad, shabby women. The policemen had to be at least 5 feet 8 inches in height, and those who were mounted had excellent horses, furnished with black saddlery and green saddlecloths.[2] The Bianconi cars were developed by Charles Bianconi, an Italian immigrant who became convinced of Ireland's need for an efficient coach service. His cars were usually open, with seats along each side, were drawn by two, three or sometimes four horses, and achieved an average speed of eight miles an hour.[3] The Galway mail coach covered the 133 miles to Dublin in fourteen and three-quarter hours, but the Bianconi cars must have taken at least seventeen hours.[4] Usually mail coaches travelled overnight, so very likely the convict women were faced with a long and nightmarish journey without a chance to sleep. By the time they reached Dublin, they must have been exhausted.

In 1824 *Pigot's Directory* described Dublin Bay as being 'equal in fine and picturesque scenery to the celebrated Bay of Naples' and referred to Dublin as: 'The noble city, crowded in the perspective with lofty spires and domes, with numerous shipping moored in the harbour, altogether so happily combined, as to form one of the most delightful of Nature's views, highly improved by affluence and taste'.[5]

According to *Thom's Almanac* in 1847, the population of the metropolitan police district was 287,729, of whom approximately 75 per cent were Catholics. As for the city, it

> is nearly surrounded by the Circular-road, 9 miles in extent, and comprises an area within the limit of 1,264 acres, which is intersected by the Liffey, the northern portion containing 478, and the southern 786 acres. The river is crossed by 9 bridges, 7 of stone and 2 of iron, and is embanked on each side along the whole range of the city, a length of 2½ miles, by quays faced with granite, affording an open and ready communication, in all parts, between the northern and southern sections. It is the residence of the Chief Governor of Ireland, the seat of the see of the Archbishop of the southern province, and the centre of all the political, ecclesiastical, educational, fiscal, commercial, and military institutions. Its principal public buildings are, Dublin Castle the seat of Government, the Courts of Law, the King's Inns, the Custom House, and the Post Office; the Cathedrals of the Holy Trinity or Christ Church and St Patrick . . . The buildings appropriate to literature, science, and the fine arts, are Trinity College, the College of Surgeons, the National Educational Buildings, Kildare-place Buildings, the Dublin Society, The Royal Irish Academy, the Hibernian Academy for paintings by native Artists, the Royal Irish Institution for ancient pictures and the Apothecaries' linen Hall and the Corn Exchange.[6]

The Richmond female penitentiary was on the right-hand side of Grangegorman Road, in the north-west quadrant of the city. As Grangegorman Road was handily situated to the entrance of the main highway to Galway, the convict women did not have much chance to see anything of Dublin. Not that it mattered, as they would have been too exhausted to appreciate their first glimpse of a real city after their long journey.

In 1849 Richmond was the only prison in the United Kingdom reserved exclusively for females, a fact which caused the administration considerable embarrassment. It was strictly laid down in the Prisons Act that it was not lawful for any woman to be keeper of a prison, as a result of which a governor had to be appointed. But the governor of Richmond was virtually a figurehead, who often clashed with the head matron who was the effective head of the institution.[7] In 1849 the governor was Thomas L. Synott, who had recently taken over from Dominic Marques, who had been a witness in the Kilmainham enquiry of 1842. The head matron was Marianne Rawlins, who had also been a witness at the enquiry. The prison was designed by Francis Johnson, whose overall plan of the building 'was somewhat fan shaped, the courts between each stick of the "fan" forming yards and exercise grounds'.[8] The solitary cells were placed at the end of each fan stick, and early in the prison's history, all new prisoners began in the solitary cells, progressing along the fan stick towards greater liberty. 'The cells in question were 12'4" square by 11' high to the ceiling, which was arched.'[9] The frontage, which is still in existence and is now used for administrative purposes, 'consists

of a central block with two balanced wings pierced by massive gateways'.[10] The
central block is crowned by a fine clock tower, which was completed in 1816.
On 1 September 1836 the penitentiary was made over to the grand jury of the
city, and it became the central depot for female convicts from all over Ireland
who were awaiting embarkation aboard convict transports.[11]

In all, the prison contained 256 cells, and in 1849 about fifty of them had been
appropriated for convicts under sentence of transportation. The only articles of
furniture permitted in the cells were heavy iron bedsteads. The convicts occupied
classrooms and yards 'distinct from the others', and they had their own laundry.
Their clothing consisted of shifts, jackets, petticoats, aprons, handkerchiefs, caps
and shoes. Each prisoner was issued with a pair of blankets, a pair of sheets, a
rug and a bed tick. A policy of work therapy was followed, and the prisoners were
kept busy at sewing, knitting, cooking, cleaning, nursing, or working in the laundry,
the hospital or the reception ward.[12]

Marianne Rawlins, who had been chosen for the head matron's job by the Quaker
prison reformer Elizabeth Fry, was a formidable woman who was responsible for
the entire management of the prison. She was assisted by a staff of assistant matrons,
which included a deputy head matron and a number of specialist matrons in charge
of the store, the hospital, the laundry, the reception area and the kitchen. There
were ten general assistant matrons, and as there were sixty-six lunatics in the prison
at the time, there was a specialist matron for lunatics.

By the standards of modern prisons, the Richmond female penitentiary served
a remarkable variety of purposes. It not only accommodated felons, misdemeanants
and those awaiting trial, but it served as a multi-purpose detention centre for vagrants,
lunatics and drunkards. During 1849, 9,567 women were committed to the
penitentiary, some of them for periods of only seven days. The average number
confined daily was 353, with 25 children. Some 3,362 prisoners, or about a third
of those who passed through the penitentiary in 1849, were felons or misdemeanants.

The following table shows the age, religion and literacy of the felons and
misdemeanants.[13]

Sentence		Religion		Literacy	
10 years and under	6	Protestants	542	Read and Write	693
14–15 years	82	Presbyterians	6	Read only	1,296
16–20 years	660	Roman Catholics	2,814	Neither	1,373
21–30 years	1,631		3,362		3,362
30–40 years	586				
41 and upward	397				
	3,362				

In 1849 the prison was facing serious administrative difficulties, and the original
plan for a female prison run by female officers had proved a difficult one to implement.

Since the Prison Act prohibited a woman from being the governor but the burden of management nonetheless fell on the shoulders of Marianne Rawlins, she often found herself in conflict with the governor. At the same time the governor found himself in the wretched position of administering a large female prison without a defined statement of duty. As proper female surveillance was considered indispensable, a committee of ladies was tried, but failed. In the report of the inspectors-general for 1850, it was recommended that two ladies, one a Protestant and the other a Roman Catholic, be selected as 'Visitors' and vested with the same powers as a local inspector. These ladies would oversee the discipline, treatment and both secular and religious instruction of the prisoners. The matron would then be strictly confined to management and the supervision of relevant staff. The governor would supervise the male staff and would act as accountant and senior storekeeper. One feels the administration was finding it difficult to contain Rawlins, as well as carry out the original charter of a 'perfect female prison governed by female officers'.[14]

The day at the penitentiary began early, at six-thirty in the summer. The assistant matrons signed their names in the 'unlocking book', a special register kept in the head matron's office, after which they received their keys and unlocked their respective wards. Any unusual occurrence during the night had to be reported to the head matron. Immediately after washing and prayers, the assistant matrons supervised the prisoners while they cleaned their cells and corridors. The prisoners were exercised in the yards for half an hour after breakfast and dinner, while the regular instruction time for reading and spelling, overseen by the assistant matrons, was from 11 a.m. to 1 p.m. When they were not exercising or at school, the prisoners were working, provided work was available. During 1849 the penitentiary did not have a trained teacher on the staff, and the report of the inspectors-general for 1850 observed: 'Experience has however shown, that the faculty of teaching is only innate in comparatively few individuals, and that an adequate portion of training is generally indispensable in this as in any other art'.[15] To this end, it was recommended that a regular schoolmistress, whose qualifications would meet the approval of the Education Board be appointed.

The return of daily diet for the gaols and workhouses of Ireland in 1848 showed the diet at the Richmond female penitentiary to consist of 7 ounces (equal parts) of oat and Indian meal stirabout, and a pint of new milk for breakfast. Dinner consisted of a pound of wholemeal bread and a pint of buttermilk. On 1 September 1849, this was changed to 7 ounces of oatmeal in stirabout, and half a pint of new milk for breakfast, while dinner was to consist of 12 ounces of brown bread and three-quarters of a pint of new milk. The cost was 2d. per day, or £3 0s. 10d. per year. It was generally held by penal officials that the prison was not a proper place for the lunatics, and as a somewhat bizarre concession they were given a better diet than the other prisoners— white bread instead of brown, and a half a pound of beef each, three times a week. As the convicts awaiting transportation at Kilmainham received white bread, it can be taken for granted the female convicts awaiting transportation at Richmond also had white bread, but they did not have any meat.[16]

What did the convicts do for work at Richmond female penitentiary? According to the evidence given by Marianne Rawlins before the Kilmainham enquiry in 1842, they were mostly employed making clothing. The costs were 1d. for coarse aprons, ½d. for check aprons, 2d. for shifts, 1d. for caps, 2d. for jackets and 1½d. for petticoats. The governor paid for the material used in making the aprons, but no records were kept of work done by the convicts. The prison administration found it difficult to find sufficient work to keep the prisoners continually occupied. An exception to this was the prison laundry, which was well fitted out and always had enough work to keep forty women occupied.

For the nine months from 6 April 1848 until 4 January 1849, Richmond female penitentiary received fifty-five female convicts from Galway. Without exception, these women were sentenced either for larceny, for stealing livestock or for killing livestock with intent to steal.[17] Ellen and Mary Lydon and their fellow prisoners from Galway were no sooner settled in the prison routine than the wheels of the administrative machinery began to turn. Thomas N. Redington, who was under-secretary for Ireland under Lord Clarendon, received the following letter from Whitehall:

> Whitehall 19th May 1849.
>
> T. N. Redington Esq.,
>
> Sir,
> I am directed by Secretary Sir George Grey to acquaint you for the information of His Excellency the Lord Lieutenant that the ship 'Australasia' has been chartered for the conveyance of 200 Female Convicts from Ireland to Van Diemen's Land.
>
> G. Cornewall Lewis.[18]

A fortnight later it was followed by another letter which informed Redington that the *Australasia* would leave Deptford for Kingstown Harbour on 6 June. On 8 June a third letter was sent, stating that Mr Alexander Kilroy had been appointed surgeon-superintendent aboard the *Australasia*. On 16 June 1849 a final letter was sent:

> I am directed by Secretary Sir George Grey to transmit to you for the purpose of being laid before his excellency the Lord Lieutenant, the accompanying copy of the Charter Party of the Convict Ship 'Australasia' engaged for the transportation of 200 female convicts from Ireland to Van Diemen's Land, also a list of the stores shipped for their use.[19]

Obviously the authorities in England kept their Irish subordinates well informed concerning the movement of convict vessels. On 16 June the Dublin newspapers reported that the barque *Australasia*, Captain J. Connell, had arrived at Kingstown to embark 200 female convicts and forty children to New South Wales. It seems the press had forgotten no convict transports had sailed for New South Wales since 1840.[20]

In the meantime, the prisoners were being prepared for their journey to Van

Diemen's Land in more ways than one. The chaplains were for the most part zealous men, who made the most of the interval at Richmond penitentiary to spiritually prepare the prisoners for both the voyage ahead and their long exile. The Catholic convicts were fortunate in having the Rev. Bernard Kirby, an experienced and dedicated chaplain who always bridged the gap between his flock and himself by addressing the convict women as his 'dear sisters'. It was Fr Kirby who created a remarkable precedent by arranging the first religious confirmation ever held at a penitentiary in Ireland. On 10 August 1841 he had taken advantage of the visit of the Right Rev. Bede Polding, the new Bishop of New South Wales, to have ninety-two of the 150 women who were to sail to Hobart in the *Mexborough* confirmed in their religion. Kirby made it a practice to try his utmost to rectify any spiritual deficits the women may have had through isolation or lack of clergy, to minister properly to them, and he had the full cooperation of the prison administration. For the confirmation ceremony the prison chapel was beautifully decorated with flowers, and the matrons' pews contained several prominent citizens, both Catholic and Protestant, thereby also making the occasion an ecumenical triumph. So unusual was this ceremony that the *Limerick Reporter* described it as 'the first under similar circumstances which took place in Ireland . . . the first we know of since the days of primitive Christianity'. The convicts also received regular visits from nuns belonging to a religious order which specialised in this work.[21]

The second quarter of 1849 was a busy time for the convict depots, as the *Maria* sailed in April, the *Hyderabad* in May and the *Australasia* in June. The mode of transportation to the transports had changed somewhat since Stephen Howard's day and the convicts were not sent direct in cars, to Kingstown, but were sent by another route:

> Yesterday one hundred male convicts . . . were conveyed from the depot in covered cars to the North Wall, where they were put on board the Viceroy steamer . . . The prisoners were mostly fine athletic young men; they were all manacled. They were under an escort of fifty constabulary . . .
>
> Soon after the above shipment, a batch of female convicts, consisting of 160, were brought in cars to the point of the wall, where they were embarked aboard a steam tug and conveyed to Kingstown harbour, and transferred to the Maria II.[22]

The 200 female convicts to sail in the *Australasia* were about to endure what could only be described as the most heart-rending week of their lives. Most of them were west-coast convicts who spoke only Gaelic, and it was the grim duty of Fr Kirby to inform them that the majority of them would never again see Ireland after the *Australasia* left Kingstown Harbour. Certainly, most of them would be free to return after their terms had expired, but few would have the resources. Most would marry in their new country and live the remainder of their lives there.

In June 1849 Kingstown was preparing for the visit of Queen Victoria early in August. Now known as Dun Laoghaire, Kingstown had become the port of Dublin and a fashionable residential area, with its rows of neat terrace houses adorning the shoreline. It consists of two huge man-made piers which enclose 250 acres of water. The east pier is 3,500 feet long and the west pier 4,950 feet. Work was began in 1817, but it was not completed until 1859. The Victoria Wharf, which is now engulfed by the ferry terminal, was constructed in 1837 and was mainly used by the government to embark troops and convicts.[23] It was here that the *Australasia* lay waiting for her human cargo.

If the convicts were burdened with grief, things were not much happier in the castle. In 1847 George Villiers, the Earl of Clarendon, had been appointed viceroy after serving a distinguished diplomatic career. He had studied the Irish question, and had several ideas he hoped to implement, but his was a most difficult term. He had to cope with the famine, the Young Ireland movement, the serious economic problems brought about by the bankruptcy of the landlords and the emigration of the peasantry. Towards the end of his term he was mixed up in an unsavoury blackmail case involving an unscrupulous newspaper proprietor. At the conclusion of his term in 1852 he had the cold comfort of knowing he had failed in a situation where no man could have succeeded.[24] Thomas N. Redington, who had given up a successful political career as MP for Dundalk for the onerous position of undersecretary, was apparently so exhausted after Clarendon's term of office he retired to his beautiful estate at Kilcornan Galway. He died in 1862, aged only forty-seven.

The press usually paid little attention to the departure of convict vessels, and the departure of Ellen Lydon and her fellow convicts on the *Australasia* was not reported. However, in August 1841 the *Limerick Reporter* had described the particularly touching departure of a female convict ship bound for Van Diemen's Land, the *Mexborough*. Immediately before its departure, the ship was visited by Fr Kirby and Miss Mary Crofton, a senior assistant matron from the penitentiary. Fr Kirby arrived on deck at 1.00 p.m.:

> They crowded around him like children who hail the appearance of a beloved parent, after a long absence, and when they understood he was about to deliver them his last discourse, before leaving their native land, wept most bitterly. He then ascended the poop, which he converted into a temporary pulpit, and here he found it impossible to proceed for some time in consequence of the bitter tears which bedewed the countenances of all, not withstanding the wretched sufferers made every effort to conceal the intensity of their grief from the eye of him to whom they looked for consolation. The scene from the deck was one eminently calculated to awaken the bitterest feelings of regret in the minds of those who were about to bid their native land an eternal adieu.[25]

Father Kirby then delivered a long address, beginning by reminding the prisoners that this would be the last time he would be able to address them as an Irish priest, and on that account he had come to take his farewell. He began by quoting from Genesis iii.15, and the main theme of his sermon was the salvation of mankind through the death of Christ at Calvary. He asked them not to regret their country, nor those they left behind, and warned them that they 'never did more than the good thief on the cross, nor of Mary Magdalene, who will prove a mother to you all'. The final part of the sermon was aimed at inspiring the women to face their future life with faith and courage, and was rounded off with a last 'farewell'. This again brought about an unrestrained burst of sobbing from the women; even those who were Protestants. With the help of Miss Crofton, Fr Kirby then distributed Prayer Books to those who could read, and rosary beads to those who could not. This was followed by the distribution of temperance medals and green ribbons. Fr Kirby and the reporter then left the vessel, amidst the tears and prayers of the women. The *Limerick Reporter* made a point of giving generous praise to the surgeon who made the ceremony possible. His name was John Stephen Hampton, and it was his first voyage as surgeon-superintendent of a convict ship.[26]

The ceremony aboard the *Mexborough* seems to be typical of the last farewells aboard convict ships, particularly those which carried women. Fr Bernard Kirby was a convict chaplain of many years experience, and he must have found such leavetaking harrowing and emotionally draining. He regarded the convicts as his brothers and sisters, and it must have been impossible to steel his feelings against these farewells to convicts who for the most part were victims of political and economic circumstances beyond their control. Indeed, because Kirby chose to identify closely with them, and because he was an educated man who understood their fundamental innocence, it must have taken every ounce of faith and strength to endure the farewells.

The ceremony aboard the *Australasia* probably followed similar lines, except there were 200 convicts on board as against 145 for the *Mexborough*. The literacy rate was low, and only thirty-nine at the most merited Prayer Books. On 26 June 1849 the *Australasia* left Kingstown, with its cargo of sad and frightened women looking back on the rows of terraces which for the vast majority would be their last glimpse of Ireland.

11

A New Destiny

The *Australasia* was built by James Laing of Southwick, Sunderland, in 1847. She was slightly smaller than the *Constant*, being 485.3 tons new measurement, 114 feet long, 25.5 feet wide, and with a depth in hold at midships of 19.1 feet. This gave her 4.47 beams per length and 5.96 depths per length—ratios that augured well for both speed and seaworthiness. A barque, her description in terms of rigging, masts and so on was identical with the *Constant*. The *Australasia* represented the new design for cargo ships which began to emerge at the beginning of the 1840s, the chief characteristics of which were 'less sheer, greater length in proportion to depth and breadth, more balanced ends, flatter floors, and less extremes of curvature in the hull'.[1]

In 1849 the *Australasia* was owned by four men, of whom Adam Riddell of Clarendon Place, Marylebone, was the principal. Her master, James Connell, had taken command of her after delivery from Laing's shipyards on 3 June 1847. It has not been possible to establish the destination of her maiden voyage, but in 1848 she sailed to Hobart with ordinary cargo, returning to London on 8 May 1849. Her voyage to Hobart with convicts was her third since launching.

A fast vessel, the *Australasia* completed the voyage to Hobart in ninety-five days, a time which in 1849 had only been equalled, or bettered, by eight other convict transports, four of which sailed from England. As a new vessel she was given a higher rating than the *Constant* by Lloyd's of London: A1 for twelve years against nine years for the *Constant*. The *Australasia* was one of the new Sunderland vessels that dominated the final years of transportation to Van Diemen's Land. According to Charles Bateson:

> The domination of Sunderland-built vessels in the convict service during the final years of transportation to Tasmania is remarkable. Almost all the newer vessels after 1841 came from the shipyards of this Durham port, and they proved excellent frigate-built vessels. They were fast and seaworthy, and their more modern design made conditions

for the prisoners far more pleasant than previously had been the case or was still the case in the older vessels.[2]

If John Hemery, master of the *Constant*, was a patrician, James Connell was a shellback. Born in Bangor County Down in 1806, he was granted his third-class masters certificate by the London Examination Board on 24 May 1849, while the *Australasia* was being fitted out for convicts. He was a veteran of the England to Australia route, and before taking over the *Australasia* he had been made master of the *Rosalind* in 1845/46 and again in the early months of 1847. The *Rosalind* was a 317-ton barque which plied between London and Launceston. Connell was a stern master, who forbade the drinking of spirits on his ships at any time and swearing or abusive language when women were present. His wife, Mary Ann, who was seven years his junior, lived in the Ratcliff area of Stepney, East London, with their children John and Jane, then aged eight and one. Connell faced the voyage as master of a female transport with great trepidation.

The surgeon-superintendent Alex Kilroy was also born in 1806. He received his London Diploma in Medicine in 1828, his London Certificate in Medicine in September 1831, and was promoted to full surgeon on 3 June 1838, as 'a deserving officer', on the recommendation of the surgeon-general of the navy. However, his earlier career had not been without its ups and downs. In April 1832 he was reprimanded by Sir William Burnett, the physician-general of the navy, for the careless way he kept his journal on the *Meteor*, and was informed his pay would be stopped if it occurred again. In January 1833 he was again reprimanded for the careless and unscientific manner in which he kept his journal aboard the *Alban*. However, the following year he received a favourable report for his service on Ascension Island and in 1835, as an enterprising young officer, he requested promotion. Burnett admitted he was a satisfactory officer but did not feel he was talented enough to warrant promotion above those higher on the seniority list, 'many of them of high professional character'.

The turning point of Kilroy's career came in February 1837, when Captain Dacies and Surgeon Bate of the *Edinburgh*, a seventy-two-gun ship of the line, sent a favourable report to the Naval Board: 'Mr Kilroy has on all occasions performed his duties in a satisfactory manner, and is a gentleman of good character and fair talent'.[3] Captain Dacies also asked for Kilroy to be appointed to the Cape of India flagship *Cara*. On 15 April he was appointed to the eighteen-gun *Favourite*, as full surgeon, and in June 1838 his promotion was made formal. He was already quite experienced as a surgeon-superintendent aboard convict ships. In 1845 he spent three months as a relief surgeon on the *China* while she was waiting at Woolwich, and later that year he was appointed surgeon-superintendent aboard the *Mayda*, a Sunderland barque 100 tons larger than the *Australasia*, which had embarked 199 convicts at Woolwich on her maiden voyage. Kilroy managed to get them to Norfolk Island with only four deaths. The convicts aboard the *China* and the *Mayda* were male and Kilroy, who was responsible for the organisation and discipline of the convicts as well as their health, must have been glad to have Mrs Lambert as matron on the *Australasia*.

The female convict ships had not carried a marine guard since 1747, when the guard of the *Lady Shore*, assisted by many of the sailors, had mutinied when the ship was four days from Rio de Janeiro and made off to Montevideo in Uruguay. The officers and those loyal to them, who had been cast adrift in a longboat off the coast of Brazil, managed to get to the Rio Grande, from where they were given passages to Rio de Janeiro. As for the mutineers, they were made prisoners of war by the Spaniards, who took the *Lady Shore* as a Spanish prize. The women they so coveted 'were distributed as servants among the Spanish ladies'.[4] After that the British government decided a ship without a marine guard was the safer course.

Because female convict ships presented serious difficulties of their own, a matron sailed with the later ships, and her duties were onerous indeed. In July 1847 the prison inspectors, writing from Millbank prison, recommended that a religious instructor should also be appointed. They warned the duties of superintending the schools and work classes were already too heavy for a single matron, who should not be burdened with religious instruction as well. By far the most telling comment concerning the matron's duties came from the Rev. R. W. Gibbs, a minister who worked his passage to Hobart as religious instructor on the *Cadet*. The *Cadet* arrived in Hobart on 12 April 1849, shortly before the *Australasia*, and Gibbs reported a matron's duties as being so arduous that two assistant matrons should be appointed to prevent prisoners engaging in intercourse with the sailors and evil combinations with each other. Gibbs felt the matrons should alternate in four-hour watches every day and night, and also recommended the provision of six solitary cells in a remote part of the ship, well away from the sailors.[5] Quite clearly, Mrs Lambert was in for a torrid time.

Clothing for the women normally consisted of a brown serge jacket and a petticoat, a couple of linen shifts, a linen cap, a neckerchief, a pair of worsted stockings and a pair of shoes. In July 1847 the prison inspectors concurred with the ladies of the convict ship committee, who said the clothing given to the female convicts was both insufficient and ill-fitting. As a result the following clothing was recommended: 2 brown serge dresses, 3 cotton shifts, 1 flannel petticoat, 2 check aprons, 2 cotton jackets, 2 cotton nightcaps, 2 neckerchiefs, 2 pairs of women's shoes and 2 pairs of worsted hose. They also recommended the clothing be made by the authorities of Millbank prison, rather than the Admiralty, so it could 'be properly fitted and strongly made'.[6] The extent to which this recommendation was implemented is not known, but as conditions on convict ships had improved considerably at this time, it was probably carried out in its entirety. Gilbert Inglis, the purser on board the female convict ship *Duchess of Northumberland*, had this to say in November 1852:

They were dressed when they came aboard in coarse brown serge petticoats, or skirts I suppose is the proper name for them, and a loose jacket of the same material which some of them wore outside the petticoat and others inside, and plain straw bonnets without any trimmings at all which they exchanged when they came on board for black calico caps made very loose behind . . . There were eight beds in the mess four on top and four underneath the two outside of the upper ones being moveable while the other two were fixtures and served as a table in the daytime while the outside ones served for seats . . . They have 2/3 of a pound of meat and bread allowed per day to each one and tea night and morning. All through the day they are allowed to walk about the decks with very little restriction they are not allowed to talk to the sailors, nor the sailors to them, but it is impossible to prevent that entirely.[7]

The ladies of the convict ship committee also pointed out the convict ships were damp, and that the bedding should be properly aired before sailing.

The crew of the *Australasia* consisted of three mates, twenty-two seamen, three apprentices and a boy, a carpenter, a cook, a steward, a cuddy servant and a butcher. The *Constant* had also carried a boatswain, seven more seamen and an extra boy. During his previous voyage to Hobart, Connell had managed with a small crew of only twenty men. He was now carrying an extra twelve seamen, a cuddy servant and a boy. In view of the problems which occurred between the seamen and the women aboard female convict ships, it is remarkable he chose so large a crew. Presumably he found the previous voyage with a small crew quite a strain.[8]

The crew engaged to sail to Hobart Town, from there to any ports or places in Australia where cargo might be found, and from Australia to any port in the Southern, Atlantic or Pacific Oceans or the Indian and China Seas. They also had to agree to inflict corporal punishment upon the prisoners, as directed by the surgeon-superintendent and the master. Any man found asleep on the lookout was to forfeit two days' pay to the Merchant Seaman's Fund.

Connell seems not to have inspired any great loyalty among his crews, as only two of the apprentices remained on board the *Australasia* from her maiden voyage, and only the first mate Hargrave and the third apprentice remained from the second voyage. Hargrave first went to sea in 1821 as an apprentice, served in the Royal Navy for three years, and received his mate's certificate at the age of thirty-seven. Five feet 9 inches in height, with dark brown hair and hazel eyes, he was aged forty-one in 1849. The second mate, Peter Peterson, was born in Heligoland in the North Frisian Islands in 1805 and first went to sea as a boy of eleven. There is no record of his ever receiving a certificate of any sort, and he could not write. He was 5 feet 9½ inches tall, with brown hair and blue eyes. Frederick Franklin, the third mate, was born in Limehouse in 1827, went to sea as a thirteen-year-old and was shown in the seaman's register as a growing boy with brown hair, dark complexion and blue eyes. He was able to write, so presumably was fully literate. William Jones, the cook, was born in Jamaica in 1808 and was described as 'a man of colour', with dark hair and dark eyes. He went to sea at the age of ten and was not able to write. The carpenter, Andrew Miller, was born in the Orkney Islands in 1815, and first went to sea in 1833. He was able to write and was 5 feet 8 inches tall, with brown hair sallow complexion, blue eyes, and a scar on the left hand. Daniel Duffy the carpenter was born in Newcastle in

1820 and first went to sea in 1849. He was not able to write, and was described as being 5 feet 9 inches tall, with a fresh complexion, brown hair, grey eyes and an anchor tattooed on his right arm. Richard Parding, a seaman who drowned on the voyage, was born in Newark, County Nottingham, in 1830. He first went to sea as an apprentice in 1847, and received his seaman's ticket in 1849. He was described as being 5 feet 5½ inches tall, with brown hair, blue eyes, tan complexion, and a scar on the left cheek. It was not recorded whether or not he could write. Most of the remaining sailors had gone to sea at a very early age. The younger ones could usually write, while the older ones could not. The cuddy servant William Naughton was born at Deptford in December 1826 and was unusually tall by the standards of the times, being 6 feet ¼ inch in height. He was described as being auburn-haired, with a fresh complexion, grey eyes and a pockmarked face. He was on his first voyage and was literate. The only other member of the crew on his first voyage was the eighteen-year-old seaman John Kennedy. When they were unemployed, most of the men lived in Stepney, Deptford or Woolwich.[9]

These then were the men who were to guide the *Australasia* on her 13,000-mile voyage to Australia. The seamen seemed to be a competent group, but the second and third mate do not inspire confidence. Peterson was illiterate and could not have been a reliable navigator, however experienced he was, while Franklin was simply too young and inexperienced.

The scale of victualling in the agreement allowed the crew a pound of bread a day for each man, 1½ pounds of beef per day, or 1¼ pounds of pork, and 1½ pounds of flour per week. Occasionally rice was allowed, a quarter of a pint of peas on pork days, and the rest consisted of half an ounce of coffee, a quarter of an ounce of tea and a pound of sugar per week, including the quantity of lime juice. Vinegar and lime juice were issued according to the Act, and three quarts of water was also issued daily. The Merchant Seaman's Bill laid down a scale of substitutes. A pound of preserved meat could be issued on Sundays, in lieu of salt meat, after being a month at sea. Molasses could be substituted for plums; potatoes and yams for flour, suet, peas or rice; cocoa for tea or coffee. Total water requirements were calculated at the rate of one gallon per man per day for the passage only. Each sailor had to provide a spoon and a tin quart pot, and lime juice, mustard and vinegar were served out every week after being ten days on salt meat. Apparently the ration of peas was not given with beef, probably because the beef measure was greater. The diet strongly reflected the faith the British authorities placed in lime juice as an anti-scorbutic agent.

Without exception, the convict women were facing their first long voyage and, as was usually the case, the first two weeks were a nightmare. According to the Rev R. W. Gibbs, the women aboard the *Cadet* in 1849 were all seriously seasick for at least a fortnight. The Rev. Robert Downing, who left Dublin in September 1848 with 304 male convicts aboard the *Pestonjee Bomanjee*, reported the convicts suffered badly from seasickness early in the voyage. The Rev. Charles Woods, who sailed from Cork on 29 July 1851 on the *Blenheim*, also reported serious seasickness among the 310 male convicts during the first few days out of harbour. The route to the Cape led across the notoriously rough seas of the Bay of Biscay, and this did not help the seasick convicts.

Nevertheless, it was a good preparation for the Atlantic at its worst, and was well summed up by an immigrant to Port Phillip in 1850, whose voyage was deceptively smooth at the outset:

> The morning broke calm and beautiful. Passed out of the Bay in the night into the 'Broad Atlantic' with wind in favour it is truly wonderful. How quiet the ocean is and yet we are sailing at the rate of 8 knots an hour, there is a beautiful swell and the ship bends to it admirably, dipping her figurehead into the water at each bound.

Twelve days later the anonymous immigrant underwent a change of heart. After describing the chaos on board ship during a storm, he observed that:

> Bad as the Bay of Biscay may be, and is, it is nothing when compared to the immense rolling waves of the Atlantic. It beggars description in comparison the one a baby— the other a giant . . . To a novice the Bay of Biscay might appear dreadful, but it is like a baby when compared with the Atlantic whilst rounding the Cape . . . The birds are still following us, at least 200 of them.[10]

Throughout the voyage of the *Australasia*, Alexander Kilroy had 155 patients, of whom all but eleven were convicts. He received his first patient on 27 June, the first day out of harbour, when he treated a convict child for obstipation, or intractable constipation. The child was discharged cured on 7 July. Two days later he treated a convict for a scald, and then went for a week without treating any convicts. This was to be his only idle period during the voyage, as the patients came almost daily after that. His busiest day was 12 July, on the third week out of port, when he treated five convict women for syphilis, discharging them as cured fifteen days later, and another suffering from fever, who was discharged after ten days. The most common complaint was obstipation, for which sixty-two patients were treated, followed by dysentery (thirty-six treated) and bronchitis (fifteen patients). There were eight cases of syphilis, seven cases of fever, six cases with sore throats or cynanche, four with diarrhoea, two each for ophthalmia, scalds and tabes, and one each for ulcerated mouth, rheumatism, dysuria, luxation, ulcer, bruise, parturition and debility. There were only three cases of scurvy, all of them in the first half of September, when the *Australasia* was only a fortnight or so away from Hobart.

Kilroy's treatment of his patients followed the standard medical procedure of the time. His first serious patient was a woman from Kings County, who took ill on 10 July, complaining of a violent headache, spinning sensations, pain in her back, debility and constipation. The constipation was treated with calomel, a heavy white powdered purgative, and the fever was treated by cutting the hair close and constant applications of a wet cloth. Kilroy was well equipped with purgatives and he followed up with pulverised jalapae, a medicinal root used as a cathartic, magnesium sulphate or Epsom salts, pulverized rhubarb, and the antacid magnesium carbonate. Eight days after taking ill, the woman recovered. In the more severe cases of fever, which were also attended with constipation, Kilroy used the diuretic potassium nitrate, a diaphoretic causing perspiration, and a variety of other medicines. He also shaved the heads of his patients and applied blisters both to the scalp and to the epigastrium (upper abdominal surface). The blistering agent was not named, but almost certainly it was cantharides. In two out of the seven cases which failed to respond, he resorted to venesection. In fact, Kilroy fared much better than Hampton had on the *Constant*, as he lost no patients after venesection or bleeding and all his fever cases eventually recovered.

Surgeon-superintendent Kilroy was fortunate that so many of his patients suffered from obstipation, as it was a complaint he was well equipped to deal with. Mary Lydon fell ill with dysentery on 20 September, or nine days away from Hobart, and was treated with pulverized ipecac (a medicinal root used as an expectorant), an emetic or a diaphoretic, pulverized jalapae, and 'pulverized ipecac et opia' (better known as Dover's powder) for the relief of pain associated with the griping. Two days after taking ill she complained of debility and was given diluted sulphuric acid as an astringent, and opium. The treatment was successful and Mary felt much better after two days. As she was rather weak she was given lemon juice with sugar daily, and the diluted sulphuric acid treatment was also continued. Kilroy did not find a great deal of favour with 'cretai praep' (prepared chalk) as an anti-diarrhoeal agent, and only used it in the more severe cases.

On 15 August an Armagh woman took ill with a severe case of dysuria, or painful urination. Kilroy used a catheter to draw out a pint of urine, as she had not passed water for several days, and prescribed 'Ol Ricine' or castor oil, potassium carbonate, infusus sennae (a medicinal root used as a cathartic), potassium nitrate (used as a diaphoretic and diuretic), opium, calomelus, magnesium sulphate and camphor. She was not cured during the voyage and was sent to hospital on arrival at Hobart.

The bronchitis cases were treated with calomel, 'infusus sennae', antimony tartrate (which was used as an expectorant and an emetic), magnesium sulphate and the severe purgative, croton oil. It is not recorded how he dealt with his syphilis cases.

Kilroy was also well equipped to deal with cough, colds and sore throats, using camphor and creosote (an oily distillate from wood tar), an antiseptic, anaesthetic and an escharotic, along with peppermint oil and zingiberis or ginger, as well as many other nostrums. For pain he only had opium, which he appears to have used effectively.

Three convicts died on the voyage, and Kilroy did not record their personal details. The first one, Honora Neill, fell ill of dysentery on 30 August. She appeared cured, but suffered a severe relapse and died on 23 September. Kilroy complained she had been without food for six days and developed scurvy. The second woman, Mary Headon, fell ill with dysentery on 18 September and died seven days later. Kilroy described Headon's case as: 'The most severe and unmanageable case I ever saw. The stools horridly offensive, the stench quite overpowering pervading the whole prison in an instant.'[11] He used solution of chloride of zinc which destroyed the stench immediately it was applied. Mary Headon was also suffering from scurvy.

The third woman, Bridget Butler, was sixty years of age and fell ill on 23 September, again of dysentery. She died five days later, only one day out of port. According to Kilroy she had been suffering from debility for nearly a month. She could not eat the normal food, and Kilroy gave her a special diet. Kilroy noted that her dysentery was brought about 'by her catching a cold in consequence of her taking off part of her clothing to have it washed'.[12]

Sixteen women were sent to hospital on arrival at Hobart Town, including one who had been ill since the third week of the journey. Three other women who fell seriously ill during the first half of the journey had to be sent to hospital. For these it must have been a wretched journey. Happily, Ellen Lydon stood up to the journey very well and there is no record of her falling ill. Her cousin Mary made a good recovery after being ill for eight days with dysentery.

Kilroy's summary of the journey is most interesting. He begins by stating the convicts were not as healthy as they looked when they first came on board, claiming that the food fed to them in Grangegorman Road was both 'insufficient and bad'. He also believed that the bread and milk diet had been deliberately supplied to them to give them 'a healthy appearance'. Soon after the convicts left Kingstown their health declined and they began to suffer from constipation, indigestion and gastric irritation. Further to this he was hampered by the fact the supply of potatoes usually given to Irish convict ships could not be procured at Kingstown, obviously because of the great famine. In his summary Kilroy also describes how he successfully used venesection, purging, blisters and 'wet and cold applications to the head' to cure his fever cases. He also complained of the slow convalescence of his patients, due to other complications such as dysentery and dysuria.

The convicts were generally in good health until they passed the Cape of Good Hope, but then dysentery set in with a vengeance. It became worse as the *Australasia* neared Van Diemen's Land, being complicated in some cases with scurvy. Three of the convict children died, two of tabes (wasting) and the third, who was born on the ship, of debility eighteen days later. During the last week at sea, preserved potatoes were served out every second day, and rice was substituted for peas. An additional quantity of lemon juice and sugar was also served. Scurvy cases were given an extra two ounces each of sugar and lemon juice and this, according to Kilroy, had 'a beneficial effect'. Kilroy's summary concluded with the opinion:

> I think a great number of cases of dysentery, that occurred latterly in the ship is to be attributed principally to cold and damp feet, for whenever they went on deck, their feet soon became damp and cold in consequence of the thinness of their shoes, which are of very little use as a means of keeping the feet dry and warm, and I think it would be a great improvement, in Female convict ships to send thicker and stronger shoes and in that case, one pair for each convict would be sufficient for the voyage.[13]

It must be remembered that medical science as we know it today was then in its infancy. Certainly Kilroy's opinions concerning the cause of dysentery were quaint, and some of his more drastic methods, including venesection and blisters for the treatment of fever, were downright dangerous. But these were the standard treatments of the day, and Kilroy seemed to have been careful to treat his patients in a graduated manner. He left the more severe methods till last, only using them when he felt he had to. At least one of the convicts had no faith in his methods of treatment and kept saying she felt well when she obviously was not. This was rare, however. Surgeon-superintendent Kilroy was an officer and a caring medico who had undertaken the finest medical training available in the world at that time.

Of the twenty-six Galway convicts, only six were ill enough to appear on the sick list although one of them—Sarah Williams—appeared on the list several times, with constipation and dysentery. This is quite a remarkable performance, considering the long period they had already spent in gaol, plus the fact they were sad frightened women on their first voyage.

On the First Fleet, which sailed in 1787 with 759 convicts, the mortality rate was a remarkably low thirty-six men and four women. However, the death toll of the Second Fleet of 1790 was horrific. At least 939 men and 78 women were embarked, and the death toll was 256 men and 11 women. It had been hard to find good surgeons, as low pay, poor status, exacting work and unpleasant conditions made convict service unattractive. Generally, there were much better opportunities on shore. Because of the death toll of the Second Fleet, naval surgeons were appointed as surgeons-superintendent, beginning with the *Royal Admiral*, which left England in 1792. This system worked well, but was discontinued after the *Earl of Cornwallis* sailed in 1800. After this the number of deaths during the voyage and of sick landed in the colony rose sharply. The Irish transports *Hercules* and *Atlas*, which sailed in 1801–02, had forty-four and sixty-three deaths respectively. In 1814, the *General Hewart* had thirty-four deaths on board, and the *Surrey* had thirty-six.

The British government then reintroduced the system of naval surgeons as surgeons-superintendent, and Joseph Arnold sailed in this capacity on the *Northampton* in 1815. The system again worked very well, although the surgeon-superintendent at first had little authority. In 1820 'more explicit and comprehensive instructions' were issued to the surgeon-superintendent. His status was thoroughly defined, as he was not only responsible for the health of the convicts, but also for their organisation and discipline, and he was advised to secure the 'cordial co-operation' of the guard commander and the master of the ship to this end.[14]

The mortality rate improved strikingly from 1821 onwards. While the *Atlas* recorded a death for every 2.7 convicts embarked in 1802 and the *General Hewart* recorded a death for every 8.8 convicts in 1814, the *Lady Kennaway* recorded one death for every 16.3 convicts in 1835. This improvement was apparently due to the appointment of naval surgeons as surgeons-superintendent and the careful delineation of their duties. As Charles Bateson has noted:

> Almost 440 shiploads of male and female convicts reached Sydney and Hobart from the beginning of 1821 until the end of 1840, but in only nine ships did the deaths from disease equal one death to every 20 prisoners embarked, or less, and in no case did the deaths exceed one to every 16.3 prisoners embarked.[15]

The death toll for male convicts aboard the Hobart-bound convict ships between

1841 and 1853 was quite low, never reaching double figures. Inexplicably, the female transports did not fare so well during this period. In 1843 there were seventeen deaths among the women on the *East London*, which gave her a mortality rate of one death to every 7.8 prisoners. Seven of the 150 female prisoners died on board the *Cadet*, which sailed from Plymouth in 1848, giving her a mortality rate of one death to every 21.7 convicts.[16] The convicts, however, had much more chance of reaching Australia than the emigrants.

> Fearful though their treatment often was especially in the earliest years—losses among them through illness at sea averaged less than four per voyage. On an emigrant ship a surgeon would not have considered it untoward had losses run to five times this number. The transportation system also lost remarkably few ships.[17]

In fact only five transports were wrecked, with a total loss of 520 convicts, including those six who died on King Island after the *Neva* foundered off its coast. No fewer than twenty-six emigrant ships failed to arrive, and at least 2,500 of their passengers and crew drowned.[18]

As the *Australasia* embarked 200 convicts and had three deaths, Alexander Kilroy's record of one death for every 66.6 convicts landed is a very good one. But Kilroy had one big ally, and that was the natural hardiness of the Irish convicts. Their ability to survive brutal masters, incompetent surgeons and extremes of temperature has been noted, and their resilience proved to be remarkable throughout the transportation era.[19]

However, women also gave more trouble aboard convict ships than men did. In 1837 Dr Morgan Price, a veteran of seven voyages on convict ships, gave evidence before the select committee on transportation. He felt there was no distinction between male and female convicts, between convicts going to New South Wales or Van Diemen's Land, or between the English and the Irish convicts, as to their expectation of punishment. In answer to the questions put before him, Dr Price said he had never had any problem in managing the convicts during their voyage out. He had used schooling as a means of classification, but had never been able to make a complete classification, founded upon the character of the prisoners. Those who could read and write were separated from the rest as much as possible. He found the convicts to be as bad at the end of the voyage as they had been at the beginning. He went on to say he had 'a considerable deal' more trouble with the females, which he attributed to the limited punishments available for them rather than their character. He also found the women were not reformed by being transported.

Most of the trouble occurred between the crew and the women, as it was very difficult for one matron and the surgeon-superintendent to enforce complete separation. 'If there ever was a hell afloat,' wrote T. Clarke, surgeon of the *Kains* in 1830–01, 'it must have been in the shape of a female convict ship—quarrelling, fighting, thieving, destroying in private each other's property from a mere spirit of devilishness, conversation with each other most abandoned, without feeling or shame.'[20]

Needless to say, not all female convicts were offenders. Indeed, some were totally innocent. In his memoirs John Nicol, the steward aboard the *Lady Juliana* when she sailed with the Second Fleet, describes how a beautiful young Scottish girl died of a broken heart before the ship left the Thames, such was the humiliation of her position.[21]

There is no evidence of any serious trouble among the female convicts aboard the *Australasia*. Nevertheless, it is obvious Kilroy and Matron Lambert did not have things all their own way. Kilroy is very qualified in his comments on convict behaviour, with the more tractable convicts described as quiet or good and the borderline cases as being indifferent. Eighteen of the convicts received negative ship reports, but no correlation has been found between their offence, their county and their shipboard behaviour. Most were described as bad, two were described as garrulous and quarrelsome, and one was described as lazy and filthy. One woman, an arsonist, described as violent and quarrelsome, had deliberately committed the offence to be transported. Ellen Lydon and her cousin Mary were rated quiet on the ship reports.

Kilroy did not record how he punished the troublemakers. Women on board transports were sometimes flogged or caned, although it is unlikely Kilroy would have needed to resort to corporal punishment. Other methods of discipline or punishment included confining troublemakers in a special confinement box, or a coal hole, in the darker part of the ship. The Rev. R. W. Gibbs records how the surgeon in the *Cadet* gave two women two hours solitary confinement for fighting and inciting others to breach discipline while the ship was still in the English Channel. Gilbert Inglis, on the *Duchess of Northumberland* in 1852, reported that no fewer than ten women were placed in the confinement box for stealing, fighting and using insulting language to superiors.[22] One particularly effective method of punishment was shaving women prisoners' heads. John G. Williams, the surgeon aboard the small 369-ton barque *Kinnear*, had so much trouble with the 144 women being transported from Dublin to Hobart he shaved the heads of nine of them. During the enquiry that followed, Williams insisted it was 'the only way of controlling women of this quality'. The Admiralty gave the opinion this did not seem to be too bad under the circumstances, but that the practice should not be encouraged.[23] It is amusing to recall how Gibbs found the women aboard the *Cadet* such a handful he felt three matrons were needed, and no fewer than six solitary cells. The Rev. Charles Woods, aboard the *Blenheim*, had serious difficulty when he tried to instruct Irish-speaking convicts in Christian doctrine, and his solution was the simple one of selecting bilingual convicts to instruct those who only spoke Gaelic in the Irish Catechism.[24] How Kilroy and Matron Lambert overcame this problem is not known, but it was a difficult one, as more than half the convicts in their care were from the west coast, and many of them spoke no English. There were no well-educated women on board, and only eight were fully literate.

Throughout the voyage every effort was made to keep the women busy. The Rev. R. W. Gibbs described how ladies of the convict ship committee came on board and distributed Bibles, tracts, workbags, needlecases and pincushions. The

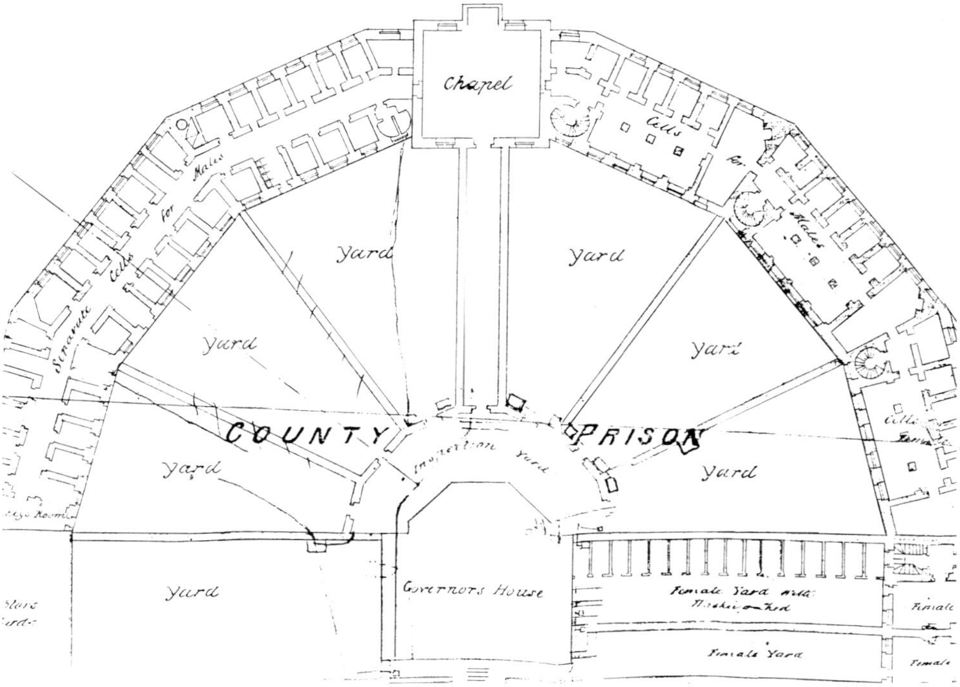

Ground plan of Galway county prison (*Galway County Library*)

Clifden Connemara, 1854 (*National Library of Ireland No. R854*)

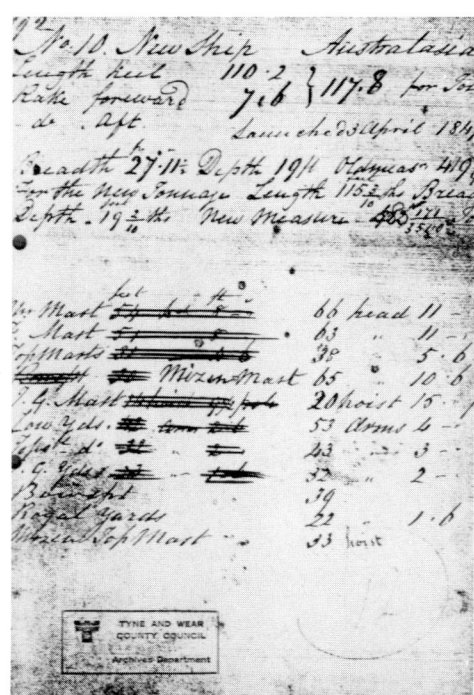

Convict record of Ellen Lydon (*Archives Office of Tasmania*)

Specifications of the *Australasia* (*By permission of the Chief Archivist, Tyne and Wear Archives Service*)

Eleanor Dixon, built on the same lines as the *Australasia* (*Trustees of the National Maritime Museum, London*)

better educated women were made monitresses and taught reading and writing to their illiterate companions. The classes continued to function, even though the matron on the *Cadet* was ill for three weeks. The women also made a lot of shifts and dresses, which were packed into bales when the ship approached Hobart. Kilroy and Matron Lambert doubtless followed a similar routine aboard the *Australasia*.

There is no evidence of prostitution, a problem which usually bedevilled female convict ships. Being a man of high moral character, Connell would not have countenanced such conduct from his crew, but eight years later, on a voyage to Port Phillip in the *Stebonheath*, the young female immigrants and the crew made a laughing stock of him. Connell, who wrote up his log books in grand style, recorded the following:

The first, second and third mates were found in the single women's quarters, after having been repeatedly warned, and were placed in irons.

The carpenter became intoxicated and molested the single women, used indecent language, and struck the chief officer who knocked him down. An all-in brawl ensued, as the boatswain assisted the carpenter against the officers, who finally secured them and sent them ashore as the boat was in port. Two seamen were placed in irons after becoming intoxicated and using the foulest language in demanding the release of the two men already in irons.

The ship's cook struck without provocation.

The ship's company complained they were short of provisions, particularly meat, because the cook was giving it to the female immigrants in return for sexual favours. The cook responded with insolence, insubordination and abusive language. 'Go to buggery and the meat too and wait my pleasure.' A wild fight with a member of the ship's company followed. Next day the cook returned to duty, but only under great pressure.

A member of the crew cut a hole in the female water closet, and was given ten days in irons for this offence.

Another member of the crew tied the tail of a pig to the bars of his cage, and kept beating it until six inches of the tail came off.

One of the crew was chastised for smoking, and he set the chief officer's clothes on fire.

The boy of the watch was struck with the cat-o'-nine-tails by the first mate for not seeing the lantern out in the fore rigging. He responded by telling the mate he would knock his brains out.[25]

No doubt Connell must have wished himself back on the *Australasia*, where a much stronger system of discipline prevailed.

Convict ships may have had few mishaps, but safe passage could still not be taken for granted, and five convict ships were wrecked *en route* to Hobart or Sydney, four of them with heavy loss of life.

The first convict ship to be wrecked was the *Amphitrite*, which went ashore in Boulogne Harbour on 30 August 1833. The ship rapidly broke up and all but three of the 136 people on board perished, including 101 female convicts. The year 1835 was a particularly bad one for wrecks, as three ships were lost. The *George III* was wrecked when it struck a 'sunken and uncharted rock' in the D'Entrecasteaux Channel on 12 April 1835. Of 294 persons on board, 134 were drowned, including 127 male convicts. A month later the *Neva* was wrecked when she struck the Harbinger Reefs off King Island on 13 May. Of 240 people on board, 218 were drowned, including 138 female convicts. Seven survivors, including six convicts, later died on King Island, making the total deaths in the disaster 225. On 10 December the *Hive* was wrecked when she ran aground south-west of Cape St George on the New South Wales coast. The boatswain was drowned, but the rest got ashore. On 28 August 1842 the *Waterloo* was wrecked in a storm while at anchor at Table Bay off Cape town. One hundred and ninety people were drowned, including 143 male convicts and fifteen soldiers of the 99th Regiment.[26]

The Rev. R. W. Gibbs, who reached Hobart in the 465-ton *Cadet* on 12 April 1849, kept a very accurate journal of the voyage. As the ship approached to within 7 degrees north of the equator he reported slow speeds of two miles per hour and very high temperatures of up to 80°F in the shade. This continued until the ship was about 10 degrees south of the line. Fifty-nine days out of port, the *Cadet* passed within a mile of the Cape of Good Hope, and twenty-three days later she began to make very fast speeds of up to 200 miles per day. On three consecutive days the *Cadet* logged 200 miles each day. When she was only two weeks from Hobart, travelling in latitude 38° and moving down to latitude 43°, she met the roaring forties. However, the *Cadet*, which was built on the Isle of Man, was a slow ship and her three voyages to Tasmania took 137, 115 and 116 days. (Although her third voyage is officially recorded as 151 days, this time includes a five-week delay at Plymouth.) Well-named, well-manned, well-founded and skippered by the experienced James Connell, the *Australasia* tore along the last stretch of her voyage at a cracking pace.

The *Australasia*'s last few days at sea in the Storm Bay area were tragic ones, as on 26 September the second convict died and a young seaman, Richard Parding, was drowned, no doubt swept overboard by huge seas. Two days later the third convict died just before the *Australasia* met the pilot boat. Almost certainly the *Australasia* encountered similar problems as the *Cadet*, which had great difficulty in entering Storm Bay, but late in the afternoon of 28 September the *Australasia* met the pilot boat.

The pilot made the following entry in his register: 'Boarded at 4.30 p.m. 28th September 1849, four guns; only passengers listed as cabin passengers were Kilroy and Mrs Lambert; tons 485 new measurement. Crew, 32, 200 convicts and 28 children. Bearings and distance of lighthouse N.N.W. 12 miles wind S.W. weather squally, pilots name Lawrence. Agent McNaughton.'[27] There is some discrepancy between the harbour master's report and the real figures, as twenty-six children were landed and there were thirty-four in the crew, excluding Connell.

On 29 September the *Australasia* arrived in Sullivan's Cove. The sick women were immediately sent to hospital, and Kilroy and Connell received instructions on how to proceed when they reached the Derwent. The ship was placed under a strict quarantine and could only be approached by authorised persons. Nobody could land until permission was received from the lieutenant-governor through the colonial secretary. The surgeon was obliged to furnish the colonial secretary with a large number of returns pertaining to the convicts, the free passengers, the sick, the property of the convicts, general cargo and unused clothing and bedding. Some idea of what happened to the women on the *Australasia* after she reached Sullivan's Cove can be gained from the observations of the Rev. Mr Gibbs on the *Cadet* and the Rev. Mr Woods, who came out on the *Blenheim*. On the second day after the *Cadet*'s arrival, Gibbs reported: 'Muster master with officers and constables came on board and continued during the day in taking down names, ages, and descriptions of the convicts'.[28] Three days later the women were disembarked and taken to the prison hulk *Anson*. Five days after the arrival of the *Blenheim*, Woods noted: 'This afternoon the Right Reverend, the Catholic Bishop strongly advised and exhorted all the Catholic prisoners; the guard being present'.[29]

Bishop Willson was away on Norfolk Island when the *Australasia* arrived at Sullivan's Cove, and the women were met by the vicar-general, Fr William Hall, whose task it was to strongly advise and exhort them. An austere and forbidding Englishman, Hall was no Bernard Kirby, but as it happens, Ellen Lydon would not have understood a word he said.

12

Probation on the *Anson*

Although the *Australasia*'s voyage had been a fast one, the last stretch had been wet and miserable and the women were very much the worse for wear when they reached Hobart Town. Only three had died, but sixteen were immediately sent to hospital. Of the remainder, 145 were sent to the prison hulk *Anson*. As the women were run down and possessed very few skills, the muster master and the principal superintendent processed them as soon as possible. On 2 October Ellen and Mary Lydon, together with Mary's twenty-one-month-old son Batholomew, were travelling upriver to the *Anson* on the small steamer *Derwent*. Doubtless exhausted, sad and confused, the huge river and the majestic Mount Wellington probably overwhelmed them. Governor Arthur's observations on women prisoners from 1837 are pertinent: 'I am sure it would excite the sympathy of any person to see them on their arrival. I have gone aboard the transports to see the women; the state of depression and agony they are in is scarcely to be described.'[1]

Hobart was named after Lord Hobart, a former colonial secretary, and is beautifully situated on the Derwent River beneath the magnificent Mount Wellington, and about thirteen miles from the mouth of the Derwent. In 1851 it had a population of 23,107 and 4,050 houses, of which 2,932 were of stone or brick. Already it was taking shape as an important provincial city, with well-laid-out streets, handsome freestone houses, extensive wharves handling a large volume of shipping and several fine public buildings. Religion was not neglected, as St David's Anglican Cathedral was a good example of Gothic architecture and there were three handsome Episcopalian churches—Trinity, St George's, and St John's. The Presbyterians boasted the spacious churches of St Andrew's and St John's, and there were two Wesleyan chapels. As for the Catholics, they had the fine church of St Joseph's, which was and remains the hub of their religious activity. There were many public institutions dedicated to scientific, religious and humanitarian pursuits. An observatory was situated in the government domain, just outside the town near Government House.

Anglesea barracks, an excellent example of well-planned military accommodation, held pride of place on the southern side of the harbour, surrounded by many beautiful residences.[2] From July 1848 it quartered the 99th Regiment, under the command of the ascetic Colonel John Napper Jackson, who had served with great distinction in the Peninsula War. His deputy was Major Edward Last, a popular and genial man who was later to become the visiting magistrate at the prisoners' barracks. Lieutenant G. J. De Winton, who came out on the *Constant*, was stationed on Norfolk Island with a strong detachment of the 99th. Indeed, Hobart seemed to have everything, but not everybody saw it this way. The exiled Young Ireland leader John Mitchell remarked on 6 April 1850, as the transport *Neptune* prepared to enter the Derwent:

> We are becalmed in the channel; but can see the huge mass of Mount Wellington, ending to the eastward in steep cliffs. In the valley at the foot of those cliffs, as they tell me, bosomed in soft green hills, bowered in shady gardens, with its feet kissed by the blue ripples of the Derwent—lies that metropolis of murderers and university of burglary and all subter-human abomination, Hobart Town.[3]

The 1,742-ton *Anson* had been built in 1812 at Paull, near Hull. Her dimensions were: length of deck, 175.5 feet; length of keel, 144.5 feet; beam, 48.3 feet; depth of hold, 21 feet.[4] She was normally classed as a third-rate ship of the line with seventy-four guns, though her description, taken from the Navy lists, shows her to carry eighty guns. The difference seems to lie in six 18-pounder carronades carried in the roundhouse. She carried 590 men as her normal complement. The *Anson* did not see any distinguished service in her prime as a warship. From 1812 to 1827 she was 'in ordinary at Portsmouth'. In 1834 she was in quarantine service at Leith, in 1837 in quarantine service at Stangate, and from 1844 to 1850 she was used for convicts at Hobart.

Lord Stanley had planned to build a female penitentiary in a healthy inland situation less than twenty miles from Hobart and with a capacity for 400 prisoners.[5] This prison was never built, and on 20 September 1843 it was decided to use the *Anson* as a convict hulk, situated in the Derwent at Risdon. The *Anson* sailed from Plymouth with 499 convicts on 1 October 1843 and arrived at Hobart on 4 February the following year, under the command of Captain Coglin. She was later fitted out in Hobart for her new role as a convict hulk, at the cost of £12,307 6s. 4d. Almost immediately after her arrival, the *Anson* was anchored in Prince of Wales Bay, on the western side of the Derwent, where she received the female prisoners from the *Woodbridge* and the *Angelina* on 25 April. As a prison hulk she was not seen in a very flattering light. Lieutenant-Colonel Munday leaves us this description:

> In the rides and drives for promenading purposes Hobart Town has greatly the advantage of Sydney. The road through the Government Domain and farm, past Cornelian Bay, the Botanical Gardens, the old hulk Anson 74, degraded to a female prison, and round by the Bishops pretty residence to Risdon Ferry, presents one good direction for a canter, or for 'riding' on wheels for those who prefer dowagering to horse exercise.[6]

The officers appointed to take charge of the *Anson* probation station were Dr Edmund Bowden, who had been surgeon to the Chelsea and Brompton dispensary, and his second wife Phillipa Bowden, who had been matron of Hanwell asylum in Middlesex. They were named as superintendent and matron, on a joint salary of £500, with a further £300 paid to Dr Bowden yearly for discharging the duties of medical inspector of the penitentiary. Mrs Bowden was the daughter of a surgeon, Thomas Powell, and had been the principal assistant of Dr John Conolly at Hanwell asylum, which was the largest in England. As superintendent of Hanwell from 1839 to 1844, Dr Conolly had discontinued widespread restraint of the inmates and introduced a program of humane treatment in its place. Conolly had given much credit for the success of his modern methods to Mrs Bowden. On the *Anson*, Mrs Bowden was responsible for the organisation and discipline of the women, and was the mainspring of penal reform. Unfortunately, the odds were against this remarkable woman.[7]

On 17 September 1844 the comptroller-general of convicts, Captain Mathew Forster, voiced serious concern about the *Anson*, and in a letter to Lieutenant Governor Eardley-Wilmot he raised six points:

First, the demand for the type of convict labour available from the *Anson* was not likely to keep pace with the supply. As the *Anson* already had 519 convicts on board, and 600 more were expected yearly, the position could become serious.

Second, more harm than good would result from large numbers of females being confined in the type of accommodation available to the department, and Foster recommended that tickets-of-leave should be given 'to as many of the old class of female pass holders as possible with due regard to propriety'.

Third, many years of experience had convinced Forster that women were not suitable as subjects for what is termed 'Prison Discipline', and each succeeding year only strengthened that impression.

Fourth, and with great deference, Captain Forster felt the best conducted prisoners should not be brought under prison discipline in Van Diemen's Land.

Fifth, the expense of maintaining the *Anson* as a prison establishment was considerable, and it could only increase as more prisoners were brought out.

Finally, as women were not fit subjects for prison discipline, given good conduct during their early stage of probation, they should receive tickets-of-leave and conditional pardons as soon as possible.[8]

Poor Forster; it seems he had become convinced it was easier to lead a thousand men, however desperate and dangerous, than it was to control ten women. The returns for 29 June 1844, including both old convicts and probationers, show there were 23,364 male and 3,894 female convicts in the colony, a ratio of nearly six to one. Even though the more hardened male convicts were steeped in every vice known to man, it is clear the women represented the vulnerable point of the system. The 'flash mob' at the female factory gave the penal system in Hobart a difficult time, as they were incorrigible and showed no dread of any sanctions. This aspect of factory life was described by a contemporary:

Three fourths of the women then under punishment had been, in the opinion of the Superintendent, there before. This illustrates what dread is entertained for the place: women smile at being sent there; some even commit offences for the purpose. When sentenced by a police magistrate to the tub for a certain time, they are often heard to exclaim 'I'll soon bowl that out!' They have the association of numbers like themselves, and the work imposed on them is uncared for.[9]

In 1844 Forster was probably still suffering from the after-effects of the behaviour of the female convicts at the female factory during the regime of Sir John Franklin. Two incidents occurred at the factory which both mocked the Convict Department and astonished Hobart Town.

The first concerned the Rev. Mr Bedford, and has been well recorded by the Rev. Robert Crooke, who had no love for his fellow minister:

The women at the factory knew the Chaplain's character well. They were quite aware that he loved roast turkey and ham with a good bottle of port to wash them down, far more than he loved his Bible, and when he put on his surplice and spoke to them of their vices and the necessity for reformation they scoffed at him in their hearts, and regarded him with mixed feelings of contempt and ridicule . . . On one occasion as he was crossing the courtyard of the female House of Correction, some dozen or twenty women seized upon him, took off his trousers and deliberately endeavoured to deprive him of his manhood. They were, however, unable to effect their purpose in consequence of the opportune arrival of a few constables who seized the fair ladies and placed them in durance vile.[10]

On another occasion, Bedford was conducting Governor Franklin and Lady Jane Franklin around the female factory. The governor addressed the women, who numbered between 300 and 400, and as he was a humane man he received a good hearing. His wife likewise was listened to with respect, even though she was not so popular. But when Bedford decided to have his say, his speech elicited the following reaction:

They had been standing in front of the vice regal party who from an elevated dais or platform addressed them. When on a sudden the three hundred women turned right round and at one impulse pulled up their clothes shewing their naked posteriors which they simultaneously smacked with their hands making a loud and not very musical noise. This was the work of a moment, and although constables, warders, etc. were there in plenty, yet 300 women would not well be all arrested and tried for such an offence and when all did the same act the ringleaders could not be picked out. The feeling of the Governor and her Ladyship may well be conceived.[11]

Despite such behaviour, and despite the pessimism of Forster, the influence of Mrs Bowden and her husband aboard the *Anson* began to bear fruit. In October 1844, when a reporter from the *Hobart Town Courier* visited the *Anson*, he was welcomed as he ascended the ship's ladder by the singing of the prisoners, who were assembled for the afternoon service. He was impressed by the rapport the Rev. Mr Giles had with the prisoners, and even more so with the courtesy and openness of Mrs Bowden, who conducted him right throughout the ship and answered all his questions. The reporter then made the following observations:

> We found that besides the necessary duties of the establishment in washing and cooking, the women were employed in various descriptions of needlework, in the manufacture of shoes, straw-hats, door mats, &c, as far as the very limited means at Mrs Bowden's command will allow. Every part of the ship exhibited remarkable cleanliness, and we could not have expected to witness such general health, and to find the ventilation so good, where so large a number are collected together in a limited space. But these physical appearances constitute the least recommendation of those who superintend the arrangements on board the Anson. We remarked with great satisfaction the subdued, respectful, and throughout proper deportment of the women, exhibiting a very striking contrast with what we have been too long accustomed to in similar establishments in this country.[12]

He also warned, however, that despite Mrs Bowden's high principles and great energy, she could not hope for too much, because of the quality of her subjects and the environment into which they are released.

Lord Stanley was a realist so far as female prisoners went. He felt they presented a special problem in that, while they were as depraved as the male prisoners, it was impossible to subject them to the same discipline. He instructed that every female convict who conducted herself properly aboard the transport, and continued to do so during the first six months of probation, should obtain a probation pass. From then on the same rules would apply to the female prisoners as to the male. In short, the Anson was a probation station.

The Bowdens brought six female nurses out from Hanwell, the most prominent of whom were the Holdich sisters, Martha, Susan and Jane. They were the daughters of Mathew Holdich, a native of the Isle of Ely and a yeoman farmer of Lincolnshire. Martha had the additional advantage of being a qualified schoolmistress. When the Bowdens took possession of the Anson on 25 April 1844 they found the ship had not undergone any special conversion for its role as a prison hulk, other than roofing over the bows. Dr Bowden immediately set his male warders to work preparing quarters for the officers, a laundry, a storeroom and an office. Each of the Anson's three decks was divided into four wards. The male warders were given the administrative functions of clerk, storekeeper, messenger and nighwatchman. The female officers came under the supervision of Mrs Bowden, and one was assigned to every prison ward. Others were assigned to the school, the hospital, the store, the workroom, the laundry and the kitchen, each of which also had its superintendent. The Anson had a staff ratio of one warder to every twenty-three prisoners, as against one to every fifty-nine at the female factory. In his report for 1 August 1846, W. Champ, the acting comptroller-general, pointed out it cost £2,391 5s. 0d. to run the Anson, as against only £1,008 for the female factory, and that the difference was due to the higher staff ratios. According to Dr Bowden: 'The principle upon which our establishment was formed was that of efficient female superintendence'.[13]

Dr Bowden praised the efforts of his wife in her zeal to reform the prisoners:

In enumerating the moral means of discipline employed, the labours of Mrs Bowden must not be passed over in silence. To admonish the careless, to reprove the hardened, to encourage the diffident, and to soothe the penitent, is her daily task. Individually and in clases, by scriptural and other influential readings, by exhortations and addresses, by encouragement and warning, by counsel and by comfort, does she daily seek to restore the lost ones to themselves, to society, and, as far as 'human' means extend, to their God.[14]

At the end of 1845 Dr Bowden was able to point to excellent records, as the visiting magistrate had awarded only twenty-seven sentences to convicts of the *Anson* between April 1844 and April 1845. Bowden expressed complete satisfaction, on behalf of both himself and his wife, with the *Anson* 'as a place of reformatory discipline for the female convicts'.[15]

Unfortunately, Dr Bowden died on 3 September 1847 and, although his wife succeeded him as sole superintendent, she complained about her salary being fixed at £400. Early in 1848 she obtained twelve months leave and sailed to England, never to return. The historian John West pointed out that early lack of employment ruined the enterprise, but he gave remarkable credit to Mrs Bowden and the Holdich sisters:

Mrs Bowden, a lady of majestic presence and enlightened mind, who had acquired considerable experience in the management of the insane, was appointed matron. Her fertility of resource, courage, and zeal, had been greatly admired at Hanwell, where many hundreds of the unfortunates were relieved from the greatest of human calamities. The reputation of this lady recommended her to the confidence of government: with her husband, Dr Bowden, the medical officer, and a chosen staff of assistants—several only inferior to herself—she arived in this colony with high expectations of success. As a temporary expedient, the Anson, a ship of war, was appropriated to the project. The decorum of the ship, and the healthy and cleanly appearance of the women, were striking to a stranger; but the early lack of employment ruined the enterprise . . . This lady and her friends and coadjutors, the Misses Holdich, found the women generally submissive and docile: they were haunted with all kinds of terrors, and had less than the ordinary courage of women. Mere children in understanding; some, such only in years; but their actual reformation, for the most part, only remained an object of confident expectation, while their true tendencies were repressed. The lady officers, who expected to reap a harvest in this field of mercy began by blaming the colonists for scepticism, and after 3,000 women had passed through their hands, they, alas! ended in becoming sceptical.[16]

Ellen Lydon and the other female convicts reached the *Anson* and climbed the ladder up to the main deck of the towering warship, which was three and a half times the size of the *Australasia*. Mrs Bowden had been gone for over eighteen months, and the chaplain and superintendent was the Rev. G. Giles, who received a salary of £350 per annum. Susan Holdich was the acting matron and assistant superintendent at £185 per annum, Jane Holdich was the schoolmistress at £80, and Martha Holdich was the prime warder at £60. There were four other female warders at £52 per annum, and three male warders at £67. The Roman Catholic catechist was Miss S. A. Troy (£60), and the visiting magistrate was Algernon Burdett

Jones, JP, who was coroner for Hobart Town and superintendent of the Queen's orphan school.

As soon as they had all reached the main deck, the women were addressed by Giles, who explained the probation system to them, and they were then allocated their wards. Miss Troy acted as interpreter for those prisoners who only spoke Gaelic.

The prisoners from the *Australasia* were quartered on the orlop deck, in the bowels of the ship, which had four numbered wards, each accommodating seventy-five convicts, a solitary cell in the bow and a bread store in the stern. The lower deck, above the orlop deck, contained wards 5 to 8, each accommodating fifty convicts, and further solitary cells in the bow. The great cabin in the stern was reserved for the matrons. The *Anson* also had four small wards for well-behaved prisoners, a surgeon's quarters and a dispensary next to the great cabin, a large guardroom, quarters for six overseers and two wards for their wives. The upper deck contained prisoners' wards 9 to 12, but the plans retain the layout the *Anson* had when it first arrived in Hobart with 499 convicts. The stern section contained accommodation for four army officers and a military mess room, while the forward section contained a sick bay for the soldiers and seamen and a separate one for the convicts. The stern also had three ladies' cabins, a military mess room and quarters for the assistant surgeon, boatswain, carpenter and clerk in charge. There were berths for troops in the area between the stern accommodation and the prison wards. The poop deck had accommodation for ship's officers, with pride of place being held by the commanding lieutenant's cabin and mess room. The forecastle was mainly taken up with galleys, cooks' quarters and sail lockers.

Ellen and Mary Lydon stuck close together, with Mary's little son Bartholomew, as for the fifth time since leaving Salrock these young peasant women found themselves learning a new prison routine. Every morning the ship's bell summoned them to rise early, and as they all slept in hammocks, these had to be brought on deck and aired with the other bedding while the wards were cleaned and the school opened. At eight o'clock the prisoners had their morning meal and received their bread for the day. After breakfast the bell was rung for prayers, Giles officiating for the Protestants while Miss Troy looked after the Catholics. At nine the bell was rung to commence the day's work. The second meal of the day was provided at noon, followed by the afternoon's duties, the evening meal and prayers. The women were locked in their wards at 7 p.m. during the winter, and an hour later in summer. The *Anson* was a big improvement on previous prisons in one respect, as three meals were provided daily, rather than two, and the women did not have to go to bed hungry.

The daily ration aboard was four-fifths of a pound of flour (12 per cent protein content) or the equivalent in bread, half a pound each of fresh meat and vegetables, half an ounce of salt, a quarter of a pint of oatmeal and half an ounce of soap. When flour was issued the prisoners also received $^1/_{175}$ part of a pint of yeast. Females undergoing solitary confinement received one and a half pounds of flour (12 per cent) or the equivalent in bread, half an ounce of soap, and yeast when flour was issued. The normal diet for the prisoners seems reasonable enough, but those who misbehaved and were placed in solitary confinement would soon feel the difference.

Every six months each female prisoner was issued with a jacket, petticoat, cap, shift, apron and handkerchief, along with a pair of stockings and a pair of shoes.[17]

A good description of a convict from the *Anson* in full dress has been provided for us by Caroline Leakey, writing as Oliné Keese, in *The Broad Arrow*:

> She had on the usual brown serge skirt, (so short as to show a masculine pair of half-boots), a jacket of brown and yellow gingham, a dark blue cotton kerchief; and a prim white calico cap, whose narrow border was kept in frill by help of a thread run through it, completed her dress.[18]

Leakey also described the attire as grotesque in its coarseness.

During their working hours many of the women were employed in washing, carding, spinning, knitting and dyeing. Others were employed in trades such as shoemaking and mending, while the kitchen and the laundry were also used as a means of instruction. The women were regularly paraded on deck for exercise, sometimes 200 at a time. As in other probation camps, the women were divided into three classes, and every effort was made to encourage the prisoners to do as well as possible by granting or withholding privileges.

Generally, the women from the *Australasia* behaved well on board the *Anson* and only three gave real trouble. On 2 November 1849 magistrate Jones gave a woman ten days in the cells for disobedience, and when the same woman again offended on 11 November she received an extra six months probation. On 11 November another was sentenced to seven days in the cells for refusing to attend the teaching of the Catholic catechism. When the third woman went on a rampage in the nursery after her child died on 4 January 1850, it was recommended that her conduct be reported when the other women from the *Australasia* were brought up for classification on 20 January. She only lost three months, and was made a third-class convict on 22 April.

Ellen Lydon became a third-class convict on 13 February 1850 and her cousin Mary did likewise on 22 March. Ellen was then ready to leave the *Anson* to go to the Brickfields hiring depot, where she would be able to enter service with a family in the Hobart area. Nevertheless, she doubtless had many qualms about leaving the *Anson*, not unlike those expressed by Caroline Leakey in *The Broad Arrow*:

> Strange and vague are the mental picturings the prisoned female forms of the land of her exile, which she knows lies little further than a stone's throw from her. Some think, on leaving the *Anson*, they are turned adrift to all the horrors of an unexplored region; others that they will be driven to market for sale. The cunning and malicious amongst them delight in filling the minds of their less gifted associates with the most terrible apprehensions of the barbarities awaiting them on their departure from their probation. It is with a thrill of cruel suspense that such prisoners first plant their foot on Tasmanian ground.

In this respect the male convicts do not suffer so acutely. Their doubts, hopes, and fears are answered, realised, or crushed almost immediately on arriving at the colony. Their probationary course does not add suspense to sorrow. At once formed into gangs, they learn the worst, and are sent to labour in the roads, or work on public buildings. The torture of suspense is not added to it.[19]

Having Mary and little Bartholomew close by must have been a comfort to Ellen, and the expectation that her brother John and cousin Michael were due in the colony soon was something more to look forward to. However, there are no surviving records of John's arrival in Van Diemen's Land.

13

Life in Van Diemen's Land

After his gang probation expired on 26 August 1845, Stephen Howard was bound by the regulations to wait at Salt Water River for at least ten days, in case anybody in the area wanted his services, and he did not in fact return to the Hobart Prisoners' barracks until 16 November. Those convicts who had completed their gang probation reported to William Gunn, who was still the principal superintendent, and were again paraded in the central yard of the prison barracks, where Gunn told them their status had changed. They were now probation pass holders, and as such they were able to engage in private service for wages. Stephen had attained the status of third-class probation pass holder, which permitted him to receive the whole of whatever he earned. Despite this, he still had to account for the expenditure of his wages whenever the comptroller-general of convicts or any person in authority required it.

Furthermore, probation pass holders were not allowed to sue their masters for any wages or entitlements owing to them, although the comptroller of convicts could do so on their behalf. Likewise, they could 'not be liable to any civil suit or action by any person'.[1] The employer could only obtain redress through the comptroller of convicts. The pass holders were supervised by magistrates in the districts where they were employed, and were to be inspected by them at least once a month. The magistrate had to submit monthly reports to the comptroller of convicts.

Stephen did not have to wait long for employment. On 29 November he and another young Limerick convict from the *Constant*, Patrick Lynch, were hired into the service of Mr John Staples, a farmer of High Sunderland. Lynch was a short, freckled man, aged twenty-three, who had been given seven years transportation for violent assault. He was rated as a good ploughman, who could also read and write.

A formal contract of service was drawn up between Staples and the comptroller of convicts, who acted on behalf of the pass holders, negotiating their terms of employment and pay. As Stephen Howard and Patrick Lynch were facing their first labour contract, with the alternative being roadwork for rations, they were hardly in a position to argue about conditions. And as the supply of labour always greatly exceeded demand during the probation era, they faced an offer they could not refuse. Up until March 1844, pass holders were engaged in service at the rate of £9 per year. After this date they were allowed to make their own agreements. Nevertheless, their rights and obligations were explained to them in front of John Staples.

William Gunn completed the formalities on behalf of the comptroller-general, and informed the prisoners they would be obliged to muster at Brighton on the first Sunday of each month for inspection by the magistrate, G. B. Forster, who would report their condition to the comptroller-general of convicts on the tenth day of every month. They had to attend Divine Service at least every Sunday if they resided within two miles of a place of worship. Upon the termination of their engagement, they had to obtain a pass from their employer, or from the nearest magistrate, after which they had to proceed to the closest hiring depot. They were informed they were 'amenable to convict law only',[2] and could only be punished by the magistrate. Those who committed a serious misdemeanour could be returned to the probation gang for a period. A pass holder had no power to break the contract by giving or receiving notice personally while a master who wished to dispense with the services of a pass holder had to pay ten days' wages to the comptroller of convicts. If a master wished to retain the services of a convict after the allotted term, he had to enter into a new contract.

The convicts were not without their rights, and it was explained to Staples that he had to provide suitable lodgings and bedding for his pass holders without making any deductions from their wages on that account. He was also required to supply them with a daily ration of a pound of meat, 1–1½ pounds of bread, 2 pounds of vegetables, an ounce each of sugar and roasted wheat, and half an ounce each of salt and of soap.[3] In addition to this the master was responsible for the medical supervision of his servant although, in the cases of protracted illness, the comptroller hospitalised the individuals concerned. Pass holders were expected to provide appropriate clothing from their wages and could be charged with misconduct if they failed to do so.

John Staples held 234 acres on the eastern bank of the Derwent, about four miles from Bridgewater, and sixteen miles upstream from Hobart. He held another sixty acres on the banks of the Jordan River and lived in a substantial stone residence, called High Sunderland, between Church and Millvale Roads on the main road between Bridgewater and New Norfolk. Staples Sugarloaf, a large hill near Broadmarsh on the far side of Mount Dromedary, is almost certainly named after him.

Stephen apparently found Staples' service congenial enough, as he stayed for over nine months, while Lynch spent his entire period as a pass holder with Staples and qualified for his ticket-of-leave at the earliest possible time. But while service with Staples obviously presented few problems, Divine Service did. There were very few Catholic priests in Tasmania at that time, and if no Catholic service was available, pass holders had to attend the Anglican Divine Service. Being a Roman Catholic was no excuse for missing Divine Service and one man from the *Constant* received ten days' hard labour for absenting himself from Divine Service on the plea he was a Roman Catholic. However, as High Sunderland was at least four miles from Bridgewater, Stephen may have been free from any obligation in this regard.

On 15 September 1846, Stephen reported to Mr W. Lavender, the superintendent of the Jerusalem hiring depot. Jerusalem, now Colebrook, is twenty-eight miles from Hobart, near the source of the Coal River. A police magistrate's court was held there once a week; there was a post office, and an Episcopalian clergyman. Of the eight hiring stations in Van Diemen's Land, Jerusalem, Fingal and Westbury were exclusively agricultural. As Stephen's skill and experience lay in the agricultural area, this was obviously why he had been sent to one of them.

The Jerusalem hiring station was experiencing severe growing pains. On 27 September 1843, a month after the *Constant* arrived, it had 225 convicts, all of whom were employed in road-making in thinly settled country. The returns for June 1846 showed Jerusalem had 140 acres, of which 100 were under crop, 20 were ready for sowing and another 20 were being cleared and prepared for sowing. It had 17 huts with accommodation for 418 men, 52 separate apartments and 10 solitary cells. The station also fulfilled a special purpose, in that it accommodated pass holders who were ill or incapacitated. As at 30 June 1846 it had thirty-two pass holders with physical defects, and forty-seven more who were incapacitated through physical or mental illness. Jerusalem was not without its disciplinary problems and 299 convicts appeared before the visiting magistrate in 1845, of whom 268 were convicted, six for felonies and larcenies and the rest for misdemeanours. The average number of convicts at the depot each year was 500. The following year did not bring much of an improvement, as 158 convicts appeared before the visiting magistrate in the first six months, and 108 convictions were recorded against them—five for felony and the remainder for breaches of discipline. The average number of convicts at the depot for that year was 520.[4]

Stephen Howard did not stay long at Jerusalem, as on 2 December 1846, after eleven weeks, he was hired out to Mr T. Walton of Uplands. Two miles from Cambridge along the Richmond Road, Uplands is a fine example of early colonial architecture. Built of large freestone blocks, with a front verandah and large attic rooms, it also had two underground cells beneath the front rooms to accommodate convict servants. Two iron grilles, protruding several inches above the verandah floor, were placed on each side of the front door. The Walton family took no chances with their convict servants, but to be fair their accommodation was no worse than the basements used by whole families in many of the world's great cities today. As for Stephen, he seems to have been contented enough, as he stayed for twelve months—a long period for a pass holder.

After concluding his contract with Walton, Stephen was stationed in the Richmond

area. Richmond is one of Australia's most historic towns, and was described by
John West in 1851:

> Richmond—a town at the mouth of the Coal River, in the parish of Ulva and county
> of Monmouth, 15 miles from Hobart, and 100 from Launceston. It contains an episcopal
> and a catholic church, a congregational chapel, a police office, post station, a gaol, and
> court house, and several inns. It has a resident police magistrate, and the population
> of the town and district, which consists of farms, is 3,144, and the number of houses
> 545, nearly half of which are of stone or brick. Richmond is an electoral district, for
> which T. G. Gregson, Esq., is the first member.[5]

Richmond also had a fine old gaol, which was built in 1825 and is now a tourist
attraction. In 1847 it was a solid all-purpose prison, serving one of Van Diemen's
Land's busiest districts. It had the usual receiving rooms, an entrance passageway,
a large airing yard which contained an almond tree legend says was planted by
a young Aboriginal boy who was brought there for the treatment of injuries. The
prison also provided sleeping accommodation for chain gangs and in 1832 forty-
two men in irons, plus others for trial, slept in a room measuring 15 feet 6 inches
by 13 feet 6 inches. It was always grossly overcrowded and in 1841 the visiting
magistrate reported that eighty-four men awaiting trial were crowded into its halls
and passageways. It had dayrooms where the prisoners were engaged in tasks such
as whitewashing, cleaning and cutting wood. Inmates were not allowed to play
card or dice games, but they cut draught boards into the floor. There was a women's
section, complete with solitary cells.

As with most nineteenth-century prisons, there was a great emphasis upon
punishment. There were separate sets of solitary cells for male and female prisoners,
each cell measuring 7 feet by 3 feet. There was a special flogging yard, and although
floggings were frequent, a magistrate by himself could only order a maximum of
thirty-six lashes. Richmond gaol was the base of George Grover, a flagellator who
was murdered by being thrown off the Richmond Bridge when he was drunk. It
was also the base of Soloman Blay, a convict who became one of the most notorious
hangmen in Van Diemen's Land and is recorded as having executed over 150 criminals.
Transported in 1836 for counterfeiting, Blay received a conditional pardon in 1850
and his certificate of freedom in 1857. When he was placed on the pension list,
he returned to England and purchased a cottage outside London, hoping for a
little tranquillity. However, his macabre reputation soon caught up with him and,
fearing for his life, he sold his cottage at a loss and, perhaps surprisingly, he returned
to Tasmania.[6]

When Stephen arrived at Richmond the keeper of the gaol was Mr G. Wise,
who had held that position since June 1847. Serious trouble was pending between
Wise and the *Javelin* men, or privileged convicts, who brought several charges against
him concerning stores and supplies. Whether Stephen slept in the gaol or was
attached to a road gang in the area is not known. Nevertheless, he had to keep
the watchhouse keeper at Richmond well informed of his movements.

On 16 May 1848 Stephen was engaged by Mr James McRay, whose family held

Alexander Kilroy, c. 1835 (*Courtesy of Commander Guy Kilroy*)

Figurehead of the *Constant* (*Courtesy of Portland Studios and Kurtzes Museum*)

Pavilion and harbour, Kingston (*National Library of Ireland, Lawrence Collection No. R4424*)

Female Factory Cascades (*Archives Office of Tasmania*)

Mother M. Xavier Williams (*Archives of the Australian Congregation of the Sisters of Charity*)

Mother M. de Sales O'Brien (*Archives of the Australian Congregation of the Sisters of Charity*)

St Joseph's Church, Hobart Town, 1844 (*Courtesy of St Joseph's Retreat, Passionist Community, Hobart*)

a large block well off the road between Hollow Tree and Bothwell. During the early years of their residence the McRays are reputed to have had a lot of trouble with hostile Aborigines. Stephen was engaged to work for McRay for three months, and it was here he got into trouble. On 30 June he was reprimanded by the magistrate at Kangaroo Point, now Bellerive, for neglect of duty. In a long penal odyssey which covered five and a half years and 13,000 miles from the bridewell of Bruff to the court at Kangaroo Point, it was the only blemish on his record. Fortunately, the authorities thought little of the offence, as on 5 September 1848 Stephen Howard obtained his ticket-of-leave, and on 8 November he was created a constable. Due to a gap in the police records, nothing is known of his police career. Perhaps Stephen was foolish or misguided enough to feel he was improving his status by becoming a policeman.

The most dignified comment on the Van Diemen's Land police came from the historian John West:

> The police constables, mostly prisoners of the crown, were selected from each ship to assist the recognition of their fellow prisoners, and they were rewarded for every runaway they arrested. They often shortened their own sentence by procuring the conviction of others; often, too, they obtained considerable sums, and even instant liberty, by the discovery of an outlaw. They were acute, expert, and, we are told by Arthur, vigilant beyond all men he ever knew. They were objects of fear and detestation.[7]

West was speaking of the assignment era, during the regime of Governor Arthur, but the only change between police under the assignment and probation systems was the later recruitment of policemen in the probation era, under which system police were not usually selected before they had reached their ticket-of-leave status, three to five years after their arrival. But in the eyes of the public, this did not legitimise their status as policemen, which the Cornwall Chronicle makes quite clear with the savage comment:

> Scarcely a week passes without a free man being made a victim to the perjury of the felon janissary corps.
>
> Gracious God! Is it to be endured that men whose characters are irreproachable are to be submitted to the control of felons, of wretches who are dead in the eyes of the law, and to be made victims of the villainy of a set of contaminated, gallows-defrauding, gibbet-deserving, sin-inoculated, devil-devoted, hell-destined scoundrels? Are these pests fit characters to be armed with a staff of authority to enforce obedience to the laws which they have grossly violated themselves.[8]

How public opinion affected Stephen is not known. He seems to have remained in the Richmond area throughout 1849 and he received his conditional pardon on 30 July 1850. A senior family member told the writer many years ago that Stephen Howard the policeman was employed as an overseer on the construction of the Hobart to Geeveston highway, which linked the orchard area of the Huon River with Hobart, and that he proved to be such a hard taskmaster he had a tombstone allocated to him for every mile of road. It is impossible to tell how much validity this story has, but by the time he was married in 1854 Stephen had reverted to the status of a labourer and was living in the Hobart area.

In February 1850, after she had completed her period of gang probation aboard the *Anson*, Ellen Lydon found herself back on the little steamer *Derwent* as she and several other females were taken to the Hobart waterfront, where brown prison vans were waiting to convey them to the Brickfields hiring depot. The Brickfields was situated off Argyle Street, between Scott and Clara Streets. These streets have since been renamed and the North Hobart football oval now occupies the site of the depot. The plan of the Brickfields was simple, being that of a hollow square. The back section had a small hospital, a surgery and a large dormitory. The two side sections consisted of large rectangular dayrooms, with storerooms on one side and cooking and washing facilities on the other. The matron's house was to the left of the entrance, while the committee room and the receiving room were to the right.[9]

The report of the comptroller-general for 1846 shows that Brickfields had accommodation for up to 200 women, although the dormitory section was divided into two wards with sleeping places for only 128 convicts. The large ward had three tiers of berths, and the lights were left on all night. There were no solitary cells or separate apartments, and the cooking and washing facilities were considered to be good. Those women who were waiting to be hired into service were employed in needlework and cut-out work. In 1850 the superintendent and matron were Mr and Mrs Williams, who both had assistants as well as a religious instructor and two constables to help administer the depot. The visiting magistrate was Mr A. B. Jones, who fulfilled the same role aboard the *Anson*.[10]

In September 1844 a dispute arose between the comptroller of convicts and two visiting magistrates who claimed the right, under the Quarter Sessions Act, to inspect the Brickfields. The comptroller refused them permission, with the backing of the governor, and gave the following definition of the Brickfields' function: 'The building in the Brickfields, however, is not used as a Penitentiary, or Factory within the spirit and meaning of the Act, neither as a place of punishment, but merely as a Depot for the accommodation of Female Pass holders awaiting service'.[11]

Seventy-two women from the *Australasia* finished up at the Brickfields. Nineteen were sent to the female hiring depot at Ross, seventy-three miles from Hobart, designed to serve the labour requirements of the midlands.

The women from the *Australasia* contributed their share of trouble to the Convict Department, and twenty-three of them behaved so badly they were not allowed to enter into service in the Hobart area. One of these was not allowed south of Oatlands, a town fifty-one miles from Hobart, and another succeeded in getting herself banned from both Hobart and the north-east district of Avoca. Several of the women were sex offenders, and as the Victorian era was puritanical in this area, they were harshly dealt with. One woman received eight months' hard labour for being caught in bed with a ticket-of-leave man in a common brothel. Another received two months' hard labour for having sexual intercourse by the side of the Risdon Road. Yet another received fourteen days in the cells for lying on the floor in an indecent manner with another woman. At least thirteen women from the *Australasia* were convicted of sex offences, for which the usual sentence was six months' hard labour.

Although few women from the *Australasia* offended on the *Anson*, twenty-four of them got into trouble at the Brickfields, and magistrate Jones did not spare them. A woman who was disobedient received ten days in the cells for her first offence and three months' hard labour for the second. Another who was drunk received three months' hard labour. One woman was charged for fighting in the yard and behaving in a disorderly manner in the dormitory and received four months on each count, to be served cumulatively. Misappropriation of clothing usually rated three or four months' hard labour. The terms of hard labour were served at the Cascades female factory, at the far end of Macquarie Street, in the south Hobart area. Here, women under punishment were employed carding, dyeing, spinning and weaving wool from government sheep farms into coarse cloth. For those who found the company rough, and Ellen was likely one such, the grand cautionary axiom of Van Diemen's Land soon became second nature to her: 'Believe every man a rogue until you have proved him to be honest'.[12]

The supply of female convict labour greatly exceeded the demand at mid century, and Ellen spent nearly twenty-one months at Brickfields before she was hired into service. In the meantime she ran foul of the penal system for the first and only time since she arrived at Clifden bridewell in 1848. On 22 April 1851 she received fourteen days hard labour for taking a hank of worsted out of her bundle in the store without leave.

The report of the comptroller-general on 30 June 1850 shows there were 556 female convicts at the depots in Hobart, Launceston and Ross awaiting hire. It is quite clear John Stephen Hampton, who became comptroller of convicts in 1846, following the death of Forster, had little regard for Irish convicts. He had supervised Irish female convicts aboard the *Mexborough* in 1841, and male Irish convicts aboard the *Constant* in 1843. In his report for 31 December 1850 he noted:

> The great increase in the number of female convicts recently transported from Ireland to this colony as shown in Return No. 15, causes considerable embarrassment, and difficulty in their management; since generally speaking their utter ignorance of every species of useful household labour unfits them for domestic service, and as a little more than half of all the female convicts who arrived here last year were from Ireland, there is reason to apprehend that they will be the means of accumulating a heavy burden on the government.[13]

Hampton also made changes to the hiring regulations for pass holders. Generally, he seems to have formalised and extended the old regulations. Nevertheless, there were some interesting innovations. He did away with the formal system of contract, and registers were kept instead. Convicts were allowed to be hired from police stations, and police officers were given similar powers, regarding convict pass holders, as visiting magistrates. Also, pass holders were not allowed to refuse an eligible service at a reasonable rate of wages. The returns for 4 January 1851 showed female pass holders received £7 16s. 0d. in Hobart, £8 18s. 1d. at Launceston, and £8 2s. 0d. at inland districts.[14]

On 19 January 1852 Ellen received her first engagement when she entered the service of Elizabeth Hogg, a blacksmith's wife who lived at 14 Kelly Street, Hobart. She only lasted sixteen days and was sent back to the Brickfields. On 30 March she entered the service of George Perriman, a yeoman who lived at 65 Argyle Street, but she was back at the Brickfields within a week, despite Hampton's regulation that pass holders could not be employed for less than a month. On 22 April Ellen entered the service of James H. Warren, a grocer of 44 Elizabeth Street. This seems to have been a more satisfactory placement, as she stayed there until she obtained her ticket-of-leave on 10 August.

At this time both transportation and the probation system were under heavy fire. As an on-the-spot observer of the probation system, the Rev. Robert Crooke, commented:

> The idea was philanthropic, but altogether Utopian and after having been tried for several years, at an enormous cost, was abandoned as being a total failure. It has been said, and with much truth, that this project was never given a fair chance, neither do I believe it was. Before the English government sent out several thousands of convicts, they ought to have made arrangements for the necessary buildings to accommodate these men, so as to ensure separation, cleanliness and decency. Proper officers accustomed to the control and management of prisoners should have been provided, and above all, it should have been ascertained whether these men could reasonably expect to obtain employment when their term of punishment should have expired. The author does not mean to assert that the project would under any circumstances have succeeded, but with the difficulties it had to contend with it was impossible that it could have done so.[15]

On 8 March 1853 Ellen Lydon was recommended for her conditional pardon, and it was approved eleven months later, on 7 February 1854. Meanwhile, on 17 January 1853 the *St Vincent* left Spithead with 212 male convicts. She reached Hobart on 26 May, and with her arrival the transportation era of Van Diemen's Land ended.

14

A Remarkable Coincidence

The voyages of the *Constant* in 1843 and the *Australasia* in 1849 were their last as convict transports. Both continued to trade between London and various ports in Australia, usually as carriers of wool and wheat.

John Hemery had purchased the *Constant* in 1843 but, short of finance, he mortgaged her to other members of his family on 1 July 1844 for £5,000. The members were Clement Hemery, Clement Hemery, Jnr, and Peter Hemery of St Helier, Jersey. On 14 June 1849, Charles Hemery of Liverpool, and Peter and Clement Hemery, Jnr, sold the *Constant* to Richard Coombes Soutter and Robert Harwood Soutter of Lower Shadwell, Middlesex. Thus the ownership of the *Constant* remained a family affair throughout her life.[1] On 5 December 1853 she sailed from London for Melbourne, with Frances Stewart as master. On 4 October 1854 she left London on what turned out to be her last voyage, with James Duncan Kerr as master.

The ownership of the *Australasia* was much more complex. She was purchased on construction by Adam Riddell of Marylebone, who held twenty-four of sixty-four shares, in company with Benjamin Draeger of Clerkenwell, Frederick Fleisch of America Square and Innes McPherson of Wick Caithness. At the time of her wreck nine years later, Fleisch had transferred his shares to the other partners, Adam Riddell had died, and the owners were William Riddell and Benjamin Draeger.[2] On 6 August 1854 the *Australasia* left London for Hobart, where she unloaded her cargo.

On 19 March 1855, both the *Constant* and the *Australasia* were wrecked at Portland in a violent gale. The *Portland Guardian* gave the following account on 22 March, under the headline 'Disaster in the Bay—Two ships Ashore':

We have to chronicle the occurrence of a disaster in this Bay last Monday night which has not its equal in the whole previous history of this port. There has very rarely been a call upon us to record even a solitary instance during a whole season of a ship at this port being driven ashore from her anchorage by the violence of the wind. Indeed vessels lying in numbers at this point have ridden out in perfect safety gales that have sent many a one ashore in Hobson's Bay. On Monday night last however, during a gale from the east ward of a violence unknown for many a year in this part, two large vessels went ashore. These were the Constant which had discharged her cargo and was about to set sail for another port in ballast, and the Australasia loading with wool for London. It had been blowing from the east ward all day Sunday. On Monday the breeze considerably freshened, and towards afternoon it increased to a violent gale, and continued so the whole of Monday night. There were altogether twelve vessels in the bay, several of them of considerable size, and a good number of lighters and small boats moored at different points. With the exception of the Cyprus which dragged, there was no other disaster to ship or boat but the going ashore of the two last named. The Constant, Captain Kerr, parted with both of her chains during the night, and about twelve o'clock was adrift. The Captain then finding he could not prevent her going ashore, had the jib set and beached her, bows on. In that position she appeared in the morning upright and steady, and warranting the expectation that she may be got off again. The Australasia, Captain Lindsay came ashore about two hours afterwards. She parted one of her chains and seems to have dragged with the other, for in the morning she appeared stern on to the beach; she had evidently lodged on a rocky bottom. By about eight o'clock, she had turned broadside on, and was rolling and bumping with great violence. At this time the beach was crowded with spectators, who were very active in lending what assistance they could. Boats were carried on men's shoulders to the scene of disaster. A line was fastened from the Constant to the beach and a boat by that means run out to the vessel, to those on board. At the first attempt the boat filled, and had to be drawn back to be bailed out. The Australasia however was most in need of assistance and several boats from other vessels were striving through a high and heavy surf to reach the vessel. The Athlete's boat got round by the stern to the lee side, and took off Mrs Lindsay the Captain's wife. Captain Lindsay accompanied her until the boat was safe through the surf and then returned in the Severn's boat to the ship; Mrs Lindsay being conducted on board the Severn. In the course of a couple of hours all hands were got off from the unfortunate Australasia which was already broken and shewed signs of soon going to pieces. The Chronometers and instruments were got safely out of the stranded vessel. A courageous feat was accomplished by Captain Anderson of the May Queen with a crew in one of the Athlete's boats. In letting Captain Lindsay's desk with his ship's papers down for the boat, it unfortunately dropped into the sea but floated. Captain Anderson ventured through the surf after it, at the imminent risk several times of the boat's being overturned, and succeeded in recovering it, and in bringing his boat safe to the beach. The Australasia had about twelve hundred bales of wool on board, the whole of which will be considerably damaged, if indeed it will be all recovered. Amongst the incidents connected with this catastrophe should be mentioned an accident to the Harbour Master's boat which was upset in the surf on the way to the Constant, and the crew precipitated into the water, some of whom narrowly escaped drowning. During the whole of this eventful night Captain Fawthrop the Harbour Master, was toiling in every possible way and at every risk to render what assistance or give what advice might be serviceable neither did he remit his exertions during the succeeding day, until all that could be done under the circumstances was tried and accomplished. The Australasia was chartered by Mr Must of this town, Mr Must's misfortune in this disaster will meet with the sympathy of all.

The *Australasia*'s last voyage had been a disaster from beginning to end. She sailed with the master and a crew of twenty-three. A young seaman had died in the Downs, soon after leaving London. Nine crew members, including the surgeon, had deserted in Hobart, leaving a skeleton crew to sail her to Portland. Another seaman, Charles Doyle, was drowned in Portland Bay two days before the wreck. Eleven deserted at Portland and the master, David Lindsay, returned to England as a passenger with the ship's boy.

The *Constant* was more fortunate at first. She sailed with a master and twenty-one crew, and did not lose any through death. Eleven deserted at Portland, and ten were paid off.[3] There is no record of how the master, James Duncan Kerr, returned to England. On 23 March the harbour master submitted his official report:

Report of the Harbour Master, Capt. James Fawthrop (23.3.1855)

I have the honour to inform you that the Barques 'Constant' and 'Australasia' have been driven on shore at this place, the circumstances attending the stranding are as follows:

On Monday the 19th inst. the wind was blowing a fresh gale from the S.E. not exceeding a force of 6, and towards sunset it freshened to be accompanied by a short heavy sea rolling into the Bay causing the shipping to ride heavily. The 'Constant' and the 'Australasia' had each parted a cable at dark, but speedily replaced the want by letting go their sheet anchors. The surf on the beach being so high that it was not practicable to board them between 9 and 11.00 p.m. Signals of distress were shown but from the darkness little could be seen from shore. At 11.40 p.m. the 'Constant' came on the beach about a quarter of a mile to the northward of the jetty and shortly afterwards the 'Australasia' about a cable's length to the northward.

From the information I have since received from the Commanders, who are both intelligent seamen, it appears that the 'Constant' parted her port chain twice with 45 fathoms ahead, and ultimately her starboard chain with 110 fathoms ahead.

The 'Australasia' parted her starboard cable with 65 fathoms and afterwards her port cable with 75 fathoms and at last, with the sheet anchor and the remaining cables bent together, slowly drifted to the breakers. She is now a complete wreck, the greater part of the cargo (1,300) bales of wool has been washed out of her and scattered along the beach for miles.

Her hull is lying across a ledge of rocks listed to seaward and broken on the midship.

The 'Constant' does not appear to have received much damage and having only ballast it is possible that by lightening she may be got off as she is upright and lies on pretty clear ground for bottom.

Both vessels were to have sailed in a few days, the remainder as per margin rode out the gale in safety.

The cause of this disaster may be traced to defective cables in both vessels as the gale was by no means heavy and both vessels were properly moored with open hawse to S.E. and as they were commanded by intelligent able seamen, it may be presumed that they did all that could be done under the circumstances and their testimony warrants this statement.

A survey has been held on the wreck of the 'Australasia' which will be sold for the benefit of those concerned; the 'Constant' will be surveyed tomorrow.

A week later, on 30 March, Captain Fawthrop wrote:

The survey has been held on the 'Constant' and the surveyors have, after a minute and very careful examination of the hull, recommended her to be sold for the benefit of all concerned. I have carefully examined the anchorage ground where they were moored and find that the bow anchors of both ships in the same position as when first moored, showing the tenacity of the holding ground and that the defective cables have been the principal cause of the disasters.

On 13 April, Fawthrop further noted:

The wreck of the 'Australasia' has completely broken up and the greater part come on the beach, about 500 bales of wool have been saved. The 'Constant' is now completely embedded in the sand and fast breaking up . . . The purchasers of the wreck have employed a party of workmen to break up the hull.

The other vessels anchored in Portland Bay that rode out the storm: 'Severn', 'May Queen', 'Eliza Cornish', 'Cape Horn', 'City of Sydney', 'Cyprus', 'Victory', 'Sarah', and 'Champion'.[4]

Three noteworthy features emerged from the accounts of the *Portland Guardian* and the harbour master's report.

First, the *Guardian* makes it clear that shipping disasters were rare in Portland Harbour. Second, the harbour master credited both Kerr and Lindsay with being 'intelligent seamen'. Third, on two occasions in his report, Fawthrop points to defective cables as the cause of the disaster. In all, it only seems to highlight what was a remarkable coincidence.

The tiny government brig *Isabella*, which took the first probation convicts to Salt Water River, had already met her doom. She was totally wrecked on King Island in July 1845.[5]

John Stephen Hampton, the former surgeon-superintendent of the *Constant*, also ran into serious trouble as comptroller-general of convicts in 1855. In July the Legislative Council set up a select committee to enquire into convict administration. Hampton was ordered to appear before the committee, but refused to do so on the ground that the penal establishment was under Imperial administration and the Legislative Council had no control over it. The speaker issued a warrant for his arrest, but the Crown law officers doubted the legality of the warrant and he was not apprehended. The new lieutenant-governor, Sir Henry Young, came to Hampton's rescue when he prorogued the Council on 20 October. Hampton seized his opportunity and left the colony, never to return to the land 'where his name had become infamous', according to James Fenton, 'by the revelations of witnesses examined during the course of the Council's enquiry into the working of the convict department'.[6]

However, 1855 was not exclusively a year of disaster, and something wonderful also happened. For many years, the name Van Diemen's Land had been associated with penal brutality and man's inhumanity to man, but on 26 November, two years later transportation ended, the more euphonious name of Tasmania was legalised by statute.[7]

15

A Living Faith

In the mid-nineteenth century, great importance was placed in formal religious observance. Rationalism was not to undermine the teaching of the Bible until nearer the century's end, and well-placed people who openly professed to be atheists or agnostics were few and far between. Lord Stanley, the architect of the probation system, felt a convict could only be restored to society by a change in moral character and that this could only be brought about by the influence of the religious instructor or catechist. Every probation station had its catechist, and every main centre had its minister. Against this strong evangelical drive was arraigned the cynicism of the convicts. In Van Diemen's Land up until 1840, most of the convicts were English, and many of them were anything but religious. As one probationer recorded: 'You old hypocrite! There's no God in Van Diemen's Land, nor shall there be!'[1]

For some reason no Irish convicts were sent to Van Diemen's Land before late 1840, although New South Wales had received 20,480 Irish convicts out of a total of 67,980.[2] Between 1788 and 1868 an estimated 30,000 men and 9,000 women were transported from Ireland, out of a total of 162,000 which included 25,000 women.[3] From 1841 onwards the position altered dramatically, and Van Diemen's Land received forty-nine Irish transports between that year and 1853. In all, 3,568 Irish women were sent to Van Diemen's Land.[4] The writer's computations, based on Bateson's appendixes, show that twenty-seven male transports arrived in Van Diemen's Land, carrying 6,008 convicts.

As at 15 April 1848, Hampton reported that there were 1,618 Catholic male convicts, out of a total of 6,487, in the probation stations in Van Diemen's Land. There were also 449 Catholic female convicts out of a total of 1,073. In the same report, Hampton stated the ratio of Protestants to Catholics to be 2.6 to 1, and he estimated that ten Catholic clergymen would be needed to give a ratio of one Catholic clergyman to every 122 convicts.[5]

This large influx of Irish caused serious concern to the administration. Matters

came to a head over the 298 convicts from the *Pestonjee Bomanjee* who were landed
in Hobart on 2 January 1849, all holding the status of ticket-of-leave men. Not
surprisingly, they were soon in trouble, and Governor Denison noted:

> These men have been, by their own confession, placed in a position as regards the means
> of acquiring the necessaries, the comforts, and . . . the luxuries of life, much better than
> they ever could have hoped to attain in their own country. Their natural indolence
> has been enhanced by the very facility of procuring a livelihood, and they have been
> led in many instances to resort to crime, instead of to steady industry for their maintenance.[6]

Later in the year Denison again complained about the Irish convicts, begging
for smaller numbers to be sent:

> As regards Irish Convicts, as there are no means in Ireland of placing them under separate
> treatment, the sooner they are removed after sentence the better both for themselves
> and us; but I would also beg to press upon your Lordship the unadvisability of sending
> more than a fixed, and that a small, proportion of Irish immigrants to this colony. Their
> general want of industry, their insubordinate habits, their subservience to their religious
> instructors, render them peculiarly unfitted for settlers in a country like this.[7]

As thirteen Irish transports arrived in Van Diemen's Land after 1849, it seems
Denison's pleas were ignored.

The great majority of the Irish convicts were Catholics, many of them devout,
and it is only natural the Catholic church has a special role to play in the history
of the convict system. In 1820 two priests, Fr John Therry and Fr Phillip Conolly,
sailed for Sydney on the *Janus*, which was also carrying 105 female convicts from
Cork. Conolly, who was born in Monaghan and trained at Maynooth, went to
Hobart Town in 1821. For fourteen years he covered the state on horseback, fulfilling
the demands of his scattered flock. A man 'of no small ability and attainments,
witty and full of dry humour', Conolly's industry even impressed Governor Arthur,
who unsuccessfully sought a higher salary for him in 1826. Conolly, who was granted
five acres of land where St Mary's Cathedral now stands, clashed strongly with
Bishop Polding of Sydney in 1835. The following year Polding had the sad task
of suspending Conolly from his priestly functions, in front of his flock. Conolly
began an action against Polding for defamation, but decided to drop it. He became
ill in 1839 and died on 3 August. Fortunately, he was reconciled to the church
before his death.[8]

Fr John Therry of Cork, who was educated at St Patrick's College, Carlow, came
to Van Diemen's Land as vicar-general in April 1838, after performing Herculean
and inspired missionary work in New South Wales for almost eighteen years. Although
he was grossly overtaxed in those years, and his administrative and financial affairs
became chaotic, Therry demonstrated a remarkable spirit of enlightenment. His
influence amongst the convicts was remarkable and he was their banker, adviser
and arbitrator as well their spiritual director. His correspondence shows the unusual
trust they placed in him. As well, he befriended the Aborigines, who became very
attached to him, and he advocated the cause of their education to the governor.
He also gained impressive status amongst the Protestant community.

Upon reaching Hobart, Therry attempted to make up the ground lost after Conolly's suspension and subsequent disaffection from his flock. On the convict side of things, he was outstanding. Often in the course of his spiritual duties, he had to comfort men in the condemned cell, and in some cases he was known to spend the whole night with condemned prisoners as they faced their execution. Unfortunately, he overreached himself financially in Hobart, as he struggled to complete St Joseph's church in Macquarie Street and another church on the present site of St Mary's Cathedral. In addition, he faced the problems of loneliness, illness and impetuosity.[9]

On 11 May 1844, Bishop Robert Willson arrived in Hobart, accompanied by Fr William Hall, who was to be the vicar-general, and three other missionary priests. There were only two priests in Van Diemen's Land at the time—Therry, based in Hobart, and Fr Thomas Butler who had charge of the Launceston parish. Willson's appointment as Hobart's first Catholic bishop came as a shock to himself and as both a shock and a disappointment to Therry, who was convinced that the post was to be his.[10] Willson and Hall were dismayed at the huge debt incurred by Therry, and the long and bitter dispute over church property that followed proved so intractable that no independent arbitrator could solve it. Even Rome failed. The quarrel lasted for fourteen years and seriously damaged Willson's early episcopate. Therry left Hobart in 1846, to serve as a parish priest in Melbourne, but he returned to Hobart in 1848 and stayed for six years. He returned to New South Wales in 1854 and spent the remainder of his life at Balmain. He died on 25 May 1864 and had the largest funeral seen in Sydney to that date.

Robert William Willson was an Englishman, born in Lincoln in 1794, the third son of a leading builder. After completing his secondary education he was placed, at his own wish, on a farm in Nottinghamshire where he gained insights into rural industry and the management of men. In 1816 he studied for the priesthood and, on his ordination in December 1824, he was stationed as a pastor at Nottingham, where he showed great energy during the eighteen years of his tenure. He built two new churches, one of which—St Barnabas—was to become the city cathedral. He did a lot of good work among prisoners and was particularly distinguished by his work among the insane. A leading figure in the reorganisation and reconstruction of the county lunatic asylum, he even got a licence to take some patients into his own home. This nearly led to a disaster when a man suffering from a mental disease sprang up and tried to plunge a knife into Willson's heart. The knife was only deflected by a prayer book. Quickly recovering his composure, Willson asked the man the reason for his action, then invited him to sit down for dinner. Willson also distinguished himself during the cholera plague of 1832 and shortly afterwards he was presented with the freedom of Nottingham.[11]

Dr William Ullathorne, the vicar-general of Australia, heard about the energetic and competent Willson and in 1842, when Hobart Town was created a diocese separate from New South Wales, he wanted Willson as bishop. Ullathorne was one of the distinguished English Benedictines who guided the destiny of the early Catholic church in Australia. Despite the opposition of Cardinal Wiseman, who wanted Willson to stay in England, Pope Gregory XVI decided in favour of Hobart. Willson was consecrated bishop, by Wiseman, at Birmingham on 28 October 1842 and he arrived in Hobart nineteen months later. If his problem with Therry hindered him in the administration of his fledgling diocese, it did not impede his work amongst the convicts. In his enlightened approach to the mentally ill, Willson resembles Mrs Philippa Bowden, who had arrived in Hobart in December 1843.

Bishop Willson prepared a summary of his pastoral duties in the colony:

> To visit ships on their arrival, address all convicts who were of my own religion—warn them of what they should avoid, —and encourage them to follow that course which experience had convinced me would prove beneficial to them; on landing again visit them in their different locations, as often as was feasible; —encourage them, remonstrate with them, hear their grievances, oftentimes too well founded, —sometimes not—and reprove sternly, when necessity required, the obstinate and hardened. These visits gave me an insight into the working of the system all over the colony, and afforded excellent opportunities for comparing the success on one station with another, and also of ascertaining what changes it would be judicious for the Government to make. I also considered it to be necessary to pay great attention to those unhappy men who fell into great crimes, and who were condemned to forfeit life for their offences. By carrying out this plan I had ample means of becoming acquainted with what was taking place, from the time a ship arrived in harbour with its freight of criminals, to the time they became free, or expiated an offence on the fatal scaffold.[12]

Every Sunday afternoon, Willson paid a visit to one of the probation stations in the Hobart neighbourhood. The convicts were always glad to see him, for they trusted him, and they listened to what he had to say.

Norfolk Island was Bishop Willson's greatest concern. In May 1846 he visited the settlement and was appalled at the conditions he found there. The major commanding the troops entreated the bishop to go home to let the British government know the truth, and Willson complied. He immediately sailed for England, where the evidence he gave before a committee of the House of Lords was printed in the *Blue Book*, 21 June 1847. It made a deep impression on the minds of the British public, who became aware for the first time of the barbarity practised on Norfolk Island and the inhuman tortures not thought to exist within the British penal system. Willson made further visits to Norfolk Island in 1849, and felt a great improvement had taken place. However, his suggestions for further reform were ignored by the officials, and Norfolk Island soon sank to the lowest depths of its shocking history. In March 1852 Willson again visited the island and afterwards laid out the facts of his investigation in a forty-eight-page letter to the British government. Lieutenant-General Denison joined forces with the bishop and Norfolk Island was closed as a penal settlement in 1855.

As in England, Willson also had tremendous influence upon the treatment of the mentally ill. In 1855 he joined the board of management at the New Norfolk insane asylum. He continued to work vigorously for a modern hospital, in cheerful surroundings, staffed by trained people. The Victorian and New South Wales governments also sought his advice concerning the treatment of the mentally ill.[13]

On 6 January 1837 Governor Arthur was succeeded by the Arctic explorer Sir John Franklin. Unfortunately, Franklin was a weak administrator who lacked the experience to cope with the powerful factions around him. His main problem was the Arthur faction, which was led by the colonial secretary, Captain John Montagu, and the comptroller of convicts, Captain Forster, both of whom were nephews of the recently departed governor. Montagu competed fiercely for power with Lady Franklin, and Sir John Franklin dismissed him in 1842, only to have Lord Stanley both reinstate Montagu and censure Franklin, who was abruptly replaced by Sir John Eardley-Wilmot on 21 August 1843.[14] Although the small Catholic community led by Fr Therry had a high regard for Franklin, they did not miss his wife, 'who could never disguise her fierce bigotry and her intense hatred of everything Catholic, influenced her distinguished husband to disregard his better feelings'.[15]

Sir John Eardley-Wilmot arrived at a most difficult time. While the free population was agitating fiercely to control its own affairs by 1843, thousands of convicts were still flowing into the colony from all parts of the Empire. Furthermore, the penal structure was not properly prepared for the newly introduced probation system. There was inadequate work for pass holders, and the colony was deeply in debt, mainly because of the huge expenditure on gaols and prisons. Eardley-Wilmot misrepresented the facts in his reports to the Colonial Office, not only by failing to report the shortcomings of the probation system, but by insisting that all was well.[16] He was suddenly dismissed in October 1846 and died in Hobart on 3 February 1847. His successor, Sir William Denison, arrived in Hobart on 25 January 1847.

Denison had had much experience with public works in England, and his main aim was to make the probation system work. To this end he worked for more effective control of convicts, and the efficient deployment of their labour. He had serious problems with the Legislative Council, which he adjourned pending instructions from Downing Street. He also quarrelled with the Supreme Court after it declared the Differential Duties Act illegal and declared that the 'Dog Act', which opened up the question of the power of a nominee council to raise direct taxes, 'was not binding and must be set aside'. Denison tried to have the judges dismissed over these issues, but was unsuccessful. Denison's term of governor from January 1847 until January 1855 also saw two changes which he disapproved. The first was the establishment New Legislative Council, which consisted of twenty-four members, four of whom were nominees of the governor, four high ranking officials, and sixteen elected. The new council, which came into being on 30 December 1851, greatly limited the governor's power.[17] The second was the ending of transportation in May 1853, despite the protestations of Denison, who had been one of its strongest supporters. Denison was not popular, and John West has supplied the following assessment of him:

> The opposition of Sir William Denison to the colonial wishes . . . his injustice to the judges, and his sarcastic delineations of colonial character, have narrowed the circle of his friends. In future times an opinion more favourable to his reputation may be expected to prevail. It will then be remembered that he promoted the advancement of science, increased the facilities of commerce, abated the practical evils of the convict department,

advocated the principles of legislative freedom, and, by a respectable private character, sustained the moral dignity of government. But even then it will not be forgotten, that in perpetuating the convict curse, he adopted any argument, however false, and tolerated any ally, however abject.[18]

With Sir Henry Young's term as governor, commencing in January 1855, came the dawn of a new era of responsible government. His term saw the continuing development of parliament, culminating with Van Diemen's Land's first ministry in October 1855. The following month the colony's name was changed to Tasmania. Young's seven-year term was only marred by the Hampton affair, soon after his arrival, and both the governor and his wife became extremely popular in Tasmania.

In dealing with authoritarian governors, and the evolving parliamentary system, the Catholic church had a big advantage. Both Bishop Willson and his vicar-general, Fr Hall, were English, on top of which Willson was a man of outstanding ability. Whenever he conferred with Denison on any issue, the governor was forced to remember he was dealing with a man of exceptional insight and humanity whose pragmatism matched his own.

William Hall was a Londoner who began his studies for the priesthood in Paris, only to be forced to leave during the 1830 revolution. He completed his studies in Britain and then spent twelve years on pastoral duties at Moorfields and Islington. When Dr Willson came to London appealing for missionaries, Hall offered his services and, while Willson concentrated on the spiritual and humanitarian side of his episcopate, Hall was responsible for diocesan administration. Hall virtually drove himself to death working for the completion of St Mary's Cathedral in Harrington Street, but he did not neglect his pastoral duties. He regularly attended the gaols and hospitals of Hobart and comforted more than fifty criminals on the scaffold. He also formed an active group of young laymen and gave spiritual guidance to numerous clubs, sodalites and religious associations. He was by nature reserved, stern and unyielding, 'with a mortified countenance'.[19] He died on 17 July 1866.

No chapter on the early Catholic church in Tasmania can be complete without mention of the Sisters of Charity. On 20 June 1847 Sisters M. John Cahill, M. de Sales O'Brien and M. Xavier Williams arrived in Hobart from Sydney. They took up residence in what was originally Fr Therry's presbytery, from then on to be known as St Joseph's Convent, and on 23 August opened St Joseph's school for girls. For the first ten years they were in Hobart, much of their time was spent visiting the numerous penitentiaries, hospitals and nurseries around Hobart. Their primary aim was to impart religious and moral instruction to Catholics. Two hours daily were spent at the female factory, where there were often up to 240 Catholic women. They also visited the government orphanage at New Town.[20] In a letter to their superior, Mother Mary Aikenhead in Ireland, Bishop Willson summed up their work:

Sensible, prudent, humble, fervent and cheerful, their holy lives are a continued lesson of edification; and my only regret is that I have not more to aid them. Not less than 500 prisoners in Hobart Town derive benefit from their visits and instructions. Fully

100 female orphans are also visited by them. Then they have their own school with an average of about 80 daily; and besides the common gaol where the poor men are executed, also the hospital, and infirmary for aged females to visit. What a harvest! My only regret is that I have it not in my power to do all for my dear Sisters that I could wish.[21]

Mother M. John Cahill was described as a woman of 'burning zeal' who achieved remarkable results. After her death in 1864 she was succeeded as leader by Mother M. de Sales O'Brien of Cork, a cultured woman who received much of her early education in Bordeaux. She died in Hobart in 1871. The last of the trio, Mother M. Xavier Williams was born in Kilkenny in 1800, the daughter of a captain of the Light Dragoons who was killed at the Battle of Salamanca in the Peninsula War. She died in 1892, shortly after the Hobart sisters were amalgamated with the mother house in Sydney. The return to central authority was quite in accord with her wishes.[22]

The influence of these nuns on the Irish female convicts can only be described as incalculable. Without inspired missionaries such as Willson, Hall, Therry and the Daughters of Charity, the lot of the Catholic convicts in Van Diemen's Land might have proved unbearable.

16

The Founding of a Family

It is not known how Stephen Howard and Ellen Lydon met, but the Catholic Church almost certainly had some system of introducing eligible bachelor convicts to suitable female counterparts. No records exist to confirm this supposition, but in Bishop Willson the church had a man with enlightened social insight who would not have been lacking in this area and who was well supported by able missionaries.

Under John Hampton's administration, the regulations for ticket-of-leave Holders were relaxed. They no longer had to report for the monthly muster, nor were they obliged to attend Divine Service every Sunday. However, they were still required to register their residence; they could not move from one district to another without a pass from a police magistrate; and they remained subject to a strict curfew from 10 p.m. until daybreak. They were required to report to the nearest police station in person every June and December and they were not allowed on the premises of any billiard room or theatre. If they were destitute, they were maintained at government expense at the hiring depots until they found employment. Finally, they were permitted both to acquire and hold personal property and to take legal action on their own behalf concerning property, damage sustained by them, or other civil matters over which magistrates had jurisdiction.[1]

As a policeman, Stephen Howard would not have been worried by these regulations, but he seems to have left the force when he received his conditional pardon on 30 July 1850. At about the same time, Ellen Lydon appears to have found employment with James Warren congenial, and it seems likely she stayed there until their marriage.

On 16 October 1854 Stephen Howard and Ellen Lydon were married at St Joseph's Church in Macquarie Street, Hobart. They may well have longed for the ministrations of a warm and sensitive priest like Bernard Kirby, but he was 13,000 miles away and their union was solemnised by none other than the ascetic William Hall. Their joy as they humbly looked up at his 'mortified countenance' and heard him pronounce them man and wife could well have been tinged with sadness. Perhaps they even longed for the homespun friendly features of Bishop Willson. Nevertheless, they were in the presence of a man whose integrity and commitment to his pastoral duties could not be faulted. Perhaps displaying the intuition Irish peasants have in discerning a good pastor, they counted themselves fortunate.

The witnesses were John Ryan and Mary Tobin. No fewer than nine John Ryans were transported to Hobart as convicts but three of them, including the one who came out on the *Constant*, had died before the marriage took place. It is virtually impossible to say which of the remaining six John Ryans was in attendance. Mary Tobin had arrived from Kingston on the *Earl Grey* in 1849, transported for a trivial offence, and she almost certainly met Ellen at the Brickfields hiring depot. On the marriage certificate Stephen's age was shown as thirty, although he was actually thirty-eight. Ellen's age was shown as twenty-eight, which tallies with other records. Much emphasis was given in the annual prison reports to the education of prisoners, both in Ireland and Van Diemen's Land, but the marriage certificate shows that Stephen, Ellen and Mary Tobin could not write their names. The fact that only John Ryan could sign the document tends to show that the educational programs for convicts were of little avail. Stephen is described as a labourer on the certificate and Ellen as a servant.

On 6 June 1855 their first child, Bridget Catherine, was born at Adelaide Street, South Hobart. The birth certificate shows that Stephen's occupation had changed, as he was now a farmer. He had taken up a ninety-two-acre block of land at Honeywood, Geeveston, shortly after his marriage. Geeveston is a town thirty-six miles from Hobart whose main industries are orcharding, fishing and timber-getting. Seven more children were born to Stephen and Ellen, at regular two-yearly intervals: Mary, (10 May 1857), James Michael (21 December 1858), Margaret (31 August 1861), Sarah (21 July 1863), Stephen (10 July 1865), Ellen (12 September 1867) and John (30 May 1869). The children were all baptised in the Catholic church at Geeveston by Fr John Murphy. One of Ellen's friends from her convict days, Ellen White, was Mary's godmother. The first-born child, Bridget, had been baptised in Hobart by Fr Charles Woods, the former chaplain aboard the *Blenheim* in 1851. Perhaps strangely, neither of her godparents had been convicts.

All the children grew to maturity, although Stephen was an asthmatic who died aged twenty-six without marrying. In 1876, when Bridget was twenty-one, she married Richard Reid, a widower who was a general dealer, in the Congregational Church in Hobart. After her marriage, Bridget and her husband moved back to the Honeywood area and it was there, on 20 January 1878, that a violent domestic quarrel took place which led to Stephen Howard being arraigned on a much more serious charge than the one for which he had been transported.

A full account of the quarrel and subsequent trial was printed in the *Hobart Mercury*:

> Stephen Howard was charged with, that he did, on the 20 January, 1878, with force of arm have in his possession in both hands a loaded gun, and attempt to discharge the same at one Richard Reid with the intention of feloniously, wilfully, and maliciously killing him.

The prisoner, who pleaded not guilty, was defended by Mr Crisp.

The following jury were sworn: Robert Mackay, Job Hayle, Henry Fenton, Edward Giles Ford, James Foster, Morris Jeffrey, Alfred Holman, John Peasgood, Thos Backhouse, Chas Gaylor (foreman), Richard Maddock, Edward Payne.

The Solicitor General opened the case, and called

Richard Reid, who deposed that he lived at Honeywood, and was married to a daughter of the prisoner, who was a farmer. Had been married two years on Sunday, the 20th January; in the evening a quarrel had taken place with reference to a visit from Sarah Howard, whom he had ordered away. He was sitting down to supper with his wife some minutes afterwards, when the father came to the door. The wife answered him, and asked him his business. As he refused to say, she would not let him in. The prisoner then burst in the door and presented a gun at witness, calling him violent names. Prisoner snapped the gun, but it did not go off. Witness did not believe it was capped. He bobbed down behind his wife, and when he got up prisoner struck him over the head with the gun, and knocked him down, wounding his face.

His Honour asked whether there was any evidence of the gun being capped; as otherwise the pulling of the trigger could not be construed into an attempt to take life, but merely an attempt to frighten.

The witness Reid stated that he did not think the prisoner had any intention to take his life.

There being no evidence as to this fact, the Solicitor General, in accordance with the direction of the Judge, entered a nolle prosequi.

The prisoner was subsequently arraigned upon the lesser charge, and pleaded not guilty. This charge was under the 18th section of the Act which refers to the infliction of bodily injury, with or without weapon, and the presenting of firearms, either of which offence is by the Act accounted as misdemeanour.

The following jury were sworn: —Morris Jeffrey, Job Hayle, Thos Riley, Richard Maddock, Michael O'Loughlin, Thos Backhouse, John Peasgood, Charles Harper, James Pearsall, Charles Gaylor (foreman), E. G. Ford, Henry Fenton.

The Solicitor General again opened the case upon the new charge,

Richard Reid repeated his evidence, and added: The gun was pointed midway at him, and the defendant struck him, whether on the ground, or while he was falling, he could not say. The blow knocked one of his teeth out, and the prisoner went outside and broke the window of the bedroom into which witness had been taken. Witness took hold of a stick in self-defence, and prisoner again came in. Witness struck him with the stick on the face, and prisoner's wife, who had arrived, struck witness on the head with the tongs, stunning him. While he was lying down, the prisoner and his wife continued to ill-treat him. Witness had given no other provocation than the one mentioned.

To Mr Crisp: Sarah Howard threatened to go tell her father that witness was murdering his wife. The girl had an illfeeling towards him. Witness had had some beer, but knew what he was doing. Was very short-tempered in the ordinary way. Had had no row with his wife on that evening. When first complaining to the police, witness had only asked for protection.

To His Honour: Was not quarrelling with his wife when the defendant came in: she was feeding the baby.

Bridget Reid, corroborated the evidence in chief of her husband, adding that she stopped the bleeding of the wounds which had been inflicted on him.

To Mr Crisp: The only disagreement that night was about the sister. There was no row between her and her husband.

Sarah Howard, daughter of the defendant, deposed to being at Reid's house. She made a statement to her father who went up to Reid's with the mother as Reid was fighting with his wife. When they got there, her father opened the door, shoving it in. Reid's wife caught hold of her father and Reid beat him. Her father had done nothing previous to this. Reid then hit witness. Her father was then going home when Reid hit him again, with another little sister, who had also come down, and was also struck. Reid also hit her brother with a bottle. The father was doing nothing all this time. Reid struck him again, and her father hit him back again with the gun in the face. Would swear her mother did not take the tongs with her.

Constable Badcock deposed to being summoned by Sarah Howard to Reid's house. He dressed and went with them. Met Reid, his wife, and two other men. Reid ran across the road to beat a little girl who was with witness and wanted to fight witness. Reid's face was bleeding. Reid laid an information on the Monday, and witness visited him the same evening and arrested the prisoner who made no remark, and gave up the gun, warning him that it was loaded.

To Mr Crisp: Reid is a madman when he has had a glass or two of beer. His face was covered with blood. He said Howard had done it.

Mr Crisp addressed the jury for the defence.

His Honour, in summing up, referred, to the two charges, the mere presentation of a loaded weapon being enough grounds for a conviction upon the first; and any unjustifiable blow being sufficient proof of the assault. His Honour referred at some length to the evidence, pointing out that one account of the affair must be untrue, as the one was diametrically opposed to the other. The jury must decide as to which was the true account, and act upon it in their verdict; if they thought neither was reliable, they would know their duty in such a case also.

The jury retired, and after an absence of ten minutes from the court, returned a verdict of not guilty.

The prisoner was thereupon released from custody.[2]

It seems from the newspaper account that the Reids had been having a domestic quarrel, probably caused by Richard Reid being a nasty drunk. Sarah had apparently reported the quarrel to her parents, who intervened. Even though they were well on in years, it is obvious that Stephen and Ellen were nasty customers in a fight and likely that their experience as convicts served them very well in such circumstances. Even though Stephen was sixty-two years old, had received a conditional pardon twenty-seven years earlier, and was found not guilty, the incident was noted on his convict record.

Bridget's marriage to Reid apparently did not last, as she appeared on the marriage certificate of one of her daughters as Bridget Catherine McKenna. Strong family groups of her descendants live all over Australia, particularly in Western Australia, South Australia and Queensland.

After taking up his block of land at Honeywood, Stephen built a crude but strong homestead, with walls of vertical timber slabs and a shingle roof. This building stood for over a hundred years. He also acquired another block of fifty-one and a half acres on the banks of the Kermandie River. This was mostly poor land with dwarf tea-tree scrub and only a small portion of the block next to the river was suitable for cultivation. The access road into his main property is still known as Howard's Road. His new status was being formalised, as he is shown in *McPhail's National Directory for Tasmania*, in 1867–68, as a farmer. He is also shown as a farmer at Honeywood in the directories for 1881–82 and 1887. Clearly the convict stain was fast disappearing.

In the meantime Stephen and Ellen's family was growing up. Bridget, Mary and Margaret had married and moved away from the family home, while the eldest son, James, is described in *McPhail's Directory* for 1881–82 as a farmer with his father. The *Post Office Directory* for 1890–91 lists James as the sole farmer at Honeywood. As they grew older, Stephen and Ellen began to suffer from loneliness and felt oppressed by the strange incongruity of their position. However comfortable they had become in their new surroundings, the fact was they were unwilling immigrants, torn forever from their families and their loved ones. Furthermore, their alienated position was made all the more distressing by their illiteracy and by their great distance from their native land. The youngest children, Ellen and John, sometimes saw their father crying to himself. One day they asked him why he was so unhappy, and he told them he was 'lonely for the green banks of Ireland'.

On 29 August 1843, the same day the *Constant* arrived at Hobart, the bushranger Martin Cash was caught. He had given the police a wild chase around the streets of Hobart and had shot and killed a policeman. On 15 September, six days after Stephen had been taken to Salt Water River on the *Isabella*, Cash was sentenced to death. The sentence was later commuted to transportation for life, the early part of which was to be spent on Norfolk Island. After finishing his gang probation, Stephen had worked as a pass holder in the Dromedary, Hollow Tree and Richmond area. This was Cash country, and the bushranger's main hideout had been on Mount Dromedary. Stephen had doubtless heard many tales of the Cash gang, and Ellen had a fear of bushrangers that was so great she hid her valuables away so they could not be found in a sudden raid. As she passed into old age and her memory began to fail her, she could not remember where she had hidden her jewellery, so it was lost forever.

On 7 August 1897, Stephen Howard died at Honeywood aged eighty, and his death was reported to the local shire council four days later. Ellen outlived her husband by eleven years and died in the New Norfolk Hospital on 17 September 1908. She was probably living with her daughter Margaret, who had migrated up there from the Huon Valley. So ended the long, strange journey through life of this Irish peasant couple.

Many years before the death of Stephen Howard, the west coast of Tasmania was transformed into one of the great mining areas of Australia. The region had proved daunting to the early settlers, and because of its high rainfall—over 100 inches per year in many parts—and dense, impenetrable forests, it was of no agricultural value. But on 8 December 1871 James 'Philosopher' Smith discovered a large lode of tin at Mount Bischoff. In fact Bischoff was nothing less than a mountain of tin, the largest lode then known to man.

A farmer, a teetotaller and a religious man who was also an expert prospector, Smith was the first to successfully penetrate the west coast. His find led to the foundation of Waratah and the floating of the Mount Bischoff Mining Company. At its height, Waratah had a population of 2,500 and in the fifty years that followed Smith's discovery, Mount Bischoff yielded tin to the value of £5,500,000.[3]

After Philosopher Smith's discovery, prospectors penetrated further south into the centre of the rugged western region. Some based themselves at the small town of Remine, at Trial Harbour, and prospected the Mount Heemskirk area, while others pushed south of the Pieman River and explored the Mount Zeehan region twenty miles south-east of Mount Heemskirk. In the 1880s several mines were working the Mount Heemskirk lodes, but generally it was a hollow boom, and few mines repaid the money invested in them. At Zeehan, however, the prospecting activity became frenzied. In December 1882 Frank Long discovered silver lead on the Zeehan field, on the bank of a small murky creek later known as Pea Soup Creek. Long was born at Perth, Tasmania, on 1 August 1842, the son of Robert and Anne (née Bailey), both of whom had been transported to Van Diemen's Land for minor offences in the early 1830s.

Frank Long's specimens assayed at 70 ounces of silver and 75 per cent lead to the ton, and samples from other lodes gave similar assays. A rush to the Zeehan field soon began, but the metal markets were depressed and risk capital was scarce, as many entrepreneurs had been hurt by earlier booms. But by the end of the decade the great mines of Broken Hill had triggered off a major silver boom, and soon Zeehan shares were favourites on the Melbourne stock exchange. Zeehan went through a fantastic boom period and even had its own stock exchange. By the end of 1891, 159 companies and syndicates had interests in Zeehan fields, but the district was hurt by the collapse of the share boom of 1891. The Bank of Van Diemen's Land, which was Zeehan's busiest business institution, collapsed in August 1891 and twenty-seven mines associated with it ceased work. Despite this, Zeehan recovered quickly. In 1894 Zeehan had its peak year, and its output in silver lead was valued at £300,000. For twenty years production from its mines averaged a further £200,000 annually. In *The West Coast Story*, Kerry Pink sums up the growth of Zeehan:

> The 1890s saw the emergence of a new Zeehan—a town built to last. A vigorous, robust, thriving young town with a population hovering around 8,000 in the early 1900s. Its two-mile long macadamised Main St was crammed on either side with shops, hotels, banks, mine offices, theatres, billiard parlours, churches, tailors, ironmongers, auctioneers, livery stables, blacksmiths. Its residential areas sprawled along the once thickly-forested flats; the imposing homes of the mine managers and the more modest dwellings of the wage workers.[4]

Zeehan's Gaiety Theatre brought stage shows direct from the Tivoli in Melbourne. These included *The Royal Divorce* and *Uncle Tom's Cabin* and possibly the most popular of all, the All Male Welsh Choir. Like any other Australian mining town of the nineteenth century, Zeehan had a large number of hotels to cater for the thirsty miners and itinerants. At its peak it is believed to have had eighteen hotels, amongst them the Grand, Cecil, Commercial, Royal Exchange, Central, Federal, Venezia, All Nations, Shelverton and Kerrigan's. The Cecil and the Central still stand. It had large railway marshalling yards which connected Zeehan with Burnie on the north-west coast and the port town of Strahan on the west coast.

However, like most mining towns, Zeehan's life was limited and by 1910 the ore bodies were starting to peter out. Production between 1915 and 1925 was only 21.5 per cent of what it had been prior to 1910. From 1893 to 1908 production from the fields was worth some £3,500,000.[5] But Zeehan declined rapidly after the 1920s. After the Second World War the opening of the Oceana and the Montana Western mines brought fresh hope, but they soon closed, and in the 1950s Zeehan's population dwindled to 650.

Zeehan and Mount Bischoff were not the west coast's only great mining discoveries of the nineteenth century. In 1883 Tom Currie and a red-haired Irish prospector, Cornelius Lynch, discovered gold on the King River, about fifteen miles south of Zeehan. This precipitated another rush by prospectors who believed there must be a large mother lode of gold ore. In November 1883 Steve Karlson and Bill and Mick McDonough found specks of gold on a large iron-ore outcrop on Mount Lyell. This turned out to be the famous Iron Blow, and the hub of the Mount Lyell copper field. Believing they had found a rich reef of alluvial gold, the three partners pegged their claim and took in another partner, William Dixon, to help them protect their discovery. A tough, brawny, cross-eyed Irishman, Dixon had previously worked as a human packhorse, carrying heavy loads on his back for fifteen miles at a penny a pound. Dixon was also an experienced miner, who had worked the New Zealand goldfields, and he soon absorbed the shares of Bill McDonough, and later those of Steve Karlson. Another Irishman, James Crotty, gained Mick McDonough's share by paying his store bills.

Crotty was a talented entrepreneur who had considerable insight into the practical side of mining, but the financial climate of the 1880s was against him and, heavily in debt, he obtained a wages job working in the sewers of Sydney.

The mining boom of the 1890s brought two wealthy mainland investors to the field, Bowes Kelly and William Orr. Kelly was a thirty-eight-year-old Irishman who had become one of the wealthiest men in Australia. He was a large man, weighing sixteen stone, with a ginger beard and a genial disposition. At first he got along well with Crotty, who had returned to Tasmania. In 1892 the Mount Lyell Mining Company NL was formed in Melbourne, and 100,000 £1 shares were issued. The Kelly group had 55,000 of these, and the Tasmanian group 45,000, of which Crotty's allocation was 3,000.

However, a bitter feud began between the Irishmen when Kelly squeezed down the price of the Iron Blow Mine from £18,500 to £5,000. Crotty was angered at his allocation of only 3,000 shares and began several unsuccessful law suits.

Meanwhile, Kelly had samples of Mount Lyell ore assayed by international experts, and their reports confirmed Mount Lyell as a great copper mine. Crotty held three separate ten-acre leases at North Lyell, and he floated the North Mount Lyell

Copper Company. His feud with Bowes Kelly was to be one of the most expensive in the history of Australian mining. In floating his company, Crotty revealed himself as an entrepreneur of great drive and talent. He also had the richest mine, with ore assaying at 24 per cent copper. But the North Lyell complex had just been completed when Crotty died suddenly, at a fashionable Piccadilly hotel, aged fifty-four. In 1903 the companies merged.

Bill McDonough received a pension from the Mount Lyell Company and when he died, aged fifty-three, the company paid for his funeral. Mick McDonough received a government pension and the Mount Lyell company bought him a small farm. He died aged fifty-eight. When Steve Karlson died of cancer in 1904, he was impoverished and was sluicing tin at Renison Bell.

By contrast, Dixon, the former human packhorse, bought a mansion in the Melbourne suburb of Hawthorn and lived to be ninety. Crotty's widow, who had once been a barmaid, was able to live out the rest of her life in luxury and provided generously for the Catholic church in her will. Bowes Kelly died in Melbourne in 1930, aged seventy-seven, having built Mount Lyell into one of the world's great copper mines. At the time of writing, the Mount Lyell mine is preparing to close, and almost certainly will never be reopened. Nevertheless, up till 1981 the mine produced 1,576,291 tonnes of copper, 716 tonnes of silver and 36.2 tonnes of gold. The value of the copper alone would be worth more than $3,000 million.[6]

The Howard family did not escape the impact of the great mining boom on the west coast, and four of Stephen and Ellen's children became involved in the rush. Jim and Jack Howard went there in the 1890s and set themselves up as contractors, cutting wood for the steam boilers which drove the mining machinery. Physically opposites, James was a small man with a sallow complexion and black hair, while Jack was a large, powerful man bordering on six feet tall and with a fair complexion. The brothers were soon to become well known and appreciated for their wood-cutting feats as contractors.

Communications had improved dramatically in the 1890s. The Zeehan–Strahan Railway opened in 1892, and 21 December 1900 saw the opening of the Emu Bay Railway, connecting Zeehan to Burnie. The Zeehan historian H. G. Hodge summed up Zeehan as it was in 1900:

> It was a land of hope and glory, a new exciting city, which with its freshly discovered mineral wealth had become an El Dorado of the West.
>
> Hundreds of miners mixed freely with bushmen, business men, singers, musicians, gamblers, boxers, stockbrokers and people of many classifications including some odd characters the type who usually become interesting components of the populace of most mining towns.[7]

Mary, who was already married, came to Zeehan with her husband and Ellen, the second youngest, later came and stayed with her. On 17 January 1900 Ellen was married at St Fursaeus church, Zeehan, and her brother Jack was one of the witnesses. She lived at Zeehan for the rest of her life and, although she only had one child, later generations proved to be more fertile and she now has many descendants in the Hobart area. On 29 October 1900 John Luke Howard, the youngest child of Stephen and Ellen, married Annie Foley at St Fursaeus church. They had three children: John Foley (4 December 1904), Ronald James (30 August 1906), and Eileen Patricia (24 March 1910).

James returned to Honeywood, probably to take over the property on the death of his father, and Mary apparently left quite early also. Jack chose to remain in Zeehan and expanded his contracting business into logging. Soon he had forty men, and a lot of plant, working in the forests on the side of Mount Dundas. His wife, who was a shrewd businesswoman in her own right, was no handicap in this area. The couple endeavoured to give their children a reasonable education, and Ronald James, the father of the writer, attended St Virgil's College, Hobart, as boarder in the early 1920s. Although he was only at St Virgil's for two years, he managed to obtain his intermediate certificate before family pressures brought him home to take part in his parents' business. After working in Zeehan for a couple of years, Ronald Howard quarrelled with his father and migrated to Adelaide, where he worked in the sawmilling industry. Finding the Adelaide climate unsuitable, he moved to Melbourne, where he once more found employment in the sawmills, gaining valuable experience as a millhand and in the office. It was the only time he was to work for wages, as his father suffered a stroke and Ronald was obliged to return to Zeehan. In 1928 Jack Howard suffered a fatal stroke in Melbourne and from then on Ronald James, or Jim as he preferred to be known, had full charge of the family business.

Aged only twenty-two, Jim faced the most difficult period of his life. The Great Depression of 1929 struck the town a devastating blow and mines closed down everywhere. Zeehan's work force was reduced to those working in shops, on the railways or for the government. Jim was one of Zeehan's largest employers at the time, with contracts to cut timber for the Mount Lyell Mines. For two years he battled it out on the wet slopes of Mount Dundas, often working up to his waist in mud. His work force, which consisted of a competent group of timber-getters, horse drivers and axemen, did not accept the young boss easily. They questioned his maturity, experience and competence in the coarsest possible terms, although in later years the same men were to show him a loyalty that was touching. Gradually, the Depression lifted and Jim expanded into the sawmilling business, first opening a sawmill on Mount Dundas, and later another at Roseberry. Dundas was about six miles from Zeehan, and Jim kept in touch with his expanding business by means of his faithful horse Tommy, which he later replaced with an Indian motorcycle. He purchased his first car, a Ford coupe, in 1935.

During the Second World War Jim enlisted for service, but he was told to stay put as he was in an essential industry. His sawmilling interests expanded to Strahan, producing Huon pine from two mills, and in the early 1940s he opened a large mill at Zeehan which cut a wide variety of timber, including hardwood, King William pine, myrtle sassafras, blackwood and celery-top pine. Ably assisted by his staff, led by George Smith the superintendent, Bill Hutchins the mill foreman and Hilda Dunkley the senior clerk, he expanded into hardware and mining. A large hardware

Mother M. John Cahill (*Archives of the Australian Congregation of the Sisters of Charity*)

Bishop Willson (*State Library of Tasmania*)

Fr William Hall (*Archives Office of Tasmania*)

Major G. J. De Winton (retired) (*Wiltshire Regimental Museum*)

R. J. (Jim) Howard (*Author's collection*)   John Luke Howard (*Author's collection*)

Howard family house at Zeehan (*Author's collection*)

Main street, Zeehan, 1902 (*West Coast Pioneers' Memorial Museum*)

Main street, Zeehan, 1910 (*West Coast Pioneers' Memorial Museum*)

John Hemery laying the foundation stone of the Masonic Temple, Canterbury, 1880
(*Courtesy of Mr G. J. H. D. Collins*)

store was opened in Zeehan soon after the war, and later stores were opened at Rosebery and Queenstown. He also became prominent in civic affairs. He was appointed to Zeehan municipal commission in 1939 and was its chairman from 1954. He became a justice of the peace in 1940 and chairman of the court in 1954. On one occasion Robert Menzies, who was then prime minister, visited the area. During his speech of welcome, Jim observed that speech-making should be no problem for the politician who had made so many in his parliamentry career. Mr Menzies, as he then was, corrected him with remarkable dignity and humility. He said, 'Mr Howard, every time I begin to make a speech I tremble', and he meant every word.

Behind the scenes, Jim Howard was becoming heavily involved in the mining industry. In 1945 he was made a director of the Renison Bell tin mine, named after its founder, George Renison Bell, who discovered the deposit now known as Bell's Lode. Bell pegged the lode, and on 22 September 1890 the Renison Bell Prospecting and Mining Company NL was officially registered. A staunch Quaker, Bell moved to Zeehan to supervise exploratory development of the field. He was there for three years, but later moved to Queensland. For over sixty years, the Renison Bell tinfield languished, and even in boom times the field never became economically viable.

In 1907 a young Irish-Australian, Michael Patrick O'Dea, came to Tasmania to become involved in mining. Strongly influenced by George Renison Bell, who was now retired, O'Dea came to the Renison Bell mining field, selected the lease he wanted, and floated the Boulder Tin Mining Co. NL. At first he was successful, but the field ran into serious problems within a decade. Manpower became scarce during the First World War, and better wages and conditions were offering at Mount Lyell and Zeehan. More than that, the company had refining problems as it was becoming necessary to recover fine tin from low-grade sulphide ores. A young Zeehan metallurgist, Ron Midson, developed a method of treating the Renison Bell ores by flotation. O'Dea worked hard at raising capital in the Renison–Bell–Zeehan area by mergers with other mining interests, as a result of which the Renison Associated Tin Mines NL was founded. A new flotation plant was installed, which proved to be reasonably successful, as did the mine, which struggled on until the end of the war. Paddy O'Dea's son Gavin became general manager in 1944 and chairman of directors in 1954. His co-directors were R. J. Howard of Zeehan, a lifelong friend, and Fred Jakins, a former Mount Lyell mine manager. The three men felt the mine had great potential. Renison Associated Tin held all the leases on the Renison Bell field, and a diamond drilling program had located large ore deposits at deeper levels. But serious problems remained, as considerable capital expenditure would be needed to develop a large-scale underground mining operation. A modern refining plant was also needed to treat the ore.

Gavin O'Dea was in the insurance business, and he made regular trips to Queenstown to review the Mount Lyell Company's employee insurance scheme. It was these trips that gave him the chance to interest Hugh Murray, the general manager, and Geoff Hudspeth, the mine manager, in the potential of Renison Associated Tin. At first it was an unofficial arrangement between friends, and in 1956 Hudspeth inspected the Renison workings in company with the Renison director, Jim Howard:

> With Jim Howard, the sandy-haired, softly-spoken Zeehan sawmiller, businessman and Renison director, Geoff Hudspeth climbed down the winze (shaft) of the Renison orebody on a Saturday afternoon. It was his first unofficial weekend trip to Renison, but certainly not his last. For the next year or more Geoff Hudspeth spent almost every weekend at the Renison Bell mine as 'honorary consultant' to Renison Associated Tin and paved the way for Renison's formal approach to the Mt Lyell board in 1958 to become a half partner in the old tin field.[8]

Since Renison Associated Tin lacked both capital and machinery, drilling equipment was borrowed from Mount Lyell on a weekend basis, and even Jim Howard's bush machinery did duty on the mining field. Sometimes the Public Works Department, which was building the Murchison Highway, was persuaded to make its plant available for a couple of days. In the meantime the mine struggled on, and the wages bill for a work force of forty men had to be met. To this end the mine had to produce 100 hundredweight bags of tin a week. 'Sometimes the week's production fell short of the target. Hudspeth and Howard would calculate the shortfall over a few drinks in the back bar of Bill Moyle's Central Hotel, Zeehan, on a Saturday night and Jim Howard would write a cheque to cover the wages bill.'[9]

Geoff Hudspeth became as enthusiastic as Jim Howard and Gavin O'Dea, and the way was now open for a merger with the Mount Lyell Mining and Railway Co. Ltd. On 23 October 1958, at an extraordinary meeting of shareholders, Gavin O'Dea announced the details of the merger. A month later the deal was ratified and the new board was reduced from seven to five. The chairman of the Mount Lyell company, with J. A. G. O'Dea, R. J. Howard, G. F. Hudspeth and E. J. Walker.

The way was open for a vigorous expansion program. Over the next few years Renison was proved to have huge reserves and also reached a profitable level of production. In fact it soon outstripped its parent company at Mount Lyell, which became the target of takeover bids from Renison. Now part of the Consolidated Goldfields Australia group, Renison Bell is Australia's largest tin mine and the world's largest underground mining operation. As Zeehan was selected for the residential and civic centre for Renison Bell, the old town has revived and now has a population in excess of 2,000.

Father became so heavily involved in the business, mining and civic interests that he grossly overtaxed himself. As early as 1958 he had been warned by his medical advisers to lighten his burdens, but he did not heed them. In 1966 he suffered a serious heart attack, but after he recovered it was business as usual. On 21 September 1968 the inevitable occurred, and the *Hobart Mercury* reported his death under the heading, 'King of the West Coast Dies in Melbourne':

> The 'King of the West Coast'—62 year old Mr Jim Howard, of Zeehan—died in a Melbourne hotel on Saturday morning.

Born Ronald James Howard at Zeehan on September 1 1906 [in fact 30 August], he operated sawmills at Zeehan and southern centres, and was the biggest exporter of timber in Tasmania.

His father was Zeehan timber merchant Mr Jack Howard, whose business was the nucleus of R. J. Howard Pty Ltd, general merchants and hardware stores of Zeehan and Queenstown. Mr Jim Howard was the company's managing director.

He was made a director of the Renison Limited Tin Mine in 1945.

Mr Howard was appointed to the Zeehan Municipal Commission in 1939 and its chairman from 1954.

Appointed a Justice of the Peace in 1940, he was chairman of the Court for 14 years from 1954.

Mr Howard was chairman of Zeehan District Hospital Board from 1943 to 1951, when he retired because of other commitments.

He was re-appointed in 1954 as chairman, a position he held at the time of his death.

He was also:

—Member of the Board of Management of the Zeehan Dispensary and Medical Union from 1952; chairman from 1954 and 1959, after which he remained on the board for a further three years.

—Member of the Zeehan School of Mines in 1948: chairman from 1951 until it closed down.

—Chairman of the West Coast Memorial Museum since its inception.

—Original member of the Western Regional Planning Committee, 1945; chairman from 1954 till it disbanded in 1960.

—Past president of West Coast Boy Scouts Association.

—Patron of most Zeehan sporting bodies.

A generous donor to charities, Mr Howard initiated countless appeals to assist people in distress.

He is survived by his wife Kathleen and sons Patrick, Fr Graeme Howard, Julian and Paul.

The funeral will take place at Zeehan cemetery tomorrow, after Requiem Mass at St Fursaeus Church at 2 p.m.[10]

Jim Howard was a man who always preferred to look to the future rather than back to the past, and he passed on very little information about his family. A proud man, he would not have found the facts of his grandparents' background very palatable. However, he would have had little knowledge of the terrible history which lay behind the enforced emigration of Stephen Howard and Ellen Lydon.

Epilogue

Stephen and Ellen Howard were only simple Irish peasants, but their lives were intertwined with those of much more influential or sophisticated people, all of whom represent remarkable segments of life as it was lived in nineteenth-century Ireland, Britain and Australia.

Patrick Hogan of Rathcannon died, still a young man, in 1846. His wife died in 1890, in the forty-fourth year of her widowhood. The family developed into a remarkable horse-racing and hunting dynasty, a tradition currently represented by Patrick and Joseph Hogan, who are both well known in racing and hunting circles.

James Lynch moved away from Granagh shortly after 1843. It is not known where he went, but in January 1846 a James Lynch was murdered for evicting his tenants at Anglesborough, County Tipperary. There is no way of knowing if the murdered man was Stephen Howard's one-time employer or merely a namesake.

Judge Joseph Devonsher Jackson went on to become the third judge of the court of common pleas. He died at Sutton House, Howth, in December 1857 aged seventy-four. Even his critics agreed that a fairer or more impartial judge never sat on the bench.

Christopher Copinger went on to become a QC and county judge for Kerry. The author of a book on civil law for county courts, he died of a painful illness in March 1864, leaving a wife and twelve children.

John Plunket, the prosecutor, went on to become the father and the chief prosecutor of the Munster Bar in 1854. He became the third Baron Plunket, following the death of his elder brother in October 1866. He died on 16 April 1871.

John Hemery retired from the sea following the sale of the *Constant* in 1849. He embarked on a banking career, and was manager of the London and County Bank in Canterbury when he died in November 1881, in his sixty-seventh year. He was lord mayor of Canterbury in 1879. A leading Freemason, he held several senior offices in the lodge and in 1879 laid the cornerstone of the Masonic temple in St Peter's Street, Canterbury.

Lieutenant Lempster Elliott saw service with the 58th Regiment during the Maori Wars of 1845–46 and was present at Okaipau, Ohaeawai, Ruapekapeka and Horokiwi. He was promoted to captain in 1854 and sold his commission in November 1860. The photograph of him was taken at Fort William, Calcutta, when he was with the 99th Regiment. Before leaving Australia, Elliot played an important part in exploring the Champion Bay area of Western Australia.

George Jean De Winton had several postings in Australia. He was stationed at Hobart, Windsor and Brisbane, as well as Norfolk Island during the regime of John Price, whom he staunchly defended in his memoirs. De Winton was also the leader of a party which founded Gladstone in Queensland. He was promoted to the rank of major and sold his commission in October 1857. For some years he was the editor of *Colburn's United Service Magazine*. He died at Wandsworth, London, on 16 September 1898, aged seventy-four, not long after the publication of his memoirs.

John Stephen Hampton continued his extraordinary career. Despite the debacle in Van Diemen's Land, he was appointed governor of Western Australia on 28 February 1862, where he was again a controversial figure, being criticised for nepotism and for cruelty to convicts. He was, however, responsible for several major public works and he left the colony in good financial shape when he returned to England in November 1868. He died at Hastings in December 1869, and is buried in Paddington cemetery, London.

John Price, the muster master at Hobart, was commandant at Norfolk Island from August 1846 till January 1853 and his regime was to become notorious for its severity. In January 1854 he was appointed inspector-general of penal establishments in Victoria. On 26 March 1857 he was stoned to death at Williamstown by convicts who were employed in public works.

William Gunn, the chief superintendent of convicts, was transferred to Launceston in 1846, following a dispute with Hampton. He was made superintendent, and visiting magistrate, of all convict establishments in the north. He became police magistrate of Launceston in 1850, a position he held until his death in June 1868.

James Jones Pringle was dismissed from the convict department in September 1848. He had lost his wife twelve months previously, after only sixteen months of marriage. Pringle applied to the secretary of state for a pension, and Hampton forwarded reports to London concerning his erratic behaviour and addiction to spirits. As far as is known, Pringle was never again employed by the government, although he was granted a small pension. He died in February 1870, aged fifty-six.

General Thomson died at Salrock, Galway, on 29 November 1856, aged seventy-one. He had proved to be the most able leader in the area during the famine. A remarkable lament, based on II Samuel iii.38, was published in the *Galway Express* on 13 December 1856.

John Dopping went on to become the resident magistrate at Arva, County Cavan. On Tuesday, 3 April 1855, he was drowned in a boating accident in Lough Gowna, near Granard, County Longford. The tragedy also claimed the lives of three officers of the Longford Rifles.

William Deane Freeman was presiding over the quarter sessions court at Galway on the morning of 20 October 1852 when he had a stroke and died that afternoon. His body was placed in a coffin of cedar, which was enclosed in another of lead, and these were enclosed in yet another coffin of oak. His remains were taken by train to Dublin and he was buried in the family vault at St Mary's Church Crumlin.

Henry O'Loughlin, the Crown solicitor for Galway, died on 13 January 1861, aged seventy-three. He was popular in the Tuam Dunmore area, and was succeeded by his son Patrick.

Anthony Donelan died at Galway in November 1863, at an advanced age. He was held in high professional esteem, but left little in the way of an estate. He was buried at the Forthill cemetery.

Columbus Rochfort, 'the defender of the faith', died at Annaville Dangan, aged only forty-seven, on 26 July 1862. His death was a loss for Galway, as he had been a colourful and pragmatic provincial leader.

James Connell, the master of the *Australasia*, went on to command bigger sailing ships on the England to Australia route. His reputation suffered badly following a disastrous voyage aboard the *Stebonheath* in 1857–58, after which he seems to have sailed mainly in the capacity of mate. He was killed in an accident on board the *Princess of Wales*, off the Isle of Wight, on 1 March 1865. He left a widow and four children at Grove Terrace, Mile End, Stepney. His eldest son, John, followed in his footsteps.

Alex Kilroy stayed in Van Diemen's Land for some months after the arrival of the *Australasia*. On 9 January 1850 he visited the prisoners barracks and his favourable comments are now part of the local history. He made one more voyage on a convict transport, sailing from Portsmouth to Perth on the *Mermaid*, with 209 convicts, on 9 January 1851. He lost only one man. He was retired on 21 January 1865, because of gout, palpitation and 'decay of the vital powers'. He died in November 1872.

The Holdich sisters married after the *Anson* was broken up in 1851. Martha married an army officer, but was widowed in 1857 and spent most of the rest of her life teaching school at Ballarat. Susan married in 1855 and died in England in the 1880s. Jane married Joe Allen Learmouth of Hobart and died in England aged ninety-five.

Bishop Willson left the Catholic church in Tasmania well established and when he left Hobart, in declining health, in February 1865, the church had a cathedral, 20,000 Catholics and nineteen priests. He died on 30 June 1866, an outstanding product of Britain's great era.

Fr William Hall died in July 1866, aged fifty-nine, having exhausted himself building St Mary's Cathedral. As he became older, he became closer to his community, who treated him as their spiritual father.

Frank Long, the prospector who discovered the Zeehan mining field, faced a penniless old age before the government came to his rescue and granted him a pension of £1 per week. He died in December 1908, aged sixty-six.

After Jim Howard's death in 1968, the family business was carried on for the next eleven years by the third son, Julian. In 1979 the business on the west coast was sold, bringing to an end a family business presence in Zeehan going back more than eighty years.

The Zeehan historian H. G. (Horrie) Hodge paid tribute to father in his account of the 'Silver City's History', during the centenary celebrations of 1982:

THE LATE JIM HOWARD—KING OF ZEEHAN

Men who created employment and assist people as the late Jim Howard did are the salt of the earth..

The telephone directory 1955 read:

R. J. Howard
A.N.A. Pty. Ltd.—Hardware Store—
Launceston Queenstown Transport Service—Paddy's Drapery Store—Sawmills and Timber Yard—Vacuum Oil Co.—Director Renison Tin Mines.

POSITIONS HELD

Chairman Zeehan Mun. Commission—Justice of the Peace—Chairman of the Court— Chairman Zeehan Hospital Board and Medical Union—Patron of nearly all Zeehan Sporting Bodies.

His 22 houses sheltered many homeless people.

In 1955 he employed 52 bushmen and mill workers—30 men supplying logs and 20 employees in his stores. He was respected and admired by his staff and most people.

His contribution of service is reflected in the words of the Missionary Archibald Naismith.

'We cannot all be heroes, and thrill a hemisphere
With some great daring venture some deeds that mock at fear,
But we can fill a lifetime with kindly acts and true
There's always noble service for noble hearts to do.'
Great men are never redundant, they live on.

Horrie Hodge, who lived through a terrible depression in his youth, valued men who create employment and his remarks reflect this. But it is difficult to suppress a wry smile when comparing his comments with the merciless tone of Judge Jackson's letter concerning the fate of Jim Howard's grandfather 139 years previously.

Appendix

PROFILE OF MALE CONVICTS ABOARD THE *CONSTANT*

Due to the complete records in the Tasmanian Archives, it has been possible to undertake a statistical analysis of the convicts on board the *Constant* and the *Australasia*. The sample is too small to allow any hard and fast conclusions to be drawn, but the statistics are not without their interesting features.

The *Constant* sailed from Dublin on 9 May 1843, before the famine, and Table 1 gives a breakdown of the convicts by county of origin (which is not necessarily the county in which they were arrested or tried). The three convicts who died on board have not been included.

It will be noted Dublin supplied the most convicts, with 40 (or nearly 20 per cent) of the whole number. Almost all the Dublin convicts were transported for stealing offences, mostly clothes of some description, although some also stole watches and rings. One even stole a cow, but this was unusual for Dublin, whose convicts seem to have been typical inner-city thieves, operating within the central city area.

It will be noted that Limerick with 20 convicts, and Tipperary with 18, are also well represented. This is not unexpected as Limerick, Clare and Tipperary were hotbeds of Whiteboy activity from 1800 until the famine. Stephen Howard and his accomplices were active in the barony of Coshma, which was a primary focus of Whiteboy unrest. Surprisingly enough, Clare is poorly represented with only two convicts on board. The six northern counties of what is now Ulster are poorly represented, with 11 convicts, and Donegal, which was then a part of Ulster, is not represented at all. The three traditional military counties of Wexford, Waterford and Tipperary are all represented, with Tipperary to the fore, but Wexford has a modest representation of only two convicts. The western province of Connaught has only 15 representatives, while the east coast province of Leinster has 84. It must be remembered that Dublin accounted for 40 of these convicts, but as Dublin was then the second city of the empire, and most of these men were thieves, the representation is not surprising. Forty-four convicts for the remaining 11 counties of Leinster was not an unduly high number, and King's County (Offaly) was not represented. Sixty-six convicts came from Munster, the most turbulent province throughout the first half of the nineteenth century. Limerick heads the list, but Tipperary, which was the most rebellious county throughout the nineteenth century, is not far behind, with Cork and Waterford well represented also. Kerry is poorly represented, as is Clare. Ulster, which then included the counties of Cavan, Monaghan and Donegal, had a modest representation with 31 convicts.

Finally, five convicts came from England. Two of these were pickpockets, transported for stealing watches and money; two were soldiers, serving with the English regiments in Ireland, who were transported for mutinous conduct; and the fifth stole some fowls.

The offences listed in Table 2 show a wide variety of crimes, but there are no murders. Desertion and mutinous conduct were soldiers' offences. Forging, counterfeiting and false pretences are white-collar offences untypical of the Irish rural convict. Two of the counterfeiters were Carlow men, while a man who forged wills came from Down, and another who uttered base coinage came from Tipperary. The man who was charged with false pretences by seducing a woman and obtaining £14 was from Dublin. The bigamists varied greatly in their backgrounds. One was a farm labourer, who was sentenced at Limerick but originally came from Cork; the other was a divinity student from Dublin. None of the 40 Dublin convicts was convicted of a violent crime: 20 were transported for stealing clothes; the others for stealing books, money, food, pawnbrokers' duplicates, watches and jewellery. Only one was transported for stealing livestock, and one each for the crimes of burglary, bigamy, false pretences, and breaking, entering and stealing.

A breakdown of the 163 offences concerned with stealing, burglary and general larceny, Table 3 shows that the theft of animals rated very highly, which is consistent with the high incidence of livestock thefts among rural convicts. Clothing was important, and half of the clothes thieves came from Dublin. Food did not rate as highly as one might have expected, but given the turbulent nature of the period, the theft of firearms is not surprising. Money rated highly, although in varying amounts, from stealing 8d. in one case to receiving £50 in another. Convicts from Limerick and Tipperary accounted for eight of the 11 assaults shown in Table 2, and these were often of a serious nature. The four assaults on habitations were all committed by Tipperary convicts, in one case with firearms, and in another with a sword. Of the 23 thefts committed by convicts from Limerick and Tipperary, five concerned firearms, and a highway robbery committed by a Limerick man involved use of a double-barrelled gun. Usually the firearms stolen were blunderbusses, pistols or double-barrelled guns. On the other hand, Limerick and Tipperary convicts did not show themselves to be unduly concerned with food, clothing or money.

The sentences varied greatly, and one suspects a great lack of uniformity in the application of the law so far as sentencing went. The prisoners transported for life included an arsonist, a rapist, a horse thief, three burglars, and one who struck a man and assaulted his habitation. The prisoner who received 21 years stole a suit and handkerchiefs. Fifteen-year sentences were handed out for robbery and assault, stealing watches and jewellery, burglary, stealing a blunderbuss, and breaking, entering and stealing. One 15-year sentence was handed out to a Kerryman who waylaid a man and stole 8d. The offence was classed as a felonious assault, but this seems to be rather unjust, given that there is no record of the victim being hurt. The 14-year sentences were for the most part given to similar categories of crime as those receiving 15-year sentences. The shorter sentences were given for the less serious crimes of theft and assault, but even these are sometimes difficult to understand. For example, two brothers who committed manslaughter received only seven years, as did a man who stole 55 rings from a jeweller, and several convicts found guilty of violent assault, including aggravated assault and a malicious assault on an old man.

One hundred and seventy-two of the men were Roman Catholic, and there were 29 Protestants. Eight of the Protestants came from Dublin, but apart from that they were remarkably well distributed throughout Ireland. Ninety-nine of the convicts were literate, 46 were semi-literate (i.e., could read only) and 56 were totally illiterate. The Protestants had a much higher degree of literacy than the Catholics, as 70.9 per cent of the Protestants were fully literate, as against 44 per cent of the Catholics. One hundred of the convicts, or nearly half, were previous offenders, but even so, surgeon-superintendent Hampton reported that only eight gave any trouble on board, and that was easily dealt with. Some 51 convicts were skilled workers, and 19 of these were Protestants. Only 20.7 per cent of the Protestants were totally unskilled. The list of skilled occupations followed by the convicts aboard the *Constant* is shown in Table 4.

The average age was 26.2 years. The youngest convicts were two boys aged 13; one from County Cavan who received seven years transportation for stealing 20 fowls, and the other from Dublin who received seven years for stealing a handkerchief. Only two men had reached the age of 64; one a man from Westmeath who stole a mace, and the other a man from Doon County, Limerick, who stole money and clothes from a Doon dwelling house. The convict from Doon appears to have had his sixty-fifth birthday aboard the *Constant*, and would have been the oldest man on board. Forty-six were under the age of 19, and 13 of these were under the age of 16. Only seven were 50 or over. The average height for physically mature men, over the age of 19, was a fraction under 5 feet 6 inches. The average height for the 41 who were under 19 was almost 5 feet 1 inch. The tallest was a 30-year-old thief from Waterford, who was 6 feet ¼ inch. The shortest convict was the 13-year-old boy from Cavan, who was only 4 feet 6 inches. Sixty-eight men were married, and 47 had children, but there were no children aboard the *Constant*. By far the largest number of convicts were assigned to Salt Water River probation station, which was the principal probation station on the Tasman Peninsular. The average probation period was 30.2 months for the 191 convicts who completed gang probation. Some died, and others were deemed incorrigible. One hundred and fifty-nine are recorded as having achieved their ticket-of-leave, and 174 are recorded as having received their conditional pardon or certificate of freedom. As 15 convicts died during their sentence, this leaves 12 convicts to be accounted for. One seems to have escaped, two or three were so incorrigible they never really achieved their freedom, and some became permanent wards of the state because of illness or insanity.

The mortality rate was fairly high, as three died on their way to Australia and a further 15 died during sentence. Twenty-seven are recorded as having died after sentence, including the 65-year-old thief from Doon who died at the Port Arthur Hospital on 7 January 1869, aged 90. Twenty convicts completed their sentences without any offences or misdemeanours, but 13 were flogged. The lashes were usually given in lots of 20, 25 or 30 for misappropriation of food and cutlery, disorderly conduct, refusing to work, and absconding. One convict, a Dubliner, received 100 lashes for insubordination. Five offended seriously while on gang probation, and two were sent to the Port Arthur chain gangs. Of the three sent to Norfolk Island, one of them was a man from Meath who murdered a fellow prisoner. He was sentenced to be hanged and dissected, but this was later commuted to transportation for life, the first ten years of which had to be served on Norfolk Island. This man received his ticket-of-leave in 1858, but it was revoked the next year and there is no record of him ever having achieved his certificate of freedom. The shortest period of probation was the 15 months served by the bigamous divinity student, who achieved his conditional pardon five years after arriving in Hobart. Finally, 13 were made constables, though for the most part they proved to be poor policemen. Seven were dismissed from the force for misconduct. A 32-year-old Dubliner transported for stealing a bank note worth £20 must have been considered an excellent prospect, as he had served eight years in the Irish Constabulary, but he only lasted six or seven months, because of drunkenness and disobedience. The policemen who were dismissed were usually charged with being drunk on duty, allowing prisoners to escape, or entertaining female convicts on police premises. One policeman who was escorting female prisoners on a journey between Hobart and Launceston conveniently got himself lost for several days. He was immediately charged and dismissed from the force.

PROFILE OF FEMALE CONVICTS ABOARD
THE *AUSTRALASIA*

The *Australasia* sailed from Dublin on 26 June 1849, in the immediate aftermath of the great famine. Two hundred women were on board, but the three women who died during the voyage are not included in this analysis. A glance at Table 1 shows that the areas most severely affected by the famine are strongly represented. Clare, Cork, Kerry and Galway were all hard hit by the famine, while the northern province Ulster had the smallest representation with 32 convicts. Down and Londonderry were not represented, and once again Donegal missed out by dint of cunning or virtue. Despite the large representation from Galway, the figures for the other counties of Connaught are surprisingly small, with Sligo missing out altogether. The 12 counties of Leinster produced only 44 convicts, as against 84 for the *Constant*. The big difference was Dublin, which was represented by only six convicts. The largest representation on the *Australasia* came from the province of Munster, which produced 86 convicts, or 43.6 per cent of the total. Clare, Cork and Kerry are also heavily represented, but the representation from Limerick and Tipperary is considerably less for the *Australasia* than for the *Constant*. This would at first suggest the influence of the famine, but the breakdown of stealing offences in Table 3 does not bear this out. Theft of clothing is the highest on the list, followed by livestock and money, in a pattern similar to that found on the *Constant*. Theft of food does not rate particularly high on the list.

Table 2 makes it clear that stealing offences of all kinds predominated once again. The stealing offences broken down in Table 3 reveal striking similarities between the men and women on the *Constant* and the *Australasia*, while Table 2 reveals a much higher incidence of arson amongst the female convicts. There are also two cases of infanticide: a 20-year-old woman from Clare was given life for throwing her ten-day-old child into a mud-hole, while a 22-year-old from Armagh received only seven years for killing her one-month-old child with a bandage. The arsonists were mostly servants who revenged themselves on their employers by setting fire to their house, although one set fire to a stable and another set fire to straw belonging to the father of her child who had refused to support her. The two cases of threatening language also concerned threats by convicts to burn the house of their employer. The counterfeiting charge involved a Dublin woman who was counterfeiting shillings; the perjury a young Monaghan woman who stole £8 from her father and then apparently perjured herself during her trial. The assaults involved two women who together assaulted the head matron of County Meath gaol.

Of the eight convicts who were sentenced to transportation for life, six were arsonists, one had used threatening language, and the eighth had been found guilty of infanticide. Four of the arsonists received 15 years, as did a woman found guilty of stealing a cow. The single sentence of 14 years was given to a woman found guilty of stealing £10 12s. 6d. Regarding the other sentences, it has not been possible to find reasons for magistrates and judges giving some convicts ten years and others seven years for almost identical offences.

There were only two Protestants aboard the *Australasia*, one a semi-literate woman from Clare, the other a fully literate woman from Waterford. Only eight women were fully literate, and 31 were semi-literate, meaning that 80.2 per cent of the women on board the *Australasia* could neither read nor write. One hundred and nineteen were previous offenders, and 18 received bad ship reports. It was notable that Kilroy seemed to have much more trouble with the women than Hampton did with the men. Of the few women who were skilled workers, most were dressmakers, needlewomen, shoe binders, stocking makers or cooks. Virtually all of the remaining women worked in service, as housemaids, laundresses and nursemaids.

There were 27 married women, and they had 19 children between them, while ten of the 16 widows also had children. Only two of the single women had children. Eighteen of the women had children on board, most of whom would have been infants since older children were usually left at home with the father and the extended family. Of the 108 women who married in Australia before receiving their conditional pardons, only 15 are recorded as marrying ex-convicts. During their sentence, 35 women had 38 illegitimate children.

The average height of women over 18 was 5 feet 1 inch, while that of the younger convicts was just over 4 feet 11 inches. The tallest woman, who was 5 feet 5½ inches, came from County Roscommon. The shortest was a 13-year-old from Clare who was 4 feet 5½ inches.

The average age was 23.7 years. The oldest convict was a Clare woman of 60 who received ten years for stealing seven sheep. She was married three and a half years later. The youngest convict was a ten-year-old girl who received seven years for stealing a gown and shoes. She was married four and a half years later.

One hundred and forty-five women were recorded as being sent to the *Anson* for their gang probation, and it is not clear where the others were sent. Thirty-three never committed any offences or misdemeanours while serving their sentence, and only 17 re-offended in Australia. One hundred and sixty-two are recorded as having achieved either a conditional pardon or a certificate of freedom.

The records of the convicts aboard the *Australasia* are much less complete than for the prisoners from the *Constant*, and there are no records of five of the women after their landing in Hobart. Many disappeared after marriage, and of the others there is little record of their placements, none of them having achieved their conditional pardon or certificate of freedom. However, as freedom certificates came automatically after they had completed their sentences, it must be assumed only those who died, or were ill or incorrigible missed out. There is no record of any women who were already married returning home to their families. One suspects some of them may have stayed in the colony and perhaps taken other partners.

Finally, the mortality rate was much lower than that of the men who came on the *Constant*, and only five died during sentence.

TABLE 1 County of origin

	Constant	Australasia
Antrim	1	5
Armagh	2	4
Carlow	4	1
Cavan	12	6
Clare	2	24
Cork	16	27
Donegal		
Down	2	
Dublin	40	6
Fermanagh	6	4
Galway	2	26
Kerry	1	12
Kilkenny	3	3
King's County (Offaly)		3
Kildare	3	8
Leitrim	5	4
Limerick	20	9
Louth	3	3
Longford	4	3
Londonderry	1	
Mayo	3	3
Meath	8	3
Monaghan	6	6
Queen's County (Laois)	3	5
Roscommon	4	2
Sligo	1	
Tipperary	18	7
Tyrone	1	7
Waterford	9	7
Wexford	2	7
Westmeath	7	2
Wicklow	7	
ENGLAND	5	

TABLE 2 Offences

Constant		Australasia	
Assault	11	Assault	2
Arson	1	Arson	13
Attacking house with firearm	1	Infanticide	2
Assaulting habitation	3	Counterfeiting	1
Bigamy	2	Killing livestock	4
Desertion	5	Perjury	1
False pretences	1	Threatening language	2
Forging/Uttering/Counterfeiting	4	Stealing and receiving and	
Highway robbery	2	larceny	171
Manslaughter	2	Vagrancy	1
Mutinous conduct	2		
Rape	1		
Threatening language	1		
Stealing and receiving and			
larceny	163		
Wilful damage	2		

TABLE 3 Breakdown of larcenies and stealing offences

	Constant	Australasia
Stealing animals	44	48
Stealing clothing	40	64
Stealing watches and jewellery	15	7
Stealing money	33	26
Stealing firearms	9	
Stealing food	10	10
General larceny	12	16

TABLE 4 Sentences

Constant		Australasia	
125	convicts received 7 years	167	convicts received 7 years
42	convicts received 10 years	16	convicts received 10 years
11	convicts received 14 years	1	convict received 14 years
15	convicts received 15 years	5	convicts received 15 years
1	convict received 21 years	8	convicts received life
7	convicts received life		

TABLE 5 Classification of skilled workers

Constant	Australasia
Baker	Cook
Blacksmith	Dressmaker
Bricklayer	Needlewoman
Butcher	Shoe binder
Brass turner	Stocking maker
Bookbinder	
Cooper	
Gentleman's servant and groom	
Hairdresser	
Millwright	
Postillion	
Sailor	
Shoemaker	
Stonemason	
Tailor	
Tanner	
Tobacco pipe maker	
Weaver	
Wheelwright	

TABLE 6 Station or gang for men of the *Constant*

Broadmarsh	15	Lovely Banks	7
Browns River	9	New Norfolk	15
Bridgewater	2	Point Puer	14
Bucklands	10	Port Arthur	1
Cascade	3	Rocky Hills	12
Deloraine	11	Salt Water River	34
Fingal	12	Southport	7
Impression Bay	3	St Mary's Vale	12
Jerusalem	14	Westbury	10
Longmarsh	10		

Notes

Abbreviations
BPP British Parliamentary Papers
PRO Public Records Office
SPO State Papers Office

Chapter 1 An Irish Heritage
1. Edmund Curtis, A History of Ireland,
   Methuen, London 1936, p. 112.
2. Ibid., p. 177.
3. Ibid., pp. 249–50.
4. Patrick Francis Moran, Persecutions of Irish
   Catholics, M. H. Gill and Son, Dublin
   1884, p. 22.
5. Ibid., p. 91.
6. Ibid., pp. 306, 323.
7. Ibid., pp. 291–92.
8. Ibid., p. 232.
9. Curtis, A History of Ireland, p. 271.
10. Mainchin Seoighe, Portrait of Limerick,
    Robert Hale, London 1982, p. 193.
11. John Mitchel, Jail Journal, M. H. Gill and
    Son, Dublin 1914, p. xxviii.
12. Charles Chenevix Trench, The Great Dan,
    Jonathan Cape, London 1984, p. 284.

**Chapter 2 Limerick and the Peasant
         Guerillas**
1. John O'Donovan, Field Name Books of the
   County and City of Limerick, No. 36,
   Ordnance Survey of Ireland, Dublin 1840.
2. Mainchin Seoighe, Portrait of Limerick,
   Robert Hale, London 1982, p. 120.
3. Slater's Directory, 1846, p. 227.
4. Samuel Lewis, A Topographical Dictionary
   of Ireland, Vol. 1, S. Lewis and Co.,
   London 1837, p. 436.
5. Seoighe, Portrait of Limerick, pp. 123, 153.
6. W. E. Vaughan, Landlords and Tenants in
   Ireland, 1848–1904, Economic and Social

History Society of Ireland, Dublin 1984, p.
5.
7. Ibid., pp. 5, 6
8. Seoighe, p. 119.
9. Michael Beames, Peasants and Power, The
   Harvester Press, Sussex 1983, p. 216.
10. Dublin University Magazine, Vol. 10,
    November 1837, Chapter IX; By-Ways of
    Irish History, December 1837, p. 706.
11. Beames, Peasants and Power, p. 64.
12. Ibid., p. 71.
13. Crime and Outrage Papers, Limerick 1852,
    17/403, SPO, Dublin.
14. BPP, Vols 31, 32, 1836: Commission of
    Enquiry into State of the Poorer Classes of
    Ireland, 1836: Supplement to Appendix D,
    p. 341; Supplement to Appendix E, p. 339.
15. Seoighe, pp. 108–12.
16. Gearoid O'Tuathaigh, Ireland Before the
    Famine, 1798–1848, Gill and MacMillan,
    Dublin 1972, p. 149.
17. Ibid., pp. 147, 148.
18. Ibid., p. 149.
19. Slater's Directory, 1857, p. 180.
20. Robert Curtis, The History of the Royal
    Irish Constabulary, McGlashan and Gill,
    Dublin 1871, p. 11.
21. Michael Scott (ed.), Hall's Ireland, Sphere
    Books, London 1984, Vol. 2, p. 440.
22. Ibid., p. 441.
23. BPP, Vol. 13, 1829: Appendix to the
    Seventh Report of the Inspectors-General,
    p. 477.
24. O'Tuathaigh, Ireland Before the Famine,
    p. 99.
25. Ibid., p. 105.
26. Crime and Outrage Papers, Limerick,
    1842, 22747, SPO, Dublin.

Chapter 3 Trial of a Whiteboy

1. *Rules and Regulations of Prisons in Ireland*, HMSO, Dublin 1827, Nos XII, XIII, pp. 29, 30.
2. *Ibid.*, pp. 42, 43.
3. *Ibid.*, pp. 31, 33, 34.
4. *Ibid.*, p. 26.
5. *Ibid.*, p. 38.
6. BPP, Vol. 28, 1844: *Appendix to Twenty-Second Report of Inspectors-General of Prisons in Ireland*, pp. 416–17.
7. .BPP, Vol. 53, 1848: *Returns of Gaols and Work Houses of Ireland*, p. 389.
8. *Rules and Regulations of Prisons in Ireland*, 1827, pp. 28, 29.
9. *Ibid.*, pp. 16, 17, 18, 19.
10. *Ibid.*, p. 39.
11. BPP, Vol. 26, 1862: *Appendix to Fortieth Report of Inspectors-General of Prisons in Ireland*, pp. 302, 303.
12. *Slater's Directory*, 1846, p. 258.
13. Mainchin Seoighe, *Portrait of Limerick*, Robert Hale, London 1982, p. 40.
14. *Slater's Directory*, 1846, pp. 258, 259.
15. *The Limerick Reporter*, 9 October 1840, pp. 1, 2.
16. Mainchin Seoighe, *A Walking Tour of Historic Limerick*, Shannonside Tourism, Limerick 1982, p. 13.
17. *The Limerick Reporter*, 9 October 1840, pp. 1, 2.
18. *Ibid.*
19. M. Lenihan, *History of Limerick*, Hodges Smith, Dublin 1866, p. 476.
20. *The Limerick Reporter*, 3 March 1843, p. 4.
21. F. E. Ball, *The Judges in Ireland, 1221–1921*, John Murray, London 1926, Vol. 2, pp. 351, 352.
22. *Ibid.*, p. 355.
23. J. Roderick O'Flanagan, *The Munster Circuit*, Sampson Low, Marston, Searle and Rivington, London 1880, p. 382.
24. D. O. Madden, *Ireland and its Rulers*, T. C. Newby, London 1844, Vol. 2, pp. 260–63.
25. Gearoid O'Tuathaigh, *Ireland Before the Famine, 1798–1848*, Gill and MacMillan, Dublin 1982, p. 101.
26. A. C. Benson and Viscount Fisher (eds), *Letters of Queen Victoria 1837–1861*, John Murray, London 1907, Vol. 1, pp. 441–45.
27. *Dublin Evening Post*, 17 December 1857.
28. Frederick Boase, *Modern English Biography*, Wetherton and Worth, Truro 1897, Vol. 1, p. 1908.
29. *Kerry Evening Post*, 30 March 1864.
30. Frederick Boase, *Modern English Biography*, Vol. 2, p. 1563.
31. *Metropolitan Magazine*, 1837: Parliamentary Portraits series.
32. *Limerick Chronicle*, 11 March 1843.

Chapter 4 Overland to Dublin

1. *Limerick Reporter*, 28 April 1843. One prisoner's name appears to have been omitted.
2. *Ibid.*
3. *Kilmainham: The Bastille of Ireland*, Kilmainham Jail Restoration Society, Dublin 1982, pp. 3–8.
4. *Ibid.*
5. *Ibid.*
6. BPP, Vol. 42, 1843 (547): *Enquiry into Corruption at Kilmainham 1842—Convict Transportation—Crime and Police*, pp. 501–603.
7. Kilmainham Prison Dublin, eighth scale survey plans, 2 May 1836.
8. *Limerick Reporter*, 21 April 1843.
9. BPP, Vol. 53, 1848 (486): *Gaols and Workhouses (Ireland), Daily Diet 1847–48*, pp. 389–400.
10. BPP, Vol. 42, 1843: *Enquiry at Kilmainham*, pp. 501–603.
11. *Ibid.*
12. *Petitions for Mitigation and Clemency*, 1843, H/22/1834, SPO, Dublin.
13. *Ibid.*
14. *Ibid.*
15. *Ibid.*
16. Charles O'Mahony, *The Viceroys of Ireland*, John Long, London 1912, p. 244.

Chapter 5 Hobart Bound

1. Charles Bateson, *The Convict Ships, 1787–1868*: Brown, Son and Ferguson, Glasgow 1969, p. 35.
2. G. J. De Winton, *Soldiering Fifty Years Ago: Australia in the Forties*, European Mail Ltd, Ludgate Circus 1898, pp. 1, 2.
3. *Ibid.*, p. 11.
4. *Ibid.*, pp. 34, 35.
5. Alexander Marjoribanks, *Travels in New Zealand*, Smith Elder, London 1846, p. 19.
6. Naval Record, J. S. Hampton, ADM. 196/8, PRO, London.
7. Peter Cunningham, *Two Years in New South Wales*, Henry Colburn, London 1827, Vol. 2, pp. 215–16.
8. Bateson, *The Convict Ships*, p. 70.
9. John Boyle O'Reilly, *Moondyne*, George

Routledge and Sons, London 1889, pp. 204–05.

10. Greenhill and Giffard, *Travelling by Sea in the Nineteenth Century*, p. 14, quoted in Don Charlwood, *The Long Farewell*, Penguin, Melbourne 1981, p. 176.

11. Cunningham, *Two Years in New South Wales*, Vol. 2, pp. 216–17.

12. Journal J. S. Hampton, ADM. 101/17/9.

13. Cunningham, Vol. 2, pp. 290–305.

14. C. A. Browning, *The Convict Ship and England's Exiles*, 2nd edn, Hamilton, Adams and Co., London 1847, pp. 274, 292–326.

15. C. Lloyd and J. L. S. Coulter, *Medicine and the Navy, 1200–1900*, E. and S. Livingstone, Edinburgh 1963, Vol. 4, p. 23.

16. *Ibid.*

17. *Ibid.*, pp. 23–24.

18. Journal J. S. Hampton, ADM 101/17/9.

19. De Winton, *Soldiering Fifty Years Ago*, pp. 35, 36.

20. H. Bolitho and J. Mulgan, *The Emigrants— Early Travellers to the Antipodes*, Books for Libraries Press, New York 1970, pp. 80, 88.

Chapter 6 The Assignment System

1. Margaret Weidenhofer, *The Convict Years*, Lansdowne, Melbourne 1973, p. 16.

2. *Ibid.*, p. 17.

3. Charles Bateson, *The Convict Ships, 1787–1868*, Brown, Son and Ferguson, Glasgow 1969, p. 114.

4. *Ibid.*, pp. 379–94.

5. Coultman Smith, *Shadow Over Tasmania*, J. Walch and Sons, Hobart 1941, p. 19.

6. Weidenhofer, *The Convict Years*, p. 8.

7. BPP, Vol. 19, 1837 (518): *Select Committee on Transportation, 1837*, pp. 285, 286.

8. BPP, Vol 22, 1838 (669): *Select Committee 1837–38*, pp. 105–108.

9. BPP, Vol 19, 1837, (518): *Select Committee 1837*, p. 290.

10. *Ibid.*, p. 283.

11. Smith, *Shadow over Tasmania*, p. 106.

12. BPP, Vol. 22, 1838 (669): *Select Committee 1837–38* p. 109.

13. *Ibid.*, p. 101.

14. John West, *The History of Tasmania*, Angus and Robertson, Sydney 1971, p. 475.

Chapter 7 Probation at Salt Water River

1. G. J. De Winton, *Soldiering Fifty Years Ago: Australia in the Forties*, European Mail Ltd, Ludgate Circus 1898, p. 38.

2. BPP, Vol. 48, 1847 (36): *Comptroller-General's Report, 1st August 1846*, p. 220.

3. BPP, Vol. 19, 1837 (518): *Select Committee*, p. 294.

4. Peter Cunningham, *Two Years in New South Wales*, Henry Colburn, London 1827, Vol. 2, p. 302.

5. BPP, Vol. 42, 1843 (159): Stanley to Franklin, 25 November 1842, *Correspondence on Convict Discipline*, p. 453–59.

6. Harbour Master's Register, 1843, Archives of Tasmania.

7. BPP, Vol. 52, 1847–48 (402): *Comptroller-General's Report, 31 December 1846*, p. 71.

8. BPP, Vol. 37, 1845 (158): *Regulations of the First Stage of Convict Probation in Van Diemen's Land, October 1843*, p. 344.

9. *Ibid.*

10. Co 280/327, PRO, London.

11. *Ibid.*

12. Tasmanian Papers, Vol. 141, Mitchell Library, Sydney.

13. Robert Crooke, *The Convict: A Fragment of History*, University of Tasmania, Hobart 1958, pp. 54–56.

14. *Ibid.*

15. *Ibid.*

16. *Ibid.*, pp. 60–69.

17. BPP, Vol. 43, 1849 (800, 811): *Regulations of First Stage of Convict Probation, Van Diemen's Land September 1847*, pp. 213–16.

18. Co 280/232, PRO, London.

19. BPP, Vol. 43, 1849 (941), p. 566.

Chapter 8 Ellen Lydon of North Galway

1. Tullycross Guild Irish Countrywomen's Association, *Portrait of a Parish*, Jaycee Printers, Galway 1985, p. 58.

2. *Seventh Report of the Congested Districts Board*, HMSO, Dublin 1898.

3. *Dublin Almanac*, 1846, p. 231.

4. William Thackeray, *The Irish Sketch Book 1842*, Smith Elder and Co., London 1872, p. 425.

5. Michael Scott (ed), *Hall's Ireland*, Sphere Books, London 1984, Vol. 2, pp. 414, 415, 416.

6. *Slater's Directory*, 1846, p. 117.

7. Cecil Woodham Smith, *The Great Hunger*, Hamish Hamilton, London 1962, p. 34.

8. BPP, Vols 31, 32, 1836: *The Commission of Enquiry into the State of the Poor in Ireland,*

1836: Supplement to Appendix D, p. 120; Supplement to Appendix E, p. 116.

9. Woodham Smith, *The Great Hunger*, pp. 411–12.

10. J. O'Rourke, *History of the Great Irish Famine of 1847*, McGlashan and Gill, Dublin 1874, pp. 2–10.

11. Woodham Smith, pp. 29–35.

12. *Ibid*., pp. 94–102.

13. *Ibid*., p. 143.

14. Tullycross Guild Irish Countrywomen's Association, pp. 35, 36.

15. *Hart's Army List*, 1854.

16. General Thomson to Sir Randolph Routh, January 1847, Salrock Papers.

17. General Thomson to John Galway, Esq., May 1847, Salrock Papers.

18. *Ibid*.

19. General Thomson to John Dopping, February 1848, Galway Outrage Papers, 1848, 164, SPO, Dublin.

20. *Ibid*., 2 March 1848, 314.

21. Woodham Smith, p. 299.

22. James Hack Tuke, *Visit to Connaught in the Autumn of 1847*, Charles Gilpin and John L. Linney, London 1848, p. 26.

23. J. Dopping to Undersecretary, 17 January 1848, Galway Outrage Papers, SPO, Dublin.

24. *Ibid*., 14 January 1848, 11/62.

25. D. Kerrigan to J. Dopping, 14 January 1848, Galway Outrage Papers, 11/62, SPO, Dublin.

26. *Galway Vindicator*, 1 April 1848, p. 3.

Chapter 9 Trial of a Peasant Girl

1. *Galway Vindicator*, 20 September 1843.

2. Crime and Outrage Papers, Galway, 1847, SPO, Dublin.

3. *Slater's Directory*, 1846, pp. 122, 123.

4. Galway County Prison Plans, 1858, Galway County Library.

5. Galway County Prison Plans, 1858.

6. *Galway Vindicator*, 6 January 1849.

7. BPP, Vol. 29, 1850: *Appendix to the Twenty-Eighth Report of Inspectors-General of Prisons in Ireland*, pp. 397, 398.

8. A. E. McClintock and C. Brady (eds), *Law Directory for Ireland: The Law and Equity Court Guide for 1846*, Hodges and Smith, Dublin 1846, pp. 71, 72.

9. J. Roderick O'Flanagan, *The Irish Bar*, Sampson Low, Marston, Searle and Rivington, London 1880, pp. 392–93.

10. *Ibid*.

11. *Galway Vindicator*, 6 January 1849.

12. James Greaney, *Dunmore*, np, June 1984, p. 88, 89.

13. *Galway Vindicator*, 16 January 1861; *Tuam Herald*, 19 January 1861.

14. *Galway Vindicator*, 21 October 1848.

15. *Galway Vindicator*, 21 October 1846.

16. *Ward v. Freeman* (1852), 2 *Irish Common Law Reports* 460.

17. *Galway Vindicator*, 17 January 1849.

18. *Galway Vindicator*, 28 October 1848.

19. *Galway Mercury*, 13 January 1849.

Chapter 10 The Richmond Female Penitentiary

1. *Galway Mercury*, 7 April 1849.

2. *Constabulary List and Directory*, 1849, pp. 121–23.

3. Gearoid O'Tuathaigh, *Ireland Before the Famine, 1798–1848*, Gill and MacMillan Ltd, Dublin 1972, p. 157.

4. *The Dublin Almanac*, 1846, p. 74.

5. *Pigot and Co's Directory*, 1824, p. 6.

6. *Thom's Almanac*, 1847, p. 582.

7. BPP, Vol. 29, 1850: *Appendix to the Twenty-Eighth Report of Inspectors-General of Prisons*, pp. 347–52.

8. Thomas King Moylan, 'The Richmond Asylum Dublin', *Dublin Historical Record*, 1945, p. 9.

9. *Ibid*.

10. *Ibid*.

11. *Ibid*.

12. *Appendix to the Twenty-Eighth Report of Inspectors-General of Prisons*, pp. 347–52.

13. *Ibid*.

14. *Ibid*.

15. *Ibid*.

16. *Ibid*.

17. Transportation Register, 1848–1849, SPO, Dublin.

18. Home Office Correspondence, HO 21/14-35979, PRO, London.

19. *Ibid*.

20. *The Limerick Chronicle*, 20 June 1849.

21. *Limerick Reporter*, 10 August 1841.

22. *Galway Mercury*, 7 April 1849.

23. Peter Pearson, assisted by Anna Brady and Daniel Gillman, *Dun Laoghaire: Kingstown*, O'Brien, Dublin 1981, pp. 23–28, 45.

24. Charles O'Mahony, *The Viceroys of Ireland*, John Long, London 1912, pp. 248–55.

25. *Limerick Reporter*, 10 August 1841.

26. *Ibid.*

Chapter 11 A New Destiny
1. David R. MacGregor, *Merchant Sailing Ships, 1815–1850*, Conway Maritime Press, London 1984, p. 88.
2. Charles Bateson, *The Convict Ships*, Brown, Son and Ferguson, Glasgow 1969, p. 293.
3. Naval Record Alexander Kilroy, 104/22, PRO, London.
4. Bateson, *The Convict Ships*, pp. 151–57.
5. Journal of Rev. R. W. Gibbs, 7 January 1849, HO 12/626/5, PRO, London.
6. Correspondence from Inspectors of Millbank Prison to Sir W. Somerville 13/7/1847, HO 45/1841, 036015 (Recommendations of Ladies of the Convict Ship Committee), PRO, London.
7. Journal of Gilbert Inglis, *Duchess of Northumberland*, 1852, JOD150, National Maritime Museum, London.
8. Crew Muster, *Australasia*, 1849, BT 98/2230–11344, PRO, London.
9. Registers of Seamen's Service, BT 113/218, PRO, London.
10. Diary of an Anonymous Immigrant to Port Phillip Bay, 1852, JOD 90 MS 70/097, National Maritime Museum, Greenwich.
11. Journal of Alexander Kilroy, *Australasia* 1849, ADM 101/6/9, PRO, London.
12. *Ibid.*
13. *Ibid.*
14. Bateson, pp. 42–52.
15. *Ibid.* p. 276.
16. *Ibid.*, p. 295.
17. Don Charlwood, *The Long Farewell*, Penguin, Melbourne 1981, p. 1.
18. *Ibid.*
19. Bateson, pp. 160, 200.
20. *Ibid.*, p. 78.
21. *Ibid.*, p. 122.
22. Journal of Gilbert Inglis, JOD 150.
23. Correspondence Concerning Surgeon John G. Williams and Admiralty re cutting of hair of female convicts, HO45/2935, PRO, London.
24. Journal of Rev. Charles Woods, No. 123/1, Tasmanian Archives.
25. Log of James Connell, *Stebonheath*, 1857/58, BT 98/6051–87680, PRO, London.
26. Bateson, pp. 246–64, 283–90.
27. Harbour Master's Register, 1849, Tasmanian Archives.

28. Journal of Rev. R. W. Gibbs, HO 12/626/5.
29. Journal of Rev. Charles Woods, No 123/1.

Chapter 12 Probation on the *Anson*
1. BPP, Vol. 19, 1837 (518): *Select Committee on Transportation, 1837*, pp. 315, 316.
2. John West, *The History of Tasmania*, Angus and Robertson, Sydney 1971, 541–42.
3. John Mitchel, *Jail Journal*, M. H. Gill and Son, Dublin 1914, p. 223.
4. Navy Lists, National Maritime Museum, Greenwich, Vol. 1.
5. BPP, Vol. 42, 1843: Stanley to Franklin, 25 November 1842, *Correspondence on Convict Discipline*, p. 461.
6. Lieutenant-Colonel Godfrey Mundy, *Our Antipodes*, Richard Bentley, London 1852, Vol. 3, pp. 177–78.
7. *Australian Dictionary of Biography*, Vol. 1, Melbourne University Press, Melbourne 1966 p. 134.
8. Forster to Governor Wilmot, 17 September 1844, HO 45/959A-36013, PRO, London.
9. R. C. Hutchinson, 'Mrs Hutchinson and the Female Factories of Early Australia', paper read before the Tasmanian Historical Research Association, 9 May 1962, p. 63.
10. Robert Crooke, *The Convict*, University of Tasmania, Hobart 1958, pp. 22, 23.
11. *Ibid.*, p. 25.
12. *The Hobart Town Courier*, 29 October 1844.
13. BPP, Vol. 29, 1846 (659): *Dr E. Bowden to Lord Stanley, 20 November 1845*, Enclosure No. 21, pp. 405–8.
14. *Ibid.*
15. *Ibid.*
16. West, *History of Tasmania*, pp. 510–11.
17. BPP, Vol. 29, 1846 (659) *Governor Wilmot to Lord Stanley*, 22 December 1845. Enclosure No. 24, p. 423.
18. Oliné Keese [Caroline Leakey], *The Broad Arrow*, Richard Bentley and Son, London 1892, p. 116.
19. *Ibid.*, p. 119, 120.

Chapter 13 Life in Van Diemen's Land
1. BPP, vol. 42, 1843: *Stanley to Franklin, 25 November 1842*, Despatch No. 175, Enclosure No. 13, p. 457.
2. BPP, Vol. 43, 1849 (800): *Regulation No.*

17 *For Hiring Probation Pass Holders May 1846–August 1847, Old Regulations*, pp. 219–23.

3. *Ibid.*, Regulation No. 12. p. 220.
4. BPP, Vol. 37, 1845: *Wilmot to Stanley Return of Probation Stations*, p. 336. BPP, Vol. 48, 1847: *23 January 1846 Report of Comptroller General*, p. 128; *29 August 1846 Report of Comptroller General*, p. 237.
5. John West, *The History of Tasmania*, Angus and Robertson, Sydney 1971, p. 546.
6. National Parks and Wildlife Service of Tasmania, *Richmond Gaol Historic Site*, Hobart 1984.
7. West, *History of Tasmania*, p. 436.
8. Quoted in Frank Clune, *Martin Cash*, Angus and Robertson, Sydney 1955, p. 71.
9. Plan of Brickfields Temporary Barrack, Archives of Tasmania.
10. BPP, Vol. 52, 1847–48 (785): *Comptroller General's Report, 31 December 1846*, p. 83.
11. Correspondence Between Forster and Visiting Magistrates Messrs Carter and Watchorn—CO280/183, PRO, London.
12. Oliné Keese [Caroline Leakey], *The Broad Arrow*, Richard Bentley and Son, London 1892, p. 79.
13. BPP, Vol. 45, 1851 (1361): *Comptroller-General's Report, 31 December 1850*, paragraph 14, p. 282.
14. *Ibid.*, Return No. XI, 6 February 1851, p. 308.
15. Robert Crooke, *The Convict*, University of Tasmania, Hobart 1958, p. 53.

Chapter 14 A Remarkable Coincidence
1. *Constant*, Transcripts Ships Register, BT 107/87—2270, PRO, London.
2. *Australasia*, Transcripts Ships Register, BT 107/96—2275, PRO, London.
3. Crew Musters, *Australasia*, BT 98/4216—2288, PRO, London.
4. Crew Musters, *Constant*, BT 98/4216—2286, PRO, London.
5. Charles Bateson, *Australian Shipwrecks, 1622–1850*, A. H. and A. W. Reed, Sydney 1974, p. 186.
6. James Fenton, *History of Tasmania*, J. Walch and Sons, Hobart 1884, p. 276.
7. *Ibid.*, p. 252.

Chapter 15 A Living Faith
1. C. A. Browning, *The Convict Ship and*

England's Exiles, Hamilton, Adams and Co., London 1847, p. 217.
2. L. L. Robson, *The Convict Settlers of Australia*, Melbourne University Press, Melbourne 1965, p. 89.
3. A. G. L. Shaw, *Convicts and the Colonies*, Melbourne University Press, Melbourne 1977, pp. 148, 166.
4. Robson, *The Convict Settlers of Australia*, p. 130.
5. BPP, Vol. 43, 1849 (941): *Denison to Earl Grey, 29 August 1848*, No 6. Enclosures 1 and 2, p. 410.
6. BPP, Vol. 45, 1850 (1153): Denison to Earl Grey, *Comptroller-General's Report, 30 June 1849*, p. 169.
7. *Ibid.*, p. 213.
8. *Australian Dictionary of Biography*, Vol. 1, Melbourne University Press, Melbourne 1966, pp. 241, 242.
9. *Ibid.*, Vol. 2, Melbourne 1967, pp. 509–12.
10. W. T. Southerwood, *Planting A Faith*, Vol. 8, np, Hobart 1981, p. 7.
11. *Australian Dictionary of Biography*, Vol. 2, Melbourne University Press, Melbourne 1967, pp. 607–08; Summary of Willson's Life and Work, Archives of Tasmania.
12. T. Kelsh, *Personal Recollections of Robert William Willson, Life and Work*, np, Hobart 1882, pp. 35, 36, 37.
13. *Australian Dictionary of Biography*, Vol. 2, pp. 607–08.
14. James Fenton, *History of Tasmania*, J. Walch and sons, Hobart 1884, pp. 158–59.
15. John H. Cullen, *The Australian Daughters of Mary Aikenhead*, Pelligrini and Co., Australia 1938, p. 85.
16. A. G. L. Shaw, 'Sir John Eardley-Wilmot and The Probation System in Tasmania', paper presented at the Tasmanian Historical Association, 14 February 1962.
17. Fenton, *History of Tasmania*, pp. 187, 188, 236.
18. John West, *The History of Tasmania*, Angus and Robertson, Sydney 1971, p. 243.
19. Cullen, *The Australian Daughters of Mary Aikenhead*, p. 87.
20. *Australian Dictionary of Biography*, Vol. 1, pp. 503–04.
21. Cullen, p. 80.
22. *Ibid.*, pp. 80, 81, 90.

Chapter 16 The Founding of a Family

1. BPP, Vol. 45, 1850 (1022): *Report of the Comptroller-General of Convicts, June 30 1849*, pp. 187, 188.
2. *Hobart Mercury*, 28 February 1878.
3. Kerry Pink, *The West Coast Story*, West Coast Pioneers Memorial Museum, Zeehan 1982, p. 46.
4. *Ibid.*, p. 63.
5. *Ibid.*, p. 65.
6. *Ibid.*, p. 66.
7. H. G. Hodge, *When Zeehan Comes Back Again*, Cox Kay Pty Ltd, Hobart 1982, p. 10.
8. Pink, *West Coast Story*, p. 99.
9. *Ibid.*, p. 100.
10. *Hobart Mercury*, 23 September 1968.

Bibliography

Publications

Australian Dictionary of Biography, Vols 1 and 2, *1788-1850*, Melbourne University Press, Melbourne 1966, 1967.

Ball, F. E., *The Judges in Ireland 1221-1921*, John Murray, London 1926.

Bateson, Charles, *The Convict Ships 1787-1868*, Brown Son and Ferguson, Glasgow 1969.

Bayley, William A., *Port Arthur Railway Across Tasmanian Peninsula*, Austrail Publications, Bulli, N.S.W. 1971.

Beames, Michael, *Peasants and Power*, The Harvester Press, Sussex 1983.

Boase, Frederick, *Modern English Biography*, Wetherton and Worth, Truro 1897.

Bolitho, H. and J. Mulgan, *The Emigrants—Early Travellers to the Antipodes*, Books for Libraries Press, New York 1970.

Brand, Ian, *Port Arthur 1830-1877*, Jason Publications, Hobart 1975.

Brand, Ian, *Penal Peninsula*, Jason Publications, Hobart 1978.

Browning, C. A., *The Convict Ship and England's Exiles*, Hamilton Adams and Co., London 1847.

Burn, David, *An Excursion to Port Arthur in 1842*, J. W. Beattie, Launceston nd.

Catholic Directory for Ireland 1848, W. J. Battersby, Dublin 1848.

Charlwood, Don, *The Long Farewell*, Penguin, Ringwood 1981.

Clune, Frank, *Martin Cash*, Angus and Robertson, Sydney 1985.

Crooke, Robert, *The Convict: A Fragment of History*, University of Tasmania, Hobart 1983.

Cullen, John H., *The Australian Daughters of Mary Aikenhead*, Pelligrini and Co., Australia 1938.

Cullen, L. M., *An Economic History of Ireland since 1660*, B. T. Batsford, London 1972.

Curtis, Edmund, *A History of Ireland*, Methuen, London 1936.

De Beaumont, Gustave, *Ireland Social Political and Religious*, edited by W. C. Taylor Ltd, Richard Bently, London 1839.

De Winton, G. J., *Soldiering Fifty Years Ago: Australia in the Forties*, European Mail Ltd, Ludgate Circus, London 1898.

Dorland's Medical Dictionary, W. B. Saunders and Company, London 1982.

Dublin Almanac, 1846.

Dublin University Magazine, Vol. X, 1837.

Fenton, James, *History of Tasmania*, Melanie Publications, Hobart 1978.

Governor of Van Diemen's Land, *Regulations for the Settlement of Port Arthur*, Auden Publishing, Hobart 1978.

Greaney, James, *Dunmore*, np, 1984.

Haley, Alex, *Roots*, Pan Books, London 1977.

Harris, Alexander ['Emigrant Mechanic'], *Settlers and Convicts* [1847], Melbourne University Press, Melbourne 1953.

Hodge, H. G., *When Zeehan Comes Back Again*, Cox Kay, Hobart 1982.

Irish Constabulary List and Directory, HMSO, Dublin 1849.

Jeffrey, Mark, *A Burglar's Life*, J. Walch and Sons Pty Ltd, Hobart nd.

Kelsh, T., *Personal Recollections of . . . Robert William Willson*, np, Hobart 1882.

Kilmainham Jail Restoration Society, *Kilmainham: The Bastille of Ireland*, Dublin 1982.

Leakey, Caroline [Oliné Keese], *The Broad Arrow*, Richard Bentley and Son, London 1892.

Lee, Joseph, *The Modernisation of Irish Society 1848-1918*, Gill and McMillan, Dublin 1973.

Lewis, Samuel, *A Topographical Dictionary of Ireland*, Vol. 1, S. Lewis and Co., London 1837.

Lloyd, C., and J. L. S. Coulter, *Medicine and the Navy 1200-1900*, E. and S. Livingstone, Edinburgh 1963.

Lubbock, Basil, *The Colonial Clippers*, Brown, Son and Ferguson, Glasgow 1975.

McClintock, A. E., and C. Brady (eds), *Law Directory For Ireland—The Law and Equity Court Guide For 1846*, Hodges and Smith, Dublin 1846.

MacGregor, David R., *Merchant Sailing Ships 1815-1850*, Conway Maritime Press, London 1984.

Madden, D. O., *Ireland and its Rulers*, T. C. Newby, London 1844.

Marjoribanks, Alexander, *Travels in New Zealand*, Smith, Alder, London 1847.

Marlow, Joyce, *The Tolpuddle Martyrs*, Granada Publishing, Frogmore St Albans, Herts 1974.

Mennel, P., *The Dictionary of Australian Biography 1855-1892*, Hutchinson, London 1892.

Mitchell, John, *Jail Journal*, M. H. Gill and Son, Dublin 1914.

Moody, T. W., and F. X. Martin (eds) *The Course of Irish History*, Mercier Press, Cork 1987.

Moran, P. F., *Persecutions of Irish Catholics*, M. H. Gill and Son, Dublin 1884.

Mortlock, J. F., *Experiences Of A Convict* [1864-65], edited by G. A. Wilkes and A. G. Mitchell, Sydney University Press, Sydney 1965.

Norman, L., *Sea Wolves and Bandits*, J. Walch and Sons, Hobart 1946.

O'Donovan, John, *Field Name Books of the County and City of Limerick*, No. 36, Ordnance Survey of Ireland, Dublin 1840.

O'Flanagan, J. Roderick, *The Irish Bar*, Sampson Low, Marston, Searle and Rivington, London 1879.

O'Flanagan, J. Roderick, *The Munster Circuit*, Sampson Low, Marston, Searle and Rivington, London 1880.

O'Mahony, Charles, *The Viceroys Of Ireland*, John Long, London 1912.

O'Neill, Judith, *Transported to Van Diemen's Land*, Cambridge University Press, Melbourne 1977.

O'Reilly, John Boyle, *Moondyne*, George Routledge and Sons, London 1889.

O'Rourke, Rev. J., *History of the Great Irish Famine of 1847*, M'Glashan and Gill, Dublin 1874.

O'Tuathaigh, Gearoid, *Ireland Before the Famine, 1798-1848*, Gill and MacMillan, Dublin 1972.

Pearson, Peter, assisted by Anna Brady and David Gillman, *Dun Laoghaire Kingstown*, O'Brien, Dublin 1981.

Pink, Kerry, *The West Coast Story*, West Coast Pioneers Memorial Museum, Zeehan 1982.

Rashleigh, Ralph, *The Adventures of Ralph Rashleigh*, Jonathan Cape, London 1929.

Robson, L. L., *The Convict Settlers Of Australia*, Melbourne University Press, Melbourne 1965.

Scott, Michael (ed), *Hall's Ireland* [1840], Sphere, London 1984.

Seoighe, Mainchin, *Portrait of Limerick*, Robert Hale, London 1982.

Slater's Directory, 1846.

Smith, Coultman, *Shadow Over Tasmania*, J. Walch and Sons, Hobart 1941.

Southerwood, W. T., *Planting A Faith*, Vol 8, np, Hobart 1981.

Thackeray, William M., *The Irish Sketch Book*, Smith Elder and Co., London 1872.

Trench, Charles Chenevix, *The Great Dan*, Jonathan Cape, London 1984.

Trench, W. Steuart, *Realities of Irish Life*, Longmans, Green and Co., London 1868.

Trustees Kilmainham Jail, *Ghosts of Kilmainham*, Elo Press, Dublin 1963.

Tullycross Guild Irish Countrywomen's Association, *Portrait of a Parish*, Jaycee Printers, Galway 1985.

Vaughan, W. E., *Landlords and Tenants in Ireland, 1848-1904*, The Economic and Social History Society of Ireland, Dublin 1984.

Vaux, James Hardy, *The Memoirs of James Hardy Vaux* [1819], edited by Noel McLachlan, William
    Heinemann, London 1964.
Villiers-Tuthill, Kathleen, *History of Clifden, 1810–1860*, np, 1981.
Villiers-Tuthill, Kathleen, *Beyond the Twelve Bens*, np, Galway 1986.
Warung, Price, *Tales of the Convict System*, The Bulletin Newspaper Co., Sydney 1892.
Weidenhofer, Margaret, *The Convict Years*, Lansdowne, Melbourne 1973.
West, John, *The History of Tasmania* [1852], Angus and Robertson, Sydney 1971.
Woodham Smith, Cecil, *The Great Hunger*, Hamish Hamilton, London 1962.

Note: Newspapers and Parliamentary Papers consulted are listed, where appropriate, in the notes.

Manuscripts
Anonymous passenger aboard the *Abel Gower* on voyage from Gravesend to Port Phillip, 1852,
    JOD 90, MS70/097, National Maritime Museum.
Connell, James, Log of Stebonheath 1857/58, BT 98/6051—87680.
Crime and Outrage Papers, Galway, 1843–52, SPO, Dublin.
Crime and Outrage Papers, Limerick, 1837–48, SPO, Dublin.
Downing, Rev. Robert, Chaplain *Pestonjee Bomanjee*, 20 September 1848 to 10 January 1849.
Gibbs, Rev. R., Chaplain *Cadet*, 4 November 1848 to 17 April 1849, HO 12/626/5, PRO London.
Hampton, J. S., ADM 101/17/9, Voyage on board *Constant*, 1843, PRO, London.
Inglis, Gilbert James, Purser, *Duchess of Northumberland*, 1852, JOD 150, National Maritime
    Museum.
Kilroy, Alex, ADM 101/6/9, Voyage on Board *Australasia*, 1849, PRO, London.
Petitions for Mitigation and Clemency, SPO, Dublin.
Salruck Papers, Thomson Family Records, Salrock, Galway.
Woods, Rev. Charles, Chaplain. *Blenheim*, 23 July to 7 November 1851, No. 123/1, Tasmanian
    Archives.

Note: Ships' indents and the Tasmanian records of the convicts from the *Constant* and the
Australasia, along with peripheral sources from the National Maritime Museum, the Public Records
Office, London, and the Archives of Tasmania, have been recorded where appropriate in the
notes.

Index